Here are some nice things people said about our First Edition of *God's Gift*:

"Oscillating between fascinating facts and witty repartee, The Midwest: God's Gift to Planet Earth! *is a blast to browse, and an excellent gift book."* — The Midwest Book Review

"For something entirely different, there's The Midwest: God's Gift to Planet Earth! ... It's definitely funny and even informative. It's highly recommended." — Richard C Longworth (author of Caught in the Middle)

"Loving RAYGUN's humorous and informative [book]. It's a side-splitting, knee-splapping read." — Best Midwest Travel

"This book is a fun read ... It melds history and humor and substance. This isn't just about geography, it's a state of mind." — Doug Hamilton (Prairie Public Radio)

"Hilarious. Moving. 100% truthful. Both of Paul Bunyan's incredibly large thumbs up!" — Sara (GoodReads.com)

"The chapters read like extended Jon Stewart monologues — wide-ranging, smart, accessible, and pretty dang funny. The book's biggest surprise has to be how truly informative it is." — The Little Hawk

"This book is a great read, and a lot of fun for this part of the country." — Don Marsh (St Louis Public Radio)

"Word-of-mouth alone could very well conquer the rest of the salt-of-the-earth Midwest. Seems like just a matter of time before RAYGUN's literary debut finds a pride of place next to the Bibles in people's homes." — Todd Erzen (The Des Moines Register)

"This book is really, really fun! ... And [Draper] is quite a researcher and writer." — Cynthia Canty (Michigan Public Radio)

"The book faithfully maintains [RAYGUN founder] Draper's persona and and unconventional." — The Daily Iov

THE MIDWEST: GOD'S GIFT TO PLANET EARTH!

WRITTEN IN DES MOINES

Writer: **Mike Draper**
In-House Editing: **Blake Crabb, John Bosley,** and **Jen Mitchard**
Outside Editor: **Dan Weeks**
Outside Proofreaders: **Kathy Roberts, Sue Dinsdale,** and **Justin Norman**
Outside Digital Format Help: **Justin Norman**

DESIGNED IN DES MOINES

Head Designer and Illustrator: **John Bosley**
Slightly Less Important Designer: **Mike Draper**
Assistant Designers and Illustrators: **Jen Mitchard** and **Joe Heuermann**
Moral Support: Everyone else at RAYGUN

PRINTED IN DES MOINES

The body paper this book is American and the cover paper
comes from **Neenah, Wisconsin**
This book was printed by union labor at **Garner Printing**
Not only our rep at Garner but also our friend: **Jay Nevins**
Bound and finished by **Finishbinders**

First Printing of the Second Edition.

QUESTIONS OR COMMENTS? FIRE AWAY!

RAYGUN, LLC
400 East Locust
Des Moines, IA 50309
5152881323
contact@raygunsite.com

This book is dedicated to:
Henry Ford, Thomas Edison, Tool, high-fructose
corn syrup, Ranch dressing, and clinging to guns
and religion.

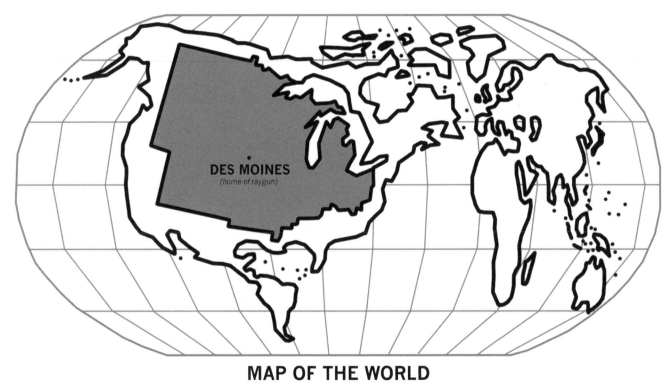

MAP OF THE WORLD

Hi there! I'm Mike Draper, founder of RAYGUN and narrator of this book, the Second Edition of our illustrated guide to the galaxy's most important region. Let's check it out together...

To give you the fullest experience possible, we've put all Midwesterners mentioned in the text — or those related to the text — in the **margins**. The city below them is their place of birth, unless it says "raised in."

LIKE THIS!

Mike Draper
Van Meter, Iowa

Blake Crabb (Lawrence, Kansas)
Editing and Curly Hair

Suzanne Corum-Rich (Pella, Iowa)
Cat Grooming

Jen Mitchard (Sheldahl, Iowa)
Assistant Designer and Assistant Curly Hair

Van Holmgren (Johnston, Iowa)
Human Resources

Lucy Shay (Chicago, Des Moines, Florida)
VP of Overreacting

Seth Nosbusch (Jackson, Minnesota)
VP of Not Knowing Book Was Being Written

John Bosley (Slater, Iowa)
Head Designer and Snake Charmer

Jessica Brinck (Moulton, Iowa)
Hot-New-Dance-Moves Coordinator

Joe Heuermann (Des Moines, Iowa)
Assistant Designer and Round Glasses

And above, you'll see the rest of the team that helped bring this Nobel-worthy work together. RAYGUN has assembled the greatest minds of our time, from exotic locales such as Sheldahl, and each person played their assigned role — our "VP of Not Knowing Book Was Being Written," for example, did a stand up job at not knowing we were all working on a book.

That's it for the introductions, now enjoy the book!

HERE'S WHAT'S IN THIS THING

PART ONE **UP IN THE SKY! IT'S A BIRD! IT'S A PLANE! IT'S A MIDWESTERNER!**

1.1 The Midwest: International Land of Mystery — pg 16

1.2 Is this Heaven? No, it's the Midwest. — pg 28

1.3 Idawahio: Home of The Iowa University, Ohio City, Idaho ... Indiana? Where are You from Again? — pg 34

1.4 We're So F**king Nice — pg 48

1.5 The Midwest: Your Most Trusted Name in Everything — pg 58

1.6 You Can't Spell "Wit" Without "Midwest" — pg 64

1.7 Where the Women Are Strong? You Bet Your Ass it Is. Even our Fictional Folk Legends are Strong. — pg 72

1.8 Politics in the Midwest: It's Raining Men and "God Hates Fags" Signs pg 82

1.9 It's Hard to be Modest When You're Perfect in Every Way ... But we Manage pg 90

PART TWO **MIDWEST SUPERPOWER**

2.1 Heartland of Domination pg 102

2.2 You Know, Rest of America, if We Don't Start Getting Some Respect, We're Gonna Secede from Your Ass. pg 114

2.3 The United States of Midwest pg 122

2.4 Hey, Rest of America: Uhhhh, You're Welcome pg 130

PART THREE **IS IT JUST ME, OR DO THE OTHER REGIONS KEEP TRYING TO KILL US?**

3.1 If You Can't Beat 'Em, Assassinate 'Em. pg 136

3.2 And if You Can't Assassinate 'Em, Send in Federal Forces. pg 144

3.3 And if You Can't Assassinate 'Em or Subdue 'Em with the Federal Military, then Take Some of Their Brightest Minds and Poison Them with Loose Women, Hard Booze, and Salt-Filled Bodies of Water. pg 148

3.4 Or Maybe Just Try to Hurt Their Feelings   pg 152

PART FOUR **MIDWEST GIVETH, AND
MIDWEST TAKETH AWAY**

4.1 Our Primary Means of Retaliation:
Passive Aggressiveness   pg 158

4.2 Our *Other* Primary Means of Retaliation:
Kicking Maximum Ass   pg 162

4.3 Killing You Softly with Type 2 Diabetes,
Car Culture, and Agricultural Byproducts.   pg 166

4.4 Controlling Young Minds with Countercultural
Smut Peddlers, Jerry Springer, and Oprah.   pg 174

4.5 If You Want an Economy Destroyed,
Let a Midwesterner Handle It   pg 180

4.6 Canada Attacks!   pg 184

PART FIVE **WE'RE #1 BY A WIDER
MARGIN THAN USUAL!**

5.1 Will the Last One Out of the Midwest
Just Remember to Extinguish the Tire Fire?   pg 190

5.2 Reports of Our Economic Demise
Have Been Greatly Exaggerated   pg 198

5.3 From Rags to T-Shirts: The Heartwarming
Mike Draper Story *(Friday, 9/8C, Only on Lifetime)*   pg 208

5.4 We're #1 by a Wider Margin Than Usual!   pg 214

5.5 The Midwest: The China Before China   pg 220

5.6 Wave The Next Time You Fly Over   pg 226

Appendix 1 Huge List of Midwesterners   pg 232
Appendix 2 Sources   pg 246
Appendix 3 Thanks and Other Stuff   pg 252

PART ONE

UP IN THE SKY! IT'S A BIRD! IT'S A PLANE! IT'S A MID-WESTERNER!

"OH HEY THERE, IT'S ME,
DON DRAPER. JUST
YOUR EVERYDAY,
HANDSOME AND
CHARMING MIDWESTERNER.

THERE'S SOMETHING
MYSTERIOUS ABOUT ME.
IS IT BECAUSE I'M FROM
ILLINOIS, BUT YOU KEEP
MIXING IT UP WITH
INDIANA AND OHIO?"

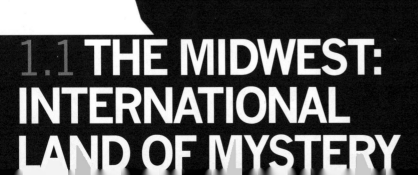

1.1 THE MIDWEST: INTERNATIONAL LAND OF MYSTERY

In the spring of 2004, I graduated with a degree in history from the University of Pennsylvania. In the fall of 2004, I was selling t-shirts out of a bag on Times Square.

By then, it was more than four years since I'd left my Iowa hometown for the bright lights of the East Coast. I had wanted to *see* the streets of Times Square, not *work on* the streets of Times Square. Now back when I left Iowa, I hadn't been totally naive about my future. I figured that the Harvard and Yale guys would mop up the top spots at America's commercial banks. Still, a degree from a second-tier Ivy like Penn would surely entitle me to a mid level position at something like the Department of the Interior, giving me a foot in the door when it came to profiting from natural gas fracking.

But by graduation it was clear that I wasn't totally cut out for the academic world. Or the corporate world. Or the government world, the nonprofit world — or really any world that required me to show up regularly, not wear flip-flops, and keep my smart-ass comments to myself.

So t-shirts it was.

The hours were reasonable, the travel was nice, and I was a walking example for parents who tell their kids that you really can't do anything with a liberal arts degree: "You wanna end up like this chump, Jackson? He studied history and now he's selling cheap shit alongside a bunch of people who learned English as a second language. Stick with a finance degree from Tuck."

"Uhh, hey man, I can hear you talking about me right now."

The t-shirt gig was going fairly well that fall. Still, I needed an angle for the designs. I had seen enough Tony Robbins infomercials as a kid to know that I had to "unleash the power within." But what was that power? What made me particularly memorable?

The answer struck me one day when, after selling shirts, I walked back to a totally empty side street that had just hours before served as a parking space for my car.

"You from Idaho?" hollered a construction worker nearby.

"Sure," I said.

"A car from Idaho got towed."

I made my way to the impound, approached the large, black woman behind bulletproof glass, and gave her my license plate number. She wrote it down under *New York* and I said, "Oh, it's an Iowa plate."

She jotted, *Ohio*, and started to get up. "Oh, it's Iowa," I said again. She stopped and looked at me, head tilted down, eyes up. It's a posture that silently conveys: "I've had enough bullshit for today, my shift's almost through, and my feet hurt. So don't start with me."

"I know," she said. "I wrote it down." She pointed to *Ohio*.

I had learned to not give big, black women a lot of guff, but I also didn't want the good folks at the impound wandering around all night looking for my car.

IOWA: WE'RE NOT IN KANSAS ANYMORE

"Actually," I said, "Ohio is spelled I-O-W-A."

"Oh, okay."

As she walked away, it struck me that I was one of the few people I knew who was simultaneously native to three states. To those I met, I had a shadowy past somewhere in Ohio. Or was it Iowa? No, no, it was Idaho. And my parents were farmers, right? Or steel mill workers? This mystique was my memorable quality. I hadn't crafted this image; rather, it came naturally to me because people outside the Midwest don't really know where it is, and don't give a shit what goes on here.

Now, this wasn't the first time something like this had happened. After four years out East, exchanges like this were so common that I hardly noticed them. "You're the guy from Ohio, right?" "Aren't you from somewhere like Indiana?"

"Pretty much."

When I first met the girl who would become my wife and told her I was from Iowa, she laughed and said, "That's hysterical ... (pause) ... Oh, you really are?"

It was a match made in heaven.

A drunk guy at a party told me, "You're not in Kansas, any more, man!"

Thanks, "bro," I'll let someone from Wichita know when I see them.

A professor once said, "Ah, Iowa, where the women are strong, the men are good looking, and all the children are above average."

At the time, I wasn't very familiar with *A Prairie Home Companion*, so I thought this was just his own observation of my home state. "Yeah," I said to myself, "that pretty much sums it up." Now, I realize that he was a Garrison Keillor fan, but not a *big* Garrison Keillor fan.

Garrison Keillor
Anoka, Minnesota

But the moment to top all others was when I went to the main Jewish sorority's formal at Penn. Five couples went out beforehand, meaning dinner was five Jewish girls from the New York area, four Jewish guys from the New York area, and me. After an hour of talking about baseball, one guy asked, "So, Mike, where're you from?"

My date lit up. Before I could answer, she lightly put her hands on the arms of the girls to either side of her to brace the table for the news: "Mike is from … *Iowa*."

"Oh my *Gawd*!"

"No way!"

"Seriously? You're seriously from Idaho?"

"What did you guys do there growing up?"

"What baseball team do you root for?"

"What do your parents do?"

"Are they farmers?"

"Yeah, I bet they're farmers, you look like a farm kid."

"Nobody is going to believe that I met a guy from Iowa tonight."

It was as though, all their lives, they had been waiting to meet a guy from Iowa, and *finally*, after almost 20 years, they had direct access.

The Midwest might as well be a foreign country to most Americans. Like most foreign countries, outsiders have heard of it, but the details of what goes on inside are pretty hazy. If you met someone from Poland, every question would be on the table. Likewise, all questions about this United States of Midwest are fair game.

"What states are there? Is Nebraska one of them? Did I just make that up?"

"What are the borders?"

"What's the weather like?"

"Do they have indoor plumbing?"

"What's it look like? Any mountains? No, wait, it's all flat. Flat. That's right."

"They speak French there, don't they? Or am I thinking of Canada?"

James T Kirk
Riverside, Iowa...eventually

Jerry Siegel
co-creator of Superman was from Cleveland, Ohio

Joe Shuster
co-creator of Superman was raised in Cleveland, Ohio

Clark Gable
part of the inspiration for Clark Kent Cadiz, Ohio

Kent Taylor
another part of the inspiration for Clark Kent Nashua, Iowa

Harold Lloyd
bespectacled silent actor who was the final part of the inspiration for Clark Kent Burchard, Nebraska

IT TAKES A SUPER ACTOR:
Brandon Routh
played Superman in
Superman Returns
Norwalk, Iowa

George Reeves
first star of the 1950s series
Adventures of Superman
Woolstock, Iowa

This country-within-a-country situation gives us a foreign-ness, a mysterious-ness, a sort of *je ne sais quoi* (as we'd say in our native Midwestern language) that has been used countless times in popular culture. Mysterious Midwesterners are everywhere, from Don Draper to Jay Gatsby, Jason Bourne to Magnum P.I., James T Kirk to Superman.

And really, where else can Superman come from? Part of his Midwestern heritage gives him his air of mystery, needing only a pair of glasses as his disguise.

"Wait, isn't that Clark Kent?"

"No, it kind of looks like Clark, but Clark is from Nebraska, Superman is from Iowa. Or is Clark from Kansas and Superman is from Minnesota?"

The other part of his Midwestern heritage gives him a goodness that eliminates the need to explain his motivation to save a crashing plane. Because being raised by the Kent family in Smallville, Kansas, automatically creates an "Aw shucks, there's no place like home, by golly, stopping that plane from crashing into all those people would just be the right thing to do" attitude.

I mean, if Superman were raised in suburban Connecticut — with a hedge-fund-managing father and a mother working her way up the corporate ladder at McKinsey — people would get confused when Superman would fly off to save the plane. "What's he wasting time with that plane for? Shouldn't he be using his super powers to create a new financial instrument with decent returns but, most importantly, high fees for his father?"

If Superman were Southern, he'd only save the non-gay passengers, who would, once saved, be open to an hour-long post-rescue soliloquy on the importance of trusting Jesus — and a couple of tips on sale items at Wal-Mart.

And if Superman were from the West, he would either be an out-of-control cowboy who would tell the plane to "Make my day, punk" before blasting it full of 45-caliber holes and crushing a shot of whiskey, or he would lazily fly out from his perch in Portland, but let the plane crash to the ground saying, "That's what those people get for using such a polluting form of travel. They should have walked or ridden a single-speed bicycle. I bet those inconsiderate bastards even used plastic bags."

Iowa-born painter Grant Wood's iconic *American Gothic* captures one major underlying

A MIDWESTERNER FOR EVERY FICTIONAL OCCASION

Hollywood can't get enough of us! With character attributes that range from extremely good looking and intelligent to kind and brave, Midwesterners can fill just about any role. And the rest of the country's poor geographic skills means that a Midwestern heritage also brings a shroud of mystery alongside a main course of kicking ass and bedding ladies. From *Superman* and *Beverly Hills Cop* to *Titanic* and *Planet of the Apes*, there are mysterious Midwesterners for any occasion.

I NEED A HERO, AND THEY'VE GOTTA BE LARGER THAN LIFE …

Superman (Smallville, Kansas) Where else is the ultimate American ideal going to be from?

Thomas "Magnum P.I." Magnum (Detroit, Michigan) Born in the 1940s in Detroit, Magnum takes his Detroit Tigers hat, mustache, and flowered shirt collection to Hawaii after the Vietnam War to solve crimes and keep America's only island state safe.

Axel Foley (Detroit, Michigan) Another Motor City savior, Axel grows up as a street tough through the 1960s before joining the police force. When his friend is killed in Beverly Hills, Axel takes his rough-and-tumble style out West. Crimes get solved. Hilarity ensues.

Jason Bourne (Nixa, Missouri) Born in 1969 as David Webb, Bourne serves in America's Special Forces before enduring behavioral modification inside the CIA's Operation Treadstone. His Midwestern goodness is too much to modify, though, when he refuses to kill a target whose children are present. The CIA sends their best Eastern operatives after him. Needless to say, it doesn't go well for anyone not from Flyover Country.

HEARTLAND GOOD LOOKS, BUT THERE'S SOMETHING THEY'RE HIDING …

Jay Gatsby (small town, North Dakota) Gatsby grows up poor as James Gatz in North Dakota during the late 1800s. He chases love to New York, redefines himself as a rich playboy, but is destroyed by rampant greed and selfishness. Just another day out East!

Edward Cullen (Chicago, Illinois) Born in 1901, this *Twilight* heartthrob was in danger of dying from Spanish Influenza at age 17. Dr Carlisle Cullen saved Edward by turning him into a vampire and taking him to Ashland, Wisconsin. Almost 80 years later, Edward moves with the Cullens to the state of Washington and finds himself in one of the most poorly written trilogies in history.

Don Draper (small town, Illinois) The lead character of *Mad Men*, Don was raised as Dick Whitman in rural Illinois during the 1920s. Like Gatsby, this mysterious man arrives in New York, but is able to wrap Manhattan around his handsome finger. He rises to the top of the advertising world while bedding scores of women in the tri-state area during the '50s and '60s.

Kate Austen (Ames, Iowa) This female lead in *Lost* has a big heart, but a criminal past (dun dun dun).

BRAVE, STRONG-WILLED, AND A LITTLE UNPREDICTABLE …

Jack Dawson (Chippewa Falls, Wisconsin) The self-proclaimed "King of the World," Jack was born in 1892 in Wisconsin before traveling to Europe. In a Paris poker game, he wins two tickets for the *RMS Titanic*, where his rough-and-tumble charm attracts the wealthy Rose DeWitt Bukater. Their brief courtship ends when Jack freezes to death in the North Sea after the *Titanic*'s sinking.

Benjamin Willard (Toledo, Ohio) When Colonel Walter Kurtz, a decorated Green Beret Officer, goes Sarah Palin and runs his own operation in Cambodia during the Vietnam War, the American military fears him more than the Vietcong. After several failed attempts to kill Kurtz, the military sends Ohio's finest: Captain Benjamin Willard. He finds Kurtz, gains his respect, and finally kills him, Midwestern style, with a machete.

George Taylor (Fort Wayne, Indiana) This courageous astronaut travels to find he is not only on a planet ruled by apes, but that planet is Earth. If someone has to see that those damned, dirty apes destroyed the Statue of Liberty, it really should be a guy from Indiana.

feeling outsiders have about Midwesterners: simpleness. The only thing we like more than standing with our pitchforks and our ladies in front of our houses is rescuing a neighbor's cat from a tree or offering a smile and some directions to a lost traveler.

Superman is unconflicted. He is good to his core. While Gotham-raised Batman is a rich playboy who runs with the city's loose women when he's not managing a multinational corporation that dabbles in weapons manufacturing, Superman resists the temptations of big city Metropolis. He subtly courts fellow Kansan Lois Lane (awww, those Midwesterners always stick together!) and still finds time to zip back to Smallville and see his "Ma" and "Pa" for a hug and some Jell-O salad.

"People from the Midwest," remarked *Daily Show* host Jon Stewart, "no matter their political stripe, never look like assholes. They just look like nice people. I know there must be assholes out there, they just never look like it."

But while our simpleness can come out as an honest work ethic, it can also be used to make us appear dumb as bricks. As if all we do is stand around with our pitchforks and our depressed wives, looking uncultured, and waiting for the second coming of Christ.

"Midwesterners: People in the 'heartland' area of America," writes Urban Dictionary, "who are known for their cultural isolation and close-mindedness."

Cold blooded, Urban Dictionary.

Their view pops up more subtly in the news. For instance, when Barack Obama was running for President in 2008, he made a trip to Europe that demonstrated his worldwide appeal. But commentators on NPR worried that this seeming no-brainer of a political move may come at a cost. Will a trip to Europe not, "play well with voters *in Middle America*?"

"Middle America!" I could almost hear Coasters screaming at their radios. "Would you get your act together?!?"

We Middle Americans were about to blow it for everyone! What was Bono doing scampering around Africa helping kids, when he should be taping public service announcements right here in the States to help the Heartland?

"Middle America needs your help," the yellow-sunglassed Irishman would say. "Every day, these simple people crouch next to their barrel fires, sharpening

SUPER AMERICAN GOTHIC

spears at both ends, delineating borders with severed pig heads, and never trusting anyone who travels to Europe, or has a passport, or has curly black hair. Because every Middle American believes that outside of Middle America is the land of Godless sodomites, Communism, and Communist sodomites.

"For only a dollar a day, well, actually more like $98 per day to account for the average cost of living in the U.S., you can adopt a Middle American like Mike here."

Cue: me looking up from my barrel fire, forlorn, drinking from a cracked pot, belly distended.

Bono would rest his famous hand on my shoulder. "With your money, Mike will be able to eat more than just skinned squirrel and methamphetamine. He'll be able to drink more than grain alcohol and rainwater, and he will finally receive an education to lift him from ignorance."

"I just wish I could listen to your music, Mr Bono," I'd say, "but the region only has one 8-track tape player and well-worn copies of John Fogerty and George Benson."

"It just breaks your heart," Bono would tell the camera. "In the election of 2004 between Bush and Kerry, 62% of Middle Americans like Mike voted for Chuck Norris because they said they, 'Like the way he takes care of business, like when he gets all pissed and kicks ass. America needs to do that to the USSR.' The remainder of Middle Americans voted for Ronald Reagan, Jesus, or the Incredible Hulk. None of whom were on the ballot, except for Reagan, whose name pops up for every Midwestern election from City Council to President.

"Don't let Middle America ruin the election of 2008. Give all you can."

> "Cue: me looking up from my barrel fire, forlorn, drinking from a cracked pot, belly distended."
>
> Ronald Reagan
> *Tampico, Illinois*
>
> Jesus Christ
> *Kirksville, Missouri...JK, LOL!*

So the mystery of the Midwest to those on the outside remains. On the one hand, we're ignoramuses voting for anyone who shoots an animal, and at the same time we are the quintessential American superheroes. In real life, I grew up with a dad who's a lawyer and a mom who's an engineer, and my knowledge of agriculture stops at realizing that corn grows upward. But to many people I went to school with, I was a trustworthy farm kid who knew the value of a dollar.

Like other Midwesterners, I am from Iowa, Ohio, Idaho, Illinois, and Indiana

GUNS 'N RELIGION GOTHIC

all at once. And living out East, I picked up on their not-so-subtle message that I was intruding.

When I once told a girl in class that I was from Iowa, she remarked, "Oh, no wonder you got into Penn."

Yes sirree! Though totally under-qualified, Penn just had to have *someone* from Iowa to broaden the life experiences for all of the New Jersey kids who deserved to be there.

"The Midwesterner by definition is a born audience member," wrote Jean Shepherd, the creator of *A Christmas Story*. "When in the outside world he feels he is eternally a guest, allowed only to participate in the proceedings because of the politeness of those around him, or because they aren't on to us yet."

And there is a lot to be on to. While the rest of America has kept up with the Kardashians, the Midwest has quietly racked up accomplishment after accomplishment with an army of intelligent, attractive, strong, and modest (which is tough to be when you're so intelligent, attractive, and strong) citizens.

The Midwest's history is among the worlds most fascinating. Our little region has produced people from Abraham Lincoln to Henry Ford. From Thomas Edison to Ernest Hemingway to Frank Lloyd Wright. You can thank us for the modern computer, modern science fiction, and modern furniture. For the skyscraper, the car, the airplane, the shopping mall, *Playboy*, McDonald's, Google, peanut butter, high-fructose corn syrup, mobility scooters, rock and roll, Anheuser-Busch, Alcoholics Anonymous, and the atom bomb. We've raised some of our country's most important figures, such as Neil Armstrong and Brad Pitt, and we've raised more presidents than any other region — the 2012 presidential race was between an incumbent hailing from Chicago, challenged by a guy raised in Michigan and his Wisconsin running mate.

The Midwest is a mystery, wrapped in a riddle, then deep-fat-fried and served on a stick at the Iowa State Fair.

From Superman to Johnny Carson, this delicacy of a region has always been at the center of America's greatness. Indeed, America's greatest accomplishments are Midwestern accomplishments, and America's greatest citizens hail from The Big Flyover.

THIS PAGE:
Jean Shepherd
raised in Hammond, Indiana

Abraham Lincoln
*raised in Perry County, Indiana,
and Coles County, Illinois*

Henry Ford
Greenfield Township, Michigan

Thomas Edison
Milan, Ohio

Ernest Hemingway
Oak Park, Illinois

Frank Lloyd Wright
Richland Center, Wisconsin

Neil Armstrong
Wapakoneta, Ohio

Brad Pitt
raised in Springfield, Missouri

Johnny Carson
Corning, Iowa

"The Midwest is a mystery, wrapped in a riddle, then deep-fat-fried at the Iowa State Fair and served on a stick."

"God is, at heart, a Midwesterner," remarked commentator George Will.

So there you have it. Not only is the Midwest God's greatest handiwork, but you shouldn't be surprised if you ever meet him and hear, "Hi there! God, from Sheboygan, Wisconsin. Boy, it sure is great to meet ya!"

By 2005, God's homeland was calling me from the East Coast. I realized that the region I'd left was the rich vein of creative material I was searching for. So I packed up my t-shirts and moved back to Iowa, opening RAYGUN in downtown Des Moines that fall. The company has grown over the years, assembling the greatest artistic minds that I happened to know or that happened to apply for jobs I posted on Craigslist. And what started as one person selling t-shirts on a street in New York has now grown into several people selling t-shirts *next* to a street in Des Moines - although from a comfortable, climate-controlled facility.

The Midwest is our primary source of material, and as we've concentrated on our home region, we've delved further and further into the mystery in which we live: What exactly is the Midwest? What are its borders? Why is it called the Midwest? What ties the people together? Why do we like Ranch dressing and Mountain Dew so much? Will we ever stop being so f-ing wonderful? Are we the final stop in human evolution's march to perfection?

In short: What makes this place tick?

Really, we can only give this our best shot. Calling the Midwest "God's gift to planet Earth" doesn't even do this place justice. Its greatness is hard to quantify, and even harder to describe.

But don't worry, NPR crowd: although New York, New Jersey, Pennsylvania, Massachusetts, and California all voted for Hillary Clinton in the 2008 primaries, 75% of the Midwest — including Iowa, Kansas, Nebraska, and Missouri — went for Obama, propelling him to later victory in the presidential race.

George Will
Champaign, Illinois

God
Sheboygan, Wisconsin

Hillary Clinton
Chicago, Illinois

NORTH DAKOTA
Grand Forks
Fargo
Bismarck

SOUTH DAKOTA
Pierre
CUSTER (John's vacay spot)

MINNESOTA
Duluth
Minneapolis
St Paul
JACKSON (Seth's hometown)
Sioux Falls
Rochester
Sioux City

Lake Superior
Great Lakes

Ishpeming
"THE U.P."
Sault Ste Marie
CORNUCOPIA
LAND O' LAKES
(Lucy's vacay spots)
Eau Claire
Green Bay
WISCONSIN

LEELANAU
(Mike's vacay spot)
MICHIGAN
Grand Rapids
Lansing
Ann Arbor
Detroit
Lake Huron
Lake Erie

Lake Michigan
Madison
Milwaukee

IOWA
Dubuque
Cedar Rapids
Iowa City
DES MOINES!
Chicago
Quad Cities
Peoria

NEBRASKA
Omaha
Lincoln

ILLINOIS
Springfield

Gary
Ft Wayne
INDIANA
Indianapolis

Toledo
Cleveland
Akron
OHIO
Dayton
Columbus
Cincinnati

MISSOURI
LAWRENCE
(Blake's hometown)
Topeka
Kansas City
Columbia
St Louis
Jefferson City

KANSAS
Wichita
Springfield
Branson

Ohio River

1.2 IS THIS HEAVEN?
NO, IT'S
THE MIDWEST.

Ah, there it is. The Midwest, in all its glory. Twelve states, some lakes, rivers, a couple of totally arbitrary borders that follow lines of latitude and longitude. It is a shape that says: I am strong, I am innovative, I celebrate REO Speedwagon's entire catalog. It brings a tear to your eye. It's not only beautiful to look at on a map, but it's beautiful to look at in real life.

"What geography can give all Midwesterners," writes Indianapolis-born Kurt Vonnegut, "along with fresh water and topsoil ... is awe for an Edenic continent stretching forever in all directions."

"Edenic" is an understatement. The Midwest isn't just "Edenic," the Midwest *is* Eden. The Bible's pretty fuzzy when it comes to details like why didn't Tyrannosaurus get on the Ark and where exactly was Eden?

That leads some to speculations: perhaps Mr and Mrs T-Rex got there right after departure and Mr T-Rex's little arms couldn't pry the door open. Perhaps Eden was the source of the Tigris and Euphrates.

Are you fucking high? You're saying that a Tyrannosaurus couldn't open the door because of his little arms? He could have just pulled the door to the Ark open with his giant death jaws! There has to be another reason he and his lady friend didn't set off on Noah's 40-day cruise.

And there is no way the Tigris and Euphrates could be the source of Eden. Those two rivers flow through a desert and have a combined average discharge of 48,381 cubic feet of fresh water.

The Midwest, by comparison, lies in the lush land that is not only between America's western continental divide along the Rockies and the eastern divide along the Appalachians, but North America's central divide, which goes right through the Dakotas, splitting north and south.

Water from this vast stretch not only flows through the Midwest, but water springs and flows out of the Midwest in all directions: the Red River of the North heading to the Hudson Bay, the St. Lawrence River flows east to the Atlantic, and the Mississippi River flows south to the Gulf of Mexico. Just those three Midwestern rivers have an average discharge of about 1.2 *million* cubic feet. That's about 25 times greater than the Tigris and Euphrates, and even twelve times greater than the

T-REX MISSED THE BOAT AND ENDED UP IN SOUTH DAKOTA
The largest T-Rex skeleton ever found was near Faith, SD

BETWEEN THE DIVIDES

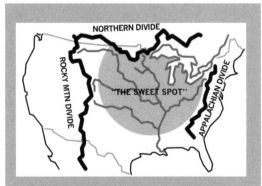

NORTHERN DIVIDE? Yessir! When you drive through the Rockies, the continental divide there really feels like a continental divide, with the peak of a mountain separating West and East. When you drive through the northern continental divide in the Dakotas, you'll pass a little road sign that doesn't even look like it's on the highest piece of ground within sight. But we're just going to have to take the geographers' word on this one.

discharge of the Nile.

And if 1.2 million cubic feet isn't enough for you, take note, the Midwest's Great Lakes hold more than 20% of the world's fresh water supply. That's 5,439 cubic miles of fresh water. If you're an American, that much fresh water not in petroleum-based plastic containers is tough to get your mind around. So to put it in a measurement you may be more familiar with, the Great Lakes is the equivalent of 4,168,181,830,000 liters of water.

This water, rich soil, and climate are so geared to agriculture that if you can't throw some seeds in the ground casually and grow something, then you're my wife.

Our dirt led to the agricultural dominance that we're most known for. Agriculture also gave us heavy industry: from John Deere's steel plow in 1837 to mechanized tractors, the Wright Brothers' airplane in 1903, and Henry Ford's mass production in 1908.

If the Midwest were its own country today, it would be the fourth-largest economy in the world, with a GDP just behind China, Japan, and Germany, and ahead of France and Brazil. That is with an extremely attractive population of only 67 million. Far smaller than China, Japan, or Germany. Meaning that of the top 5 economies, we would be tied with Germany for the second highest GDP per person.

Mid-west! Mid-west! Mid-west!

In the beginning, God handpicked a couple folks for this Eden, but not every Tom, Dick, and Harry could hack it.

Adam and Eve are prime examples of how *not* to behave if you want to stay in the Midwest. Eve was a gullible bitch who just had to have fruit from *every* tree. She was cast out and is now one of the *Real Housewives of Orange County*.

Her man-friend, Adam, wasn't much better. When God caught Adam in his fig leaf undies, this not-so-chivalrous dude tried to save himself by throwing Eve under the bus. "The woman whom you gave to be with me, she gave me of the tree." This "not-my-fault" fella was cast out and started working as an investment banker for Goldman-Sachs.

Those who remained and prospered in Eden are today's Midwesterners.

And in an odd combination of Darwin and Jesus (Jerwin? Darsus?), those Midwesterners have evolved into far more advanced, far more attractive beings. It's our defining quality. God's no slouch. He's not going to fill Eden with a bunch of homely bums. He's handcrafted every lady and gentleman himself, and sent them into a world with a certificate of authenticity that guarantees they will not go down in value.

Today, Hollywood doesn't just mine the Midwest for mysterious and handsome leading characters for its plot lines, it mines the Midwest for the chiseled features and glowing personalities of the actors necessary to play those roles. We are indeed certainly a sight to gaze upon: there's Harrison Ford, Don Cheadle, and Brad Pitt on the guys' side. Then Halle Berry, Cindy Crawford, and Christie Brinkley on the ladies' side.

The rest of the country has produced a few good-looking people. There's Massachusetts-born Matt Damon, Texas-born Eva Longoria, and ... hmmm ... wow, I'm blanking on a third ... Marlon Brando? No, he's from Omaha. Rock Hudson? No, he's from Winnetka. Terrence Howard? No, he's from Chicago.

The point is, if you need someone who's really really really ridiculously good looking, then you need someone from Team Flyover. Case in point, *Sopranos*-writer Matt Weiner created a screenplay for a show about fictional 1960s New York advertising agency, Sterling Cooper. At the center of the plot was Sterling Cooper's creative director, Don Draper, a man of genius, calm control, and chiseled features who needed to bed women across the greater tri-state area.

With so much riding on whom Weiner picked for this role, there was only one clear choice: St Louis native Jon Hamm. Weiner and director Alan Taylor had initially worried that Hamm was too handsome for the role of Don Draper, but as they say, "Go Midwest or go with some not-nearly-as-handsome person from another region."

PREVIOUS PAGES:
REO Speedwagon
Champaign, Illinois

Kurt Vonnegut
Indianapolis, Indiana

John Deere
settled in Grand Detour, Illinois, moved to Moline, Illinois

Wright Brothers
Dayton, Ohio

Harrison Ford
Chicago, Illinois

Don Cheadle
Kansas City

Brad Pitt
Springfield, Missouri

Halle Berry
Cleveland, Ohio

Cindy Crawford
DeKalb, Illinois

Christie Brinkley
Monroe, Michigan

Marlon Brando
Omaha, Nebraska

Rock Hudson
Winnetka, Illinois

Terrence Howard
Chicago, Illinois

Jon Hamm
born in St Louis, Missouri raised in Ladue, Missouri

With one Midwesterner secured, Weiner needed another to play Don's beautiful wife, Betty. So South Dakota's January Jones got the call.

In 2007, the show came to life as *Mad Men* on AMC, becoming one of the most critically acclaimed TV shows of all time. In its first four seasons, the show won four Golden Globes and fifteen Emmys, including Outstanding Drama Series four years in a row.

But *Mad Men* **isn't winning Emmys** just using the good looks of a few Midwesterners. What makes the show so successful is that the Midwest's overall mysteriousness is central to the plot. Don Draper's character grew up in Illinois in the 1920s. For people from New York, Illinois could be anywhere between Pittsburgh and the easternmost In-And-Out Burger.

For the other New Yorkers at Sterling Cooper, it's entirely possible that Don spent his formative years as a farmer or rancher or lumberjack or steel mill worker or all four at the same time while holding a pitchfork. A Midwesterner, at heart, must be good. You may not be able to put your finger on it, but having flashbacks to barns and horses and hay silently signals to the audience that this man can be trusted to do the right thing. No one who has been near hay can tell a lie. So while native New Yorkers on *Mad Men* lap up the drinking and adultery, there is a quiet tension, a goodness, about Don – he promotes the first female copywriter, he hires a black secretary, and he tries to put aside his hedonistic ways.

> "having flashbacks to barns and horses and hay silently signals to the audience: this man can be trusted"

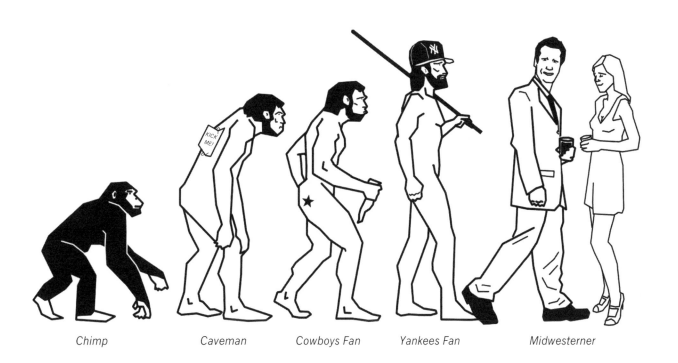

Chimp   *Caveman*   *Cowboys Fan*   *Yankees Fan*   *Midwesterner*

THE EVOLUTION OF THE MIDWESTERN MAN

POP QUIZ COASTAL FOLKS!
Fill in the Midwestern States and Cities:

1.3 **IDAWAHIO: HOME OF THE IOWA UNIVERSITY, OHIO CITY, IDAHO ... INDIANA? WHERE ARE YOU FROM AGAIN?**

There it is: The unfortunate reality we face in the eyes of so many. Toto? Idaho? Mittigan? Snow? C'mon! We're not getting the street cred we deserve. From a marketing standpoint, if you were in a nonprominent section of the country, a flashy name or marketing gimmick would help.

Kickassistan, perhaps. Or we could add some flashing lights and rename the place Girlsgirlsgirlsland. Or paint the whole thing bright yellow and call it Zero-Credit-Checks-Plus-You-Get-to-Keep-Your-Car-ia. At least we'd get to repo a lot of Trans Ams with that one.

But flashy names are not our forte. Confusing names are. I can't fault the folks who mixed up my state with others. (Except for the guy who told me, "You're not in Kansas anymore." There is simply no excuse for that.) I'll admit it: we don't make it easy for you to tell states apart. There are only two states in the country with four letter names where three letters are vowels: Iowa and Ohio.

Not only are both of those in the Midwest, but they are bookends for the longest vowel-covered stretch of real estate in the world. Ohio, Indiana, Illinois, and Iowa cover 900 horizontal miles, house more than 32 million people, but use only nine letters: A, D, H, I, L, N, O, S, and W.

Of those letters, vowels are used fourteen times, the consonants only nine times. Just I and O account for almost half of the letters. It's as though the early 1800s reversed *Wheel of Fortune* rules: vowels were damn near free, but consonants cost an arm and a leg.

Our overuse of vowels isn't the only thing that confuses. Our placement of cities can be haphazard at best. Michigan City is in Indiana. Kansas City is mostly in Missouri. The city of Indiana is actually in western Pennsylvania. Here in Iowa, while Dubuque sits in Dubuque County and Clinton is in Clinton County, we buck the trend and put Des Moines in Polk County and Des Moines County 140 miles to the east. Marion is a city in Northeast Iowa, but Marion County is in Central Iowa.

Then there's landform-induced confusion: Michigan is two big, noncontiguous peninsulas, the "Upper" and the "Lower." That doesn't seem particularly confusing until you're driving over the Mackinac Bridge

THE MIDWESTERN TRAIL

"WATCH OUT FOR THE DYSENTARY, NOW YA HEAR?"

GENERAL STORE

A FREE!	J OUTTA STOCK	S $2
B ONE LEFT!	K $7	T $1
C $7	L $1	U TWO LEFT!
D $2	M $4	V NO WAY
E $1	N $2	W $3
F $432	O FREE!	X OUTTA STOCK
G $14	P OUTTA STOCK	Y NO SIR
H BEST OFFER	Q $673	Z OUTTA STOCK
I FREE!	R $3	

"WHAT 'CHU THINK, MA? SHOULD WE STOCK UP ON THEM I'S AND O'S?"

"YUP, AND WITH THE MONEY WE SAVE WE CAN BUY AN EXTRA

SHOPPIN' AT THE GENERAL STORE

SPEAKING OF VOWELS:
Pat Sajak
host of Wheel of Fortune
Chicago, Illinois

from south to north, and are told that "upper" and "lower" are also the adjectives chosen to delineate sections of those peninsulas: you're heading from the *upper* Lower Peninsula to the *lower* Upper Peninsula.

What would make Michigan's Lower Peninsula seemingly unmistakable, though, is its uncanny resemblance to a mitten, with a "thumb" on the right side. But then along comes the state of Wisconsin, right across the lake, which also has a peninsula jutting out to the east that it calls "the thumb."

What? Look how thin that thing is! It's a pinky at best, Wisconsin! It's like you're just *trying* to confuse people.

But Wisconsin and Michigan don't stop at thumb confusion. Say you're looking for a city pronounced "Sheh·boy·gen." Well, you may be on your way to *Cheboygan* in Northern Michigan, or *Sheboygan* in Eastern Wisconsin. Sheboygan, Wisconsin, is just south of "the thumb," but in what may be a subtle message from Michigan, their Cheboygan is right on top of what would be the middle finger.

"OH HEY, IT'S ME, WISCONSIN. YOU — KNOW, THE STATE WITH THE 'THUMB' ON ITS EAST SIDE."

"YOU ASSHOLE."

THUMB CONFUSION

"Grand Rapids" puts you in either Grand Rapids, Michigan, or Grand Rapids, Minnesota (or the smaller Grand Rapids, Ohio). Wisconsin Rapids used to also be called Grand Rapids, but changed its name in the 1920s because it was so often being confused with Grand Rapids, Michigan. Grand Rapids, Minnesota, however, just charges along, not giving a shit if some of its mail ends up on the other side of the Great Lakes. If someone tells you to meet them at "Burger King in Grand Rapids" you may end up shoveling French fries in your mouth by yourself, 724 driving miles from your friend.

This geographic complexity may be the reason that in 1634, after arriving on the eastern shore of Wisconsin, French explorer Jean Nicolet was convinced it was China.

"Excuse moi, is this China?" he asked, adjusting his beret and ashing his cigarette.

"No, it's Sheboygan."

"Cheboygan? But I just sailed from Cheboygan. You people need to straighten out your place names if you want to gain national respect. This place is downright confusing."

"Sorry, man."

"It's not a big deal. Hey, do you know where a brother could find some American ladies who will fall for my French accent, striped shirt, and foreign cigarettes?"

When it comes to pronunciation, the Midwest sets the bar for confusing. Toledo (toe·lay·doh) is an ancient Spanish city; Toledo (toe·lee·doh) is on the shores of Lake Erie. But do you think we just have a thing against long "ay" sounds? Think again. Neva-

RAPID CITY

★ PIERRE

SIOUX FALLS

SOUTH DAKOTA: GREAT FACES AND GREAT ... OTHER STUFF

CAPITAL: Pierre **SIZE:** 77,116 square miles **POPULATION:** 824,082 **ADMISSION TO THE UNION:** November 2, 1889 **STATE INSECT:** Honey bee **IS THIS KANSAS?** Laura Ingalls Wilder settled in the Dakota Territory in 1879, when she was around 12 years old. She helped make the Dakotas famous when she later wrote *Little House on the Prairie,* but based it on her life in Kansas. On the flip side, L Frank Baum made Kansas famous when he wrote *The Wizard of Oz,* but based it off his life in Aberdeen, South Dakota, around 1888. **LEATHER:** Sturgis, South Dakota, has been home to a motorcycle rally since 1938, and now draws a collection of more than 500,000 leather jackets and mustaches annually. **SURPRISE! I'M FROM SOUTH DAKOTA:** Sparky Anderson, MLB manager who won the World Series with the '75 and '76 Reds, and the '84 Tigers, was born in Bridgewater, South Dakota. Other South Dakotans include January Jones, Sitting Bull, Crazy Horse, Hubert Humphrey, and Tom Brokaw.

da (nuh-vah-duh) gets you legal gambling and prostitution; Nevada (nuh-vay-duh) gets you a little closer to Ames, Iowa.

Pierre (pee-air) comes with a beret, cigarette, smug attitude, and a date-rapey style when picking up women. Pierre (peer) comes with the capitol of South Dakota. The odds of Pierre, South Dakota, date-raping anyone are pretty low.

"OH, EXCUSE MOI FOR STARING, BUT I CANNOT TAKE MY EYES OFF SUCH A BEAUTIFUL WOMAN. SO EXQUISITE! A WOMAN LIKE YOU SHOULD NOT BE DINING ALONE. MAY I JOIN YOU? HAVE MORE WINE. CAN I LIGHTLY PLACE MY HAND ON YOUR INNER THIGH? NO?! BUT YOU ARE SO BEAUTIFUL, I DO NOT WANT YOUR BEAUTIFUL THIGH TO BE CHILLY."

PIERRE (PEE-AIR), SD

Des Moines is mispronounced French that comes out "duh-moyn." Des Plaines is mispronounced French that comes out "dez-playnz." But almost no city can really top Beaucoup, Illinois. Pronounced "buck-up," it is the perfect blend of regionalized French and upbeat Midwestern attitude!

But above all of these small infractions, when it comes to locating our part of the world, our regional name doesn't do us any favors. If an American tells you they're from the East Coast or West Coast, or just from "out East" or West, you can mentally just travel either direction on the map and stop once you hit saltwater.

Because East, West, North, and South are all directions.

Midwest is not a direction. It's not even an in-between direction like Southwest or Northwest. It's an almost direction. Try to tell someone, "Just get in your car and head Midwest."

"What? You mean drive nicely and with a pitchfork?"

The most common explanation is that the Midwest is so named because it is about midway between the East Coast and the West Coast. But the term Midwest actually predates the full settlement of the West, and was not so much a regional term; rather, it was a term first used in the 1890s to describe Nebraska and Kansas, which were the "Middle West" at the time - the Dakotas being the "Northern West" and Texas being the "Southern West."

Much of what is now considered The Midwest – Ohio, Indiana, Illinois, Wisconsin, and Michigan – was originally called "The Northwest," since it grew out of the Northwest Ordinance in 1787, just outside the original thirteen colonies. This is why

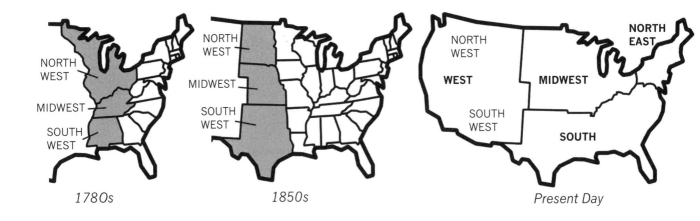

1780s

1850s

Present Day

Case Western University (formed on the site of the Western Reserve in 1826) is in Ohio, why the University of Michigan (founded in 1813) fight song proclaims the team "The Champions of the West," and why Chicago's Northwestern University (founded in 1851) is in the Central Time Zone.

By the 1880s, The West had shifted, and the edge of the country was along the line from the Dakotas to Texas. That's when "Middle West" really popped into the American lexicon.

But The West is a fickle slut, and as settlers moved all the way to the Pacific, California became the West, Oregon and Washington became the Northwest, and Arizona and New Mexico became the Southwest. Those lucky states on the ocean or the Mexican border never have to worry about their identifying direction leaving them for greener pastures (well, unless Mexico retakes Southern California and calls it Northwestern Mexico).

The middle of the country was left without a directionally based name. By the early 1900s, "Midwest" started to apply to everything from Kansas to Ohio.

It doesn't make sense to take a specific, small regional identifier and stretch it over a large area, but what else are we going to go with? For a while, much of the region referred to itself as the "Old Northwest," but that has an even more depressing connotation – the people who remained behind while everyone else went on. Wisconsin writer Hamlin Garland called the region the "Middle Border" in the late 1800s. In the mid-1800s, Ohio dropped the idea that it was Western and used "interior" and

Hamlin Garland
West Salem, Wisconsin

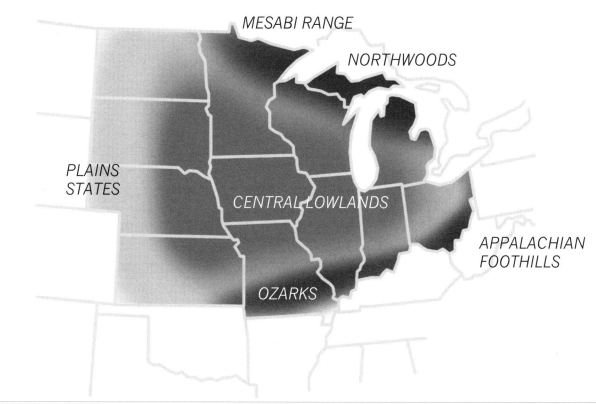

MESABI RANGE

NORTHWOODS

PLAINS
STATES

CENTRAL LOWLANDS

APPALACHIAN
FOOTHILLS

OZARKS

**FROM APPALACHIAN FOOTHILLS
TO THE PLAINS STATES**
The Midwest covers a range
of topography, from the
stereotypical Central Lowlands
to the Ozarks or Northwoods

"Great Lakes" as identifiers, but nothing seemed to stick.

"Central" is a more positive word for our location. Being "the center" of things isn't so bad. The center of attention. The central figure. Central to the plot. But even with "central," our region always has to be subjugated by something greater. You can't say, "I'm from The Central." "I'm from out Central." You'd have to say, "I'm from the Central United States."

The worst is "Middle America," or just "The Middle." These come with a vaguely derogatory connotation, because, deep down, there's something shitty about being "The Middle."

It's not really all that great to be in the middle of anything. In the middle of a custody battle. In the middle of the pack. What's worse than being nowhere is being in the middle of that aforementioned nowhere. The middle is often someplace you're in against your will –"Stuck in the Middle with You," for instance.

"I'M FINE RIGHT HERE IN THE MIDDLE. I FIND THE LACK OF LEGROOM AND MY NEIGHBORS' ELBOWS ON MY LAP TO BE VERY COMFORTING."

"ARE YOU SERIOUS? THEY LET THIS DIP-SHIT VOTE FOR THE PRESIDENT TOO?"

WOULD YOU TRUST A GUY WHO PICKED THE MIDDLE SEAT TO VOTE FOR PRESIDENT?

The middle seat is not choice seating. I mean, on an airplane, if the window or aisle opened up, who would say, "I think I'll stay here in the middle seat."

"Really?"

"Yeah, I find my neighbors' elbows in my face very comforting."

I wouldn't want to do business with someone who made those choices.

So when they ask, "But will this play in Middle America?" everyone on the Coasts knows they're really saying, "Those folks who can tolerate elbows in their face, even though they could leave the middle seat if they wanted, are at it again, voting for elected officials. God help us!"

In the end, "Midwest" won by default. But it has never had full commitment from all parties. The stretch from Ohio to Wisconsin often calls themselves "The Great Lakes States" or the "Upper Midwest." The stretch from Kansas to North Dakota call themselves "The Prairie States" or "Plains States." Missouri is a little more Southern than Midwestern, Oklahoma is more Midwestern than Southern, and Pittsburgh is economically and culturally closer to Ohio than to Philadelphia. Even a few years ago, Michigan native John Austin wrote a paper for the Brookings Institution that suggested rebranding the region as America's "North Coast."

With such identity issues, the Midwest's therapy bills must be sky high.

Some states have trouble identifying as "Midwest" because the term is more associated with the type of land you'll find stretching out in a wide band from eastern Ohio to eastern Nebraska. This land is green, rolling, agricultural, and not particularly dramatic – the whole state of Ohio has no point higher than 1,549 feet. It starts at the foothills of the Appalachian Mountains in Ohio and runs all the way to the dry land that starts sloping up toward the Rockies in Nebraska.

Corn and soybeans, corn and soybeans, soybeans and corn, cows, Mississippi river, more corn and soybeans, soybeans, corn, corn, corn, pigs, cows, corn, Missouri River, corn and hayfield, soybeans and corn, and on and on and on for almost twenty hours of driving. You'll cover more than 1,000 miles, and Eastern Nebraska will still look a lot like Eastern Ohio.

This is the stereotypical "Midwestern" stretch, with farms and white people and some cities that sound like where white farmers would take the Mrs. for a night at Applebee's: Lincoln, Omaha, Des Moines, Toledo, India-napolis, or Peoria.

Applebee's
*Headquartered in Kansas
City, Missouri*

Yet even within this main band there are heavily industrialized cities like Cleveland, Detroit, and Chicago – the third-largest city in the U.S. The northern border of the central lowlands gives way to the beaches and forests surrounding the Great Lakes.

As you head north, the population thins, corn and soybeans are replaced by evergreens and more evergreens, and lakes make their presence

**SOMETIMES A REGION
JUST NEEDS TO TALK**

"*I DUNNO DOC. I MEAN, WHERE DO I START? WHERE DO I END? AM I AN AGRICULTURAL REGION WITH INDUSTRY? OR AN INDUSTRIAL REGION WITH AGRICULTURE? SHOULD THE PLAINS STATES REALLY BE COUNTED AS MIDWESTERN? I THINK THIS ALL GOES BACK TO MY OVERBEARING MOTHER.*"

"*MM HMM, YES, I SEE.*"

MEOW MEO

felt in a big way (10,000 in Minnesota alone, the way their license plate tells it). Midwesterners call this region of northern Michigan, northern Wisconsin, and northern Minnesota, "Up North." The term "Up North" is so synonymous with going to your cabin, that here in the store we met a guy from Michigan who had a vacation place near Boyne, Michigan, and still called it "Up North," although he traveled southwest to get there.

Generally, most people in the Midwest like to head fairly straight north, so Iowa and Illinois go up to Minnesota and Wisconsin, Indiana and Ohio go up to Michigan. My grandparents grew up in small Iowa towns, but eventually moved to Southwestern Michigan, so "Up North" for us was at the family cabin in Leelanau County — Michigan's pinky.

Up there, the summer weather is perfect – with warm, humidity-free days, cooler nights – and the water is fresh. For people who haven't seen them, the Great Lakes are hard to believe. They are really vast, inland seas that can be just as volatile as oceans.

In *Moby Dick*, one of captain Ahab's most able sailors trained on the Great Lakes. In 1970, Ted Turner, founder of CNN, and "The Mouth From the South" — signed up to sail in the Chicago-Mackinac race. When told there was a chance of storms, he feigned fear and replied, "Yeah, I'm *really* scared." He didn't see that sailing on a "mill pond" was going to be much of a challenge.

But when a northerly gale started blowing more than 60 knots that year, 88 of the 167 boats dropped out, and the entire rigging on Turner's *American Eagle* fell into the water. "I publicly retract anything and everything I have ever said about inland sailing," Turner told his crew.

Great Lakes: 1. Ted Turner: 0. Your move, Dixie.

You can watch massive fronts roll across Lake Michigan from some of the nicest beaches in the world — smooth sand on cold, blue water. Forests, parks, trails,

Mike's Grandpa
Laurens, Iowa

Mike's Grandma
Chariton, Iowa

Ted Turner
Cincinnati, Ohio

**TED TURNER VS
LAKE MICHIGAN**

"YOU'RE JUST AN OVERGROWN MILL POND!"

"COME GET A TASTE!"

wineries, sailing, water skiing, Northern Lights, Euchre, bonfires.

I spent every summer living with my maternal grandparents in Leelanau, teaching sailing on Lake Leelanau and hanging out on Lake Michigan beaches. Having been to very few places beyond America, Canada, and Western Europe, I can say with absolute certainty that there is no better place in the world to be than Up North in the summer.

The farther north you go, the more rugged the terrain gets. By the time you hit northern Minnesota and Michigan's Upper Peninsula, you're in one of only two mountain ranges (technically speaking) in the Midwest — the iron and copper-rich Superior Upland that houses the Mesabi, Cuyuna, Gogebic, and Marquette Ranges.

The copper deposits in the northern Midwest are some of the oldest rocks in the world, dating back more than three billion years — three quarters of Earth's history. Rib Mountain in northern Wisconsin is part of this geological formation. It is home to one of the oldest ski resorts in the United States, and is composed of such hard rock — a quartzite resistant to erosion — that it split the southward marching glaciers. So while those massive piles of ice were walking all over Eurasia and the rest of North America, Rib Mountain said, "WTF, man? Go around."

If you head farther north in Minnesota, the increasing volume of Nickelback's shitty music tells you that you're getting closer to Canada and you'd better hang a left into North Dakota.

Fargo, North Dakota, with a population of about 100,000 not-particularly-famous residents and one very famous wood chipper, is, as a bridge over the Red River of the North explains, "the largest metropolitan area between the Twin Cities and Spokane." Yikes. So once you head west from Fargo, it'll be another 1,146 driving miles before you see another 100,000 people.

The land starts to dry out as you head west from Fargo. The cities look more Western — with saloon-themed bars and lots of freight trains.

The states from North Dakota down to Kansas are called the "Great Plains" or "Prairie" states. Their eastern edges have the green, lush, rolling hills watered by 16 to 32 inches of rain annually. But the western half of the Dakotas and Nebraska see 16 or less — "Sometimes it rains, and sometimes it doesn't." This area is home to The Badlands, a 244,000-acre national park made up of rugged carved rocks, rich fossil beds, and the largest prairie wilderness in the country.

Once you're down in Kansas, at the bottom of the plains, the landscape is flat and dry. This is where The Dust Bowl was centered and where tornados are an occasional method of travel. Kansas also straddles the fishy southern border of the Midwest, running along Oklahoma and over to Missouri, a state whose northern half is typically Midwestern, but whose southern half has the second mountain range in the Midwest: the Ozarks.

When it comes to vacationing, southern Missouri is kind of the exception to the Up North rule. With Table Rock Lake and the Lake of the Ozarks, a lot of folks from St Louis head south for their freshwater fix.

Paul Henning
Independence, Missouri

Andy Williams
Wall Lake, Iowa

This is hillbilly country. Literally. It's been documented. The Jed Clampett family made the term "hillbilly" world famous in *The Beverly Hillbillies*, and the Clampetts are said to hail from somewhere near Branson, since the show's creator, Paul Henning, grew up in Independence, Missouri. During the last 40 years, Branson has developed into a kind of redneck Las Vegas, with its own "strip." There's the Roy Clark Celebrity Theater, Andy Williams' Moon River Theater, Dolly Parton's Dixie Stampede, and permanent performances by Box Car Willie starting in 1987. The city hosts what they claim is "the largest Veterans' Homecoming celebration" in the country, "world-class festivals with special happenings" ("special happenings" must be a code the locals understand), and boasts 200 outlet stores in four malls for "shop-til-you-drop fun." Now, given how many old folks make it to Branson every year, I'd be cautious when hosting any "til-you-drop" events.

The Midwest is so big, it's the only region in the U.S. to cover three time zones — Eastern, Central, and Mountain — and the dialect moves from Southern in Missouri to alarmingly close to Canadian in northern Minnesota. One benefit of this is that we're good at math from having to subtract 1's from our TV programs' listed airtime.

MULTIPLE TIME ZONES REQUIRE MORE REFINED MATH SKILLS

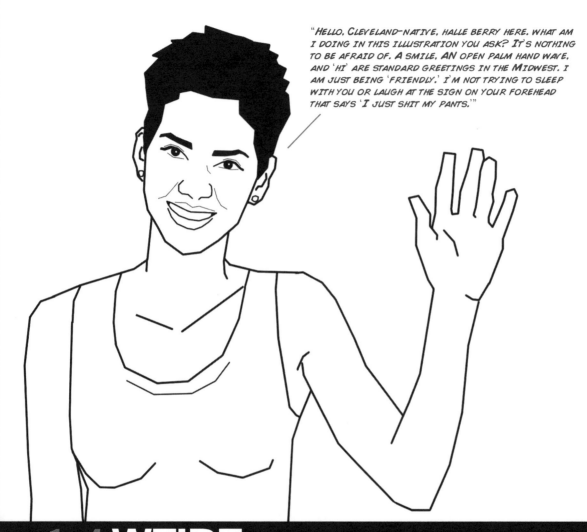

1.4 WE'RE SO F**KING NICE

Most people can tell just by looking at the smiles on our faces how happy we are. A New Yorker in Sioux Falls will get more smiles and friendly "Hellos" from strangers in South Dakota than he would get from his friends in New York.

It can be disorienting. Out-of-towners either think that every woman is trying to sleep with them or that there is a sign taped to their forehead that reads, "I just shit my pants."

We know we're lucky. I come from Iowa, but starting life anywhere in Eden puts you among the chosen few. In 1910, Wright brother Wilbur remarked that, to succeed in life you need to "pick out a good father and mother, and begin life in Ohio."

Now for the bad news. Although 67 million people are lucky enough to call this region home, almost 7 billion people live on Earth. So approximately 6.933 billion people wake up each day not living in Indiana or South Dakota or Michigan. To be faced with that every day? And the wave of disappointment that must come with it? No wonder there is so much war and unhappiness on the globe.

The Midwest gives some much-needed relief from the rest of the world. Now, it's hard to stereotype 67 million people, but since we are kind of rushing this book along and don't have money for excess pages, we use stereotypes pretty liberally. Still, while 100% of the people here in the Midwest may not be nice, by our estimates, it is about 99% of the population, with a 4% margin of error. So it may only be as low as 95% or it could be as high as 103%.

After our good looks, this niceness is what we're known most for. Little industries have popped up around this quality, with "Minnesota Nice" t-shirts, "Iowa Nice" t-shirts (like most things we in Iowa have, Minnesota claims to have thought of it first), and countless online handbooks trying to school the unfamiliar in "Midwest Nice."

Niceness in other parts of America isn't quite the same.

"SOUTHERN NICE: THAT'S A REALLY NICE JACKET. BTW, HAVE YOU FOUND JESUS?"

Robert Zemeckis
Director of Forrest Gump
Chicago, Illinois

Take Southern nice. When I was in Dallas with my wife, we were killing twenty minutes in a Starbucks one Sunday morning, waiting for their Museum of Art to open, when an old guy inquired about my camera and if I knew how to move photo files around on his computer. I set my pitchfork down and was happy to assist him.

He then sat down, started in on us with idle chit-chat, but within six minutes asked us if we had "found Jesus." At first I thought of Forrest Gump's "I didn't know I was supposed to be looking for him" reply, but instead just smiled, forgetting to say anything. "Are you Christians?" he persisted. I pondered my options.

Having gone to Penn, I can pass for a Reform Jew pretty easily (after one particularly wild night in Philly, I woke up with a yarmulke in my possession and still have it). But maybe he'd *really* try to convert me to help fill his monthly Jew-conversion quota needed to keep on track for triggering the Rapture. Having grown up Irish Catholic, I can say I'm Catholic without much trouble. And I figured this might be my best bet: church of Peter and Paul, the chosen few, kind of scary to Evangelical Christians but not going to get me into as much trouble as being a homosexual Muslim.

But when I told him I was Catholic, he pulled out his "How to convert a Catholic to Southern Baptism" playbook, telling me about how his Catholic friend's wife had an aneurism years before, and this Catholic friend asked our newfound Southern Baptist buddy to pray, because Catholic prayers only go to the Pope, but a Southern Baptist's prayers go straight to God.

I nodded. "I see," I thought to myself, "streamlining prayer delivery by cutting out the Papal middle man. I can see how this kind of thinking led the South to invent Wal-Mart."

So he prayed for his Catholic friend's wife, and guess what?! She lived! This not-so-surprising end (I mean, the direct-to-God hotline sales tactic has less power if the friend's wife dies) brought on the waterworks. Eleven minutes since sitting down with us, only five minutes after asking about our religion, he was at our table crying. In a Starbucks. At 10:55 in the morning. I was only halfway through my iced tea (but now *chugging* it).

I never thought I'd wish so much that the Dallas Museum of Art opened at 10:45 AM instead of 11:00 AM on Sundays.

Then there's West Coast nice. It's similar to Southern nice only it's slightly patronizing in tone. Instead of a niceness that masks a "come to Jesus" talk, West Coast nice comes with a large helping of consumerism or totally-out-of-touch dreaming.

While spending some time in LA, I mentioned to three different people that I had always enjoyed writing, and they told me that I should write a screenplay.

"You would do an awesome screenplay! You've got a great story, a great personality. Plus, I was at a party with my cousin, and her friend had just had coffee with Aaron Sorkin. Or his P.A. Whichever. But I can ask my cousin's friend to ask Aaron Sorkin's P.A. to look at the script."

After the first person told me something like that, I felt pretty good about myself: "Wow, though this person has only known me for twelve minutes and has never seen anything I've ever written, and doesn't even seem to have any practical connection to someone who can help me ... I'm going to win an Academy Award!"

By the third person, I thought maybe everyone in LA had called one another just before my plane landed and planned this massive, practical joke.

East Coast nice has a personality all its own, though. Its distinguishing feature is that it's not nice at all. I was once back in Philly for Penn's homecoming, and I stayed in the fairly upscale Sofitel downtown. At two AM I woke up to some ladies, locked out of their room, talking loudly in the hallway. I wondered if I should broach the subject with them. My Midwestern polite timidness took hold of me: How would I do it? What should I say?

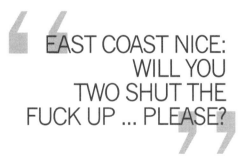

EAST COAST NICE: WILL YOU TWO SHUT THE FUCK UP ... PLEASE?

Then I heard the door across the hall open and a New York accent say, "Will you two shut the fuck up!? Please."

"It's good to be back in Philly," I thought.

Sofitel
First American location was in Minneapolis, Minnesota

"... YEAH THAT'S A COOL STORY BRO. BUT YOU'RE NOT IN KANSAS ANYMORE."

"YOU'RE LUCKY I'M FROM NEBRASKA. OTHERWISE I WOULD SLICE YOUR WEINER OFF RIGHT NOW."

YEAH, I KNOW I'M NOT IN KANSAS ANYMORE

L. Frank Baum
creator of The Wizard of Oz
*lived in Aberdeen, South Dakota,
and Chicago, Illinois*

Midwest nice is a true niceness. Not a pitch for conversion, not just adding a "please" after "shut the fuck up." Part of our niceness comes out of being genuinely happy with our lives. But part of it comes from having to build a steely exterior to brave the barrage of questions we get whenever we leave our region.

There is an upside, though, to coming from an unassuming state: people end up being a little nicer to you. Partly because you're being nice to them, but perhaps part is out of the same urge to speak slowly and softly to foreigners or mentally challenged kids.

As an Iowan, I got a lot of strange or geographical questions. But nothing like my Kansan compatriots. Even other Midwesterners stand in awe of the ability of a Kansas expatriate to hear, "You're not in Kansas anymore!" every time they tell someone where they grew up. They could say, "I know, *The Wizard of Oz* is 85 years old, one of the most famous movies of all time, Dorothy is from Kansas, and someone — I can't even fucking remember who — tells her she's not in Kansas anymore, and since I've been in Boston for the last 22 years you're about the millionth person to tell me that." But they instead just smile and say, "I'm sure not."

They may even be able to withstand follow-ups like, "Did you bring your dog Toto?" "Did you get here on a tornado?" "You didn't land on a witch, did you?" "Where's Auntie Em and Uncle Henry?"

To hear that for your entire life and not head to the top of a bell tower is almost beyond nice. It's a niceness wrapped in steel and dropped into an M-1 Abrams.

Midwest nice has an almost Zen-like serenity, a laidback air you expect on the West Coast more than the Midwest. People walk a little slower here. They take their time. Cooler heads often prevail. In 1857, just after the founding of Fergus Falls, Minnesota, a small log cabin served as a the post office. Since the German man appointed postmaster couldn't understand English, he didn't bother sorting the mail. Instead,

"When anything is going to happen in this country, it happens first in Kansas. Abolition, Prohibition, Populism ... the exit of the roller towel ... these things came popping out of Kansas like bats out of hell!" – William Allen White

TOPEKA ★

WICHITA

DODGE CITY

YOU *ARE* IN KANSAS ANYMORE

CAPITAL: Topeka **SIZE:** 82,277 square miles **POPULATION:** 2,871,238 **ADMISSION TO THE UNION:** January 29, 1861 **MOST FAMOUS KANSAS CITY THAT IS IN ANOTHER STATE:** Kansas City, Missouri **WE CAN REALLY BLOW:** Dodge City, Kansas, is the second-windiest city in America (behind only Blue Hill, Mass.) Goodland, Kansas, is eighth. **RIVAL:** Missouri. Ever since Kansas and Missouri literally slugged it out in the 1850s, these two states have viewed each other with suspicion. The KU/UM athletic rivalry is actually called "The Border War." And just like Bleeding Kansas in the 1850s, this one comes with a corporate sponsorship! **MOVIE THIS PLACE COULD DO WITHOUT:** *The Wizard of Oz.* It's been almost 100 years, people! Can we move on from the "You're not in Kansas anymore" thing? **STEVE DOOCY?** The guy on *Fox & Friends* who looks most like a talking penis is from Abilene, Kansas. **SURPRISE! I'M FROM KANSAS:** Steve Doocy aside, this state has some doozies for expatriates, like Dwight Eisenhower, John Steuart Curry, William S Burroughs, Charlie Parker, Amelia Earhart, Dennis Hopper, Don Johnson, Buster Keaton, Erin Brockovich, Jeff Probst, Wyatt Earp, and Bob Dole.

when bags came in, he would dump the mail onto the floor and let the locals find what was theirs. You would think someone would have pointed out that being familiar with the Latin alphabet would allow him to at least sort mail by name, but there's no record of complaint, and that guy kept his job for more than ten years.

Years later, during the Civil War, there was a pro-slavery newspaper editor named Mark Pomeroy in La Crosse, Wisconsin. After the assassination of Lincoln, a small mob formed to attack Pomeroy's offices, but along the way, they stopped at the bar for a beer, and after several drinks apparently forgot to go on.

In 1896, presidential nominee Ohio-born William McKinley reached a laid-back zenith as he conducted his "Front Porch Campaign." While his opponent, William Jennings Bryan, gave more than 600 speeches across the United States, McKinley never left his home in Canton, Ohio. Instead, he addressed people's questions from his porch (even taking Sundays off completely) and conducted daily phone calls with his campaign managers around the country. McKinley raised twice as much money as Bryan and won the election in a landslide.

Such level heads means millions entrust the Midwest with a crucial product: the greeting card. The Hallmark Company was founded in 1916 in Kansas City by Nebraska native Joyce Clyde Hall.

Hall and his brother were in the wholesale postcard business when they devised a plan to make cards with generic greetings for holidays and birthdays. Their Midwestern graciousness assisted generations of New Yorkers, who on birthdays could only manage to tell their loved ones, "Happy Birthday, Sweet-Cheeks, you gotta ass that won't quit, now make me a turkey sandwich, badda-bing!"

The Halls' laidback Midwestern temperament meant people in hot-headed, high-strung regions could get a calming

Hallmark card to smooth things over, instead of writing something like, "I'm sorry about our argument last night, I shouldn't have gotten that mad, but you shouldn't have pissed me off! You know I don't like it when you tell me how to get downtown when *I know how to get downtown*! I just like to go my own way! Who died and made you 'Queen of How to Get Everywhere and How to Drive?!' Fuck. Sorry."

The Hall brothers created an entire market, pioneered the use of the free-standing display rack, and helped give credence to dozens of bullshit holidays — literally called Hallmark Holidays — such as: Grandparent's Day, Boss's Day, Secretary's Day, and Sweetest Day.

Turning to the Midwest for advice goes back further than Hallmark. In the 1880s, St Louis' Eugene Field moved to Chicago and wrote the first newspaper advice column, "Sharps and Flats."

In 1936, Missouri's Dale Carnegie wrote *How to Win Friends and Influence People*. Buying a book about influence from a Midwesterner is a natural. It'll help you a lot more than 1935's Manhattan-based advice book, *Who Gives a Shit About Other People, We Gotta Move These Mortgage-Backed Derivatives if We All Want Bonuses This Year*. That one was less popular, but really ahead of its time.

GREETING CARDS FROM OTHER PLACES

SORRY I WAS LATE

BUT IT WAS FUCKING PACKED IN THE LINCOLN TUNNEL. THE CITY WASN'T ANY BETTER. THERE WAS GRIDLOCK ON 34TH. FUCKING NEW JERSEY PLATES EVERYWHERE! I DON'T KNOW WHY WE LET THEM INTO THE CITY!

NEW YORK

HAPPY WEDDING!

A WEDDING IS SUCH A BLESSED EVENT. WE WISH WE COULD HAVE ATTENDED YOURS, BUT WHEN WE SAW THERE WAS A NONDENOMINATIONAL MINISTER PRESIDING, WE JUST THOUGHT THAT WOULD BE CONFUSING FOR LITTLE ANNA BELLE AND PETER, AND WE HAVEN'T REALLY DISCUSSED HELL WITH THEM YET. CONGRATULATIONS!

ALABAMA

GRACIAS!

IF YOU CAN UNDERSTAND THIS CARD, THEN I'M AFRAID I NEED TO SEE PROOF OF YOUR CITIZENSHIP OR LEGAL STATUS.

ARIZONA

Esther and Pauline Friedman
Sioux City, Iowa

Both "Dear Abby" and "Ask Ann Landers" were penned by Iowa sisters Esther and Pauline Friedman in the 1950s. Their columns gave comfort to thousands of people over the years with simple, homespun — but not too preachy — advice. Contrast that with Brooklyn-born and Southern California-based Dr Laura Schlessinger. She has written such uplifting gems as *Ten Stupid Things Women Do to Mess Up Their Lives*, gives Bible-based advice, once used the word "nigger" eleven times during a radio show (because sometimes using the word "nigger" nine times just isn't enough!), and in the late 1990s battled a scandal involving nude photos of herself from the 1970s when she had been having an affair with a married radio mentor, Bill Ballance.

With advice-givers like Schlessinger, it's no wonder so many Californians opt for Prozac.

In the spring of 1999, Midwestern advice went global when Australian film director Baz Luhrmann took a *Chicago Tribune* column called "Wear Sunscreen" and turned it into a spoken-word song called "Everybody's Free (To Wear Sunscreen)." The song reached #1 on the UK's pop charts, #1 in Ireland, #8 in Norway, #10 in the U.S., #15 in Sweden, and by the end of the summer was certified Gold in the U.K. An impressive feat for a song that was merely a beat behind Australian voice actor Lee Perry reading the *Tribune's* column word for word.

"In Chicago's rich journalistic history," the *Tribune* wrote in March of 1999, "newspaper columns have nailed corrupt politicians, freed innocent prisoners and won Pulitzer Prizes. Not until this month, however, had one cracked the Billboard Hot 100 pop music charts."

Oddly, at the time, there was an urban legend that the advice was really that of an MIT commencement address by Indianapolis' writer Kurt Vonnegut. So when people hear some of the most inspirational advice of their time, they know it has to come from *somewhere* in the Midwest.

WE'RE ALMOST A PERFECT PARALLELOGRAM!

CAPITAL: Bismarck **SIZE:** 70,700 square miles **POPULATION:** 683,932. North Dakota's population peaked in 1936, and now only Vermont and Wyoming have fewer people. But Vermont and Wyoming blow. **ADMISSION TO THE UNION:** November 2, 1889 **STATE GRASS:** Seriously, 17 states have a "state grass." North Dakota's is Western Wheatgrass. **QUADRANGLE?** Not quite. That goddamn Red River of the North means Colorado and Wyoming are the only states with 4 right angles **MULCHED CRIMINALS:** Fargo, North Dakota, has been associated with humans stuffed in wood chippers since the Coen brothers' 1996 film, *Fargo*. But most of the movie's crazy shit goes down in Minnesota (typical). To date, no real or fictional people have been stuffed into wood chippers in Fargo or the rest of North Dakota. **BAD NEWS FOR PEOPLE WHO DON'T LIKE EXTREMELY VARIABLE WEATHER:** In 1936, North Dakota set America's record for widest temperature range in a single year, with a high of 121 and a low of *minus* 60. Fargo is the biggest city with the largest annual temperature variation (87 degrees). And in 1918, Granville set a record when it warmed 83 degrees (from *minus* 33 to 50) in only 12 hours.

1.5 THE MIDWEST: YOUR MOST TRUSTED NAME IN EVERYTHING

I watched a lot of TV as a kid, so memories of my youth involve a desire to create inspired by *Ren and Stimpy* plot lines, a sense of real introspection during particularly engrossing topics on *The Phil Donahue Show*, and a rush of utter elation whenever someone finally said "One dollar, Bob" on *The Price is Right*. So it's only natural that a rerun of *Magnum P.I.* in the late 1980s helped establish my sense of self as an Iowan.

In the episode, Magnum is hired by a lady to investigate a horse theft. She can only give him $100, but promises him $200 later.

"How can I be sure you'll pay me?" Magnum inquires.

"You know you can trust me," she replies, "I'm from Iowa."

And throughout the show, whenever Magnum doubts the situation he's in, or starts to think that maybe he's being double-crossed, he reassures himself by saying, "and besides, she's from *Iowa*."

It was like saying, "Of course my roommate couldn't have stolen my refrigerator by carrying it across the room and out the window. My roommate is *Stephen Hawking*, who is *wheelchair-bound* and almost *completely paralyzed* due to amyotrophic lateral sclerosis."

Trustworthiness is a hallmark of the Midwest, forever enshrined by "Honest Abe" Lincoln, and reinforced by "the most trusted man in America" through the 1960s and 1970s: Missouri-born Walter Cronkite. Through the assassination of JFK, the Vietnam War, and the oil embargo, America flailed. We needed someone to guide us. Cronkite's steady, Midwestern hand and his nonregional diction and accent were just what the doctor ordered.

The *CBS Evening News* was an American network's first nightly half-hour news program in 1963. It turned its anchor chair over to Cronkite. Through the 1960s, NBC put up Montana-born Chet Huntley and North Carolina-born David Brinkley, but this non-Midwestern duo didn't stand a chance. In 1970, NBC replaced them with Chicago's John Chancellor, who anchored *NBC Nightly News* until 1982.

According to Cronkite's biographer, Douglas Brinkley, Cronkite defined his medium. "If something quirky happened in Chicago or San

"WHAT THE HECK?! DID YOU STEAL MY FRIDGE, STEVE?"

"IT WAS NOT ... ME ... I DO NOT ... HAVE ... THE ... PHYSICAL ... ABILITY."

STEPHEN HAWKING COULDN'T CARRY A FRIDGE OUT, BUT HE DOES OWE A GUY IN ANN ARBOR $100
Hawking bet Michigan prof Gordy Kane $100 that the Higgs particle would never be found. It was found in 2012.

PREVIOUS PAGE:
Bob Barker
raised in South Dakota and Springfield, Missouri

Drew Carey
Barker's replacement-Cleveland, Ohio

Tom Selleck
Detroit, Michigan

Phil Donahue
Cleveland, Ohio

THIS PAGE:
Walter Cronkite
St. Joseph, Missouri

John Chancellor
Chicago, Illinois

Douglas Brinkley
Perrysburg, Ohio

Tom Brokaw
Webster, South Dakota

Gene Siskel
Chicago, Illinois

Roger Ebert
Urbana, Illinois

Francisco," he writes, "Huntley and Brinkley laughed. Cronkite, by contrast, *reported* that something funny had happened." That's what America *needed* back then. They didn't need some Montana/North Carolina dog and pony show, they needed Missouri in the worst way. Even Lyndon Johnson knew who was top dog after Cronkite delivered the damning "Report From Vietnam" in February of 1968. After that, Johnson reportedly said, "If I've lost Cronkite, I've lost the country."

That's why I stay on the Show Me State's good side, Lyndie.

In 1981, Cronkite stepped down, and the CBS spot went to Dan Rather, a Texan who decades later admitted (like most Texans) to using heroin and making up stories about George W Bush. At ABC, Canada-born Peter Jennings took the anchor's seat, and for people who liked getting American news from a Canadian, he did a pretty good job.

NBC, however, saw an evening news time-slot ripe for a Midwestern takeover. In 1982, they put South Dakota's Tom Brokaw in the saddle and never looked back. He shot to the top of the ratings and inherited Cronkite's mantle as the steady Mid-western hand at the wheel of American news.

Those were good years. While South Dakota was guiding American opinion on world events through the 1980s, Chicago made sure we were using our opposable thumbs to judge what we liked at the movie theater when Gene Siskel and Roger Ebert launched their show *At the Movies* in 1982. Their knowledgeable advice, humorous banter, and thumb-based rating system was such a success that the show ran through 2010.

And what America needed to listen to was directed by Detroit-born Casey Kasem, who hosted *American Top 40* until 1988 — and after that, *Casey's Top 40* until 1998. His smooth voice and winning personality belted out the hits, and he would end every show with a practical Midwestern yarn: "Keep your feet on the ground and keep reaching for the stars."

Today, sadly, New Jersey-born Brian Williams, Texas-born Scott Pelley, and Kentucky-born Diane Sawyer hold down the fort at NBC, CBS, and ABC respectively, which is why network news now drifts aimlessly, losing ground to Fox News and CNN.

MIDWESTERN ENGLISH:
THE TRUEST AND MOST PUREST VERSION OF ENGLISH.

Cronkite and Brokaw reinforce the idea that Midwestern English is the *real* American English. If you don't talk like us, well it's you that has the accent, Bub, because folks on TV sound like we do!

People from around the world call random Heartland phone numbers just to listen to our accent-less diction on answering machines. It's poetry.

But what exactly makes Midwestern English sound the way it does? That can be a little tricky. To the right are some mapped highlights for you.

Still, we can say once and for all that our terms are the correct terms, even if we contradict ourselves. So carbonated beverages can be pop, "vacation" can be "up north," ground squirrels can be squinnies, water fountains can be bubblers, port-a-potties can be kybos, "come with" can be "come along," "the" can be "dah," and "fuuuuuuck!" can be "uff-da."

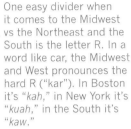

One easy divider when it comes to the Midwest vs the Northeast and the South is the letter R. In a word like car, the Midwest and West pronounces the hard R ("kar"). In Boston it's "*kah*," in New York it's "*kuah*," in the South it's "*kaw*."

In the Midwest, there are four main dialects: North Central, North, Midland, and Inland North. North dialect covers northern Iowa, southern Minnesota, and is standard "Midwestern." Midland is a little more southern, it still has the hard R but does have "cee-ment" and "dintist." North Central and Inland North start sneaking a Y-sound in, so rapids can be "*reeapids*" and car can sound a little like "*kyar*."

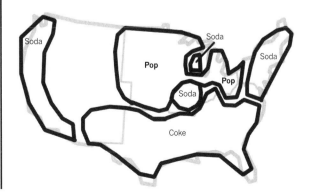

Handiest of all may be the pop versus soda, map, though. Almost the entire Midwest uses the word pop in place of carbonated beverage. For some reason, though, eastern Wisconsin and the St Louis area say soda. Southern Indiana, with its redneck tendencies, uses the Southern term, Coke instead of pop.

Siskel and Ebert no longer give out movie advice on TV, and pop radio is under the guise of Georgia-born Ryan Seacrest. Good luck, America.

Our honesty makes it easier to hire private investigators on credit and to anchor major network news shows, but there is a downside. That lady from *Magnum P.I.* only had $100 to give because she had been swindled out of the rest of her money by an unscrupulous uncle.

Damn our honesty-based gullibility!

We can be the honest friend in a time of need, or we can be the small-town tuna accepting a dinner invitation from the big city "Chicken of the Sea" can (and who was the model on that Chicken of the Sea can? Grace Lee Whitney from Ann Arbor, of course!).

In ABC's show *Don't Trust the Bitch in Apartment 23*, Chloe is the eponymous New York bitch who takes on roommates, charges them too much, then drives them so crazy they move out early, leaving their deposit.

When the show starts, Chloe is roping the perfect victim: June Colburn from Indiana. June is friendly, perky, has just moved to the city, and remarks that she once wrote a rap song at Christian camp called, "Jesus is Right, *Word*." Chloe describes June to James Van Der Beek: "She's just another small-town trusting doormat ... She'll be happier back in Ohio, or wherever."

The lesson here? Our trustworthiness gives us power, but it's also our kryptonite.

Even in the face of the overwhelming need to fib a little bit, we stand paralyzed: "Can ... not ... tell ... lie ... Trustworthy ... Midwestern ... disposition ... too much ... Being ... swindled ... by ... fast-talking ... Easterner."

This blind honesty is a historical quality that has both lost some of our expatriates some money, and undercut our marketing strategies. In 1838, Pierre "Pig's Eye" Parrant built a cabin

NOT SO FAST YOU INGRATES: PUBLIC NEWS TEAM IS TAKING A BREAK FROM ITS PLEDGE DRIVE TO KICK SOME ASS! With no commercials or bullshit filler, all PBS has is level-headed, well-written content. That doesn't get you very far in America, so they put a Midwestern face in the saddle to give the program a little sex appeal. In 1983, PBS added Jim Lehrer (Wichita, Kansas) to their news show, *News Hour*, and he carried the mantle until 2009.

WHY THE TRUSTING
MIDWESTERN
TUNA WENT EXTINCT

"OKAY, BUT YOU PROMISE YOU'RE ACTUALLY MADE UP OF SWIMMING CHICKENS?!"

"COME WITH ME, I HAVE SOMETHING I WANT TO SHOW YOU."

and store on the site of present-day St Paul. He decided to name the two-building town after himself. But he didn't pick Parrant or Pierre. Instead, he named the town Pig's Eye.

Welcome to beautiful Pig's Eye, Minnesota!

In a description of the town that a modern-day Convention and Visitors Bureau may want to avoid, it was said that Pig's Eye, "Had but three or four log houses, and was a mixture of forests, hills, running brooks, ravines, bog mires, lakes, whiskey, mosquitos, snakes, and Indians."

Fun for the whole family!

In 1841, after building and dedicating a chapel to St Paul, the city changed its name from Pig's Eye to St Paul.

There's no shortage of honesty in the Midwest. In 1881, Jesse Hiatt grew fantastic apples on his family farm in Peru, Iowa. They were juicy, they were big, and they were delicious. So what to call them? The Really Good Apple? The Fantastic Apple? No, Hiatt instead chose to call his new fruit, "The Hawkeye Apple." Sales were slim until he sold the rights to another company, which changed the name to: "The Delicious Apple." The Secretary of Agriculture at the time, Iowa-born Tama Jim Wilson tried one, and let the modesty train keep chugging when he proclaimed that he thought it was a "promising new fruit."

The Delicious Apple went on to become the mostly widely distributed apple species, and one of the most popular fruits in the country.

James Wilson
settled in Traer, Iowa

Apples
Michigan is now the country's third-largest producer of apples

1.6 YOU CAN'T SPELL "WIT" WITHOUT "MIDWEST"

"ON SCREEN, ON PAPER, OR ON STAGE, WE HAVEN'T JUST PRODUCED THE FUNNIEST PEOPLE IN AMERICA, BUT THE FUNNIEST PEOPLE ON THE PLANET."

From 1962 until 1992, Johnny Carson hosted *The Tonight Show*. During those 30 years, he taped 4,531 episodes, interviewed more than 23,000 guests, and was seen by millions of Americans every night. During his career, he was seen by more people on more occasions than anyone else in American history.

As Paul Block, *The Tonight Show*'s talent coordinator, recalls, Johnny walking onto stage, "was the coronation of the king over and over and over again. It was a show business cathedral and Johnny was the king. And he entered, and he got his royal greeting every time." He was imitated by contemporary comedians, inspired generations of comedians after him, and epitomized American comedy.

He was confident. One evening after walking out and letting the applause die down, Carson remarked, "Look, you don't have to stop, this is America, you have the right to worship."

But he was modest and allowed his guests to really shine. He wasn't always the center of attention on his show, and certainly wasn't the center of attention outside of his show. By 2010, the director Peter Jones had been trying for fifteen years to make a documentary about Carson. For the first eight years, his appeals to Carson went unanswered. In 2003, Carson finally called Jones to tell him, "You write a damn fine letter, Peter, but I don't have anything more to say." Only after Carson's death in 2005 did his family agree to let Jones film, worrying that Carson would be forgotten.

The final part of Carson's style was his short, dry wit. It wasn't obscene or over the top, but cool. When talking about a study that explained how to find your life expectancy, Johnny set up the joke by noting that the researchers have someone start at 72. From there, if you're a man, you subtract three. Women add four. "That's right," Johnny says, "apparently, women on average live longer than males. Now, it says that if you live in a big city and your next-door neighbor is a doctor, add three years. If you live in the Midwest and your next-door neighbor is a quiet man who always keeps to himself, subtract fifteen years."

This style wasn't one that Carson necessarily invented, although it's one that pervades the Midwest. Born in Corning, Iowa, in 1925 and raised in Norfolk, Nebraska, Carson is part of a long line of Midwestern wit. Carson's dry wit can be seen almost 70 years earlier in the writings of Missouri's Mark Twain.

Born in 1835, Twain grew up in Hannibal before the Midwest was fully formed, before "Midwest" was even in use. Yet the region Twain grew up in has much in common with the modern Midwest. Even then, it was as much something to pass through as it was a destination. With north-south traffic along the Mississippi River and east-west traffic along trails, Twain hailed from an ignored section of the country. He thought the other regions, especially the East, held themselves in higher regard, writing in 1869, "Tomorrow night I appear for the first time before a Boston audience — 4,000 critics."

He observed a wide swath of life, and he was the first significant example of short, Midwestern wit.

Twain's style was emulated by many outside the Midwest. It came out through Midwestern writers such as James Thurber, Calvin Trillin, and Garrison Keillor. In the 1990s, when *The Paris Review* devoted an entire issue to humor, it picked three living writers it believed put the best humor on paper, and two — Trillin and Keillor — were Midwestern.

Even Twain relied on other Midwesterners to flesh out his style. His editor, William Dean Howells, helped craft Twain's stories and advanced his writing career as an editor of *The Atlantic* and *Harper's*.

Howells had a feel for humor, similar to Twain, and their observations continue through today. Twain's comment that, "Clothes make the man – naked people have little or no influence in society," is part of a line that carries on all the way to Iowa and Nebraska-born and -bred Johnny Carson, who observed, "For days after death, hair and fingernails continue to grow, but phone calls taper off."

Traditional Midwestern humor focuses less on regional stereotypes used in Southern humor, and the rapid delivery of Northeastern humor. Instead, Midwestern humor is a mix of self-deprecation, slight sarcasm, and deadpan delivery.

It is common throughout conversation and jokes across the region. When writer Roger Welsch remembered visiting the small town of Dannebrog, Nebraska; he

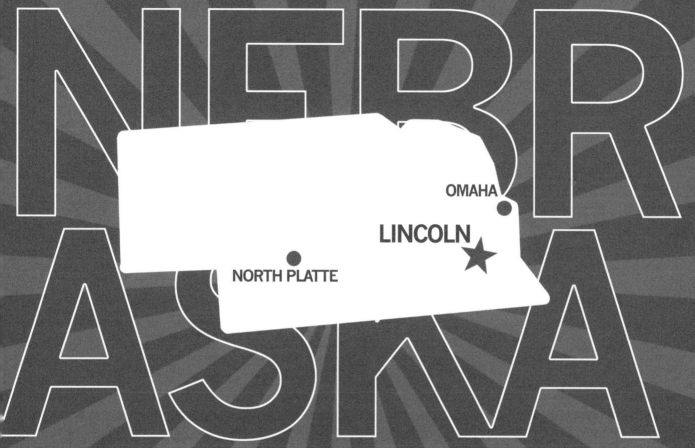

L RON HUBBARD TESTED, MARLON BRANDO APPROVED!

CAPITAL: Lincoln **SIZE:** 77,354 square miles **POPULATION:** 1,842,641 **ADMISSION TO THE UNION:** March 1, 1867 **STATE BEVERAGE:** Milk. **SLOGAN:** Nebraska, possibilities ... endless. **YOU MIGHT REMEMBER ME FROM OREGON TRAIL:** Fort Kearny, Chimney Rock **BEST ALBUM CALLED "NEBRASKA" BY A GUY FROM NEW JERSEY:** *Nebraska* was a 1982 Bruce Springsteen release. During the recording sessions, Springsteen demo'd "Born in the U.S.A." **SERIOUSLY, ALL THESE WERE BORN IN NEBRASKA?** Yup, and it's quite a list. L Ron Hubbard, Malcolm X, Gerald Ford, Marlon Brando, Crazy Horse, Fred Astaire, Bright Eyes, and Wade Boggs. **HARDEST PART FOR A COUPLE OF GUYS FROM IOWA WRITING ABOUT NEBRASKA:** Saying nice stuff about Nebraska.

MIDWESTERN COMEDIANS AND HUMORISTS THROUGH THE YEARS

On screen, on paper, or on stage, we aren't the funniest people in America, we're the funniest people on the planet.

Mark Twain (Florida, Missouri)

William Dean Howells (Martins Ferry, Ohio)

George Ade (Kentland, Indiana)

Finley Peter Dunne (Chicago, Illinois)

James Thurber (Columbus, Ohio)

Jack Benny (Chicago, Illinois)

Buster Keaton (Piqua, Kansas)

Langston Hughes (Joplin, Missouri)

Bob Hope (raised in Cleveland, Ohio)

LaWanda Page (Cleveland, Ohio)

Jean Shepherd (raised in Hammond, Indiana)

Redd Foxx (St Louis, Missouri)

Ed McMahon (Detroit, Michigan)

Johnny Carson (Corning, Iowa)

Bob Newhart (Oak Park, Illinois)

Gene Wilder (Milwaukee, Wisconsin)

Calvin Trillin (Kansas City, Missouri)

Lily Tomlin (Detroit, Michigan)

Roy Blunt, Jr (Indianapolis, Indiana)

Richard Pryor (Peoria, Illinois)

Garrison Keillor (Anoka, Minnesota)

Gilda Radner (Detroit, Michigan)

David Letterman (Indianapolis, Indiana)

P.J. O'Rourke (Toledo, Ohio)

John Belushi (Wheaton, Illinois)

Bill Murray (Wilmette, Illinois)

Robin Williams (Chicago, Illinois)

Al Franken (raised in St Louis Park, Minnesota)

Tom Davis (St Paul, Minnesota)

Tim Allen (raised in Birmingham, Michigan)

Bernie Mac (Chicago, Illinois)

Drew Carey (Cleveland, Ohio)

Tim Meadows (Highland Park, Michigan)

David Spade (Birmingham, Michigan)

Chris Farley (Madison, Wisconsin)

Jim Gaffigan (Chesterton, Indiana)

Andy Richter (Grand Rapids, Michigan)

Seth Meyers (Evanston, Illinois)

looked down the quiet main street and asked a local, "What do you folks do in this town for excitement?" The local replied, "We don't get excited in this town."

When Michigan's license plates used to call the state a "Winter Wonderland," Michiganders would tell a joke about a visitor who asked a local what they did in the summer. "If it falls on a Sunday," the local would answer, "we have a picnic."

Even in the book *Methland*, Nick Reding recounts a story of a meth addict who was cooking his amphetamine in a pop bottle attached to his bicycle. While he waited for it to finish, he decided to occupy his time by taking apart and putting back together the bicycle. This caught the attention of neighbors, who called the police. "A Fayette County sheriff's deputy pulls up," writes Reding. "The boy asks the deputy why he stopped. 'I got a call,' says the deputy in the bone-dry wit endemic to the Midwest, 'that you needed to borrow a screwdriver.'"

Nick Reding
St. Louis, Missouri

Bob Hope
raised in Cleveland, Ohio

Bob Newhart
Oak Park, Illinois

I've grown up surrounded by Midwestern humor, but so has most of America. Nearly all of the great American comedians hail from the Midwest. Carson shared the stage with contemporary greats like Bob Hope and Bob Newhart, and he helped inspire the likes of Bill Murray and David Letterman.

Midwestern humor has also had a major impact on today's comedic land-scape. David Letterman is straight from the Midwest, and both *The Daily Show* and *The Colbert Report* have ties to Midwestern humor.

The Daily Show's current host, Jon Stewart, took over hosting from Craig Kilborn in 1999. At the time, Stewart had trouble trying to change the direction of the show, but noted that things "started to take shape" when he was joined by Ben Karlin and David Javerbaum, who had both written for *The Onion,* a satirical newspaper founded in Madison in 1988 by two students at the University of Wisconsin.

For the first several years, *The Onion's* reach was limited to Madison, Milwaukee, Chicago, and the upper Midwest. Their popularity expanded in the late 1990s, becoming a major force in comedy writing, though it moved much of its operation to New York City.

In 2012, after becoming less funny out East, *The Onion* decided to move back to the Midwest, putting its entire operation in Chicago, and bringing back founding editor Scott Dikkers. Dikkers thought the comedic talent pool would be better in Chicago where writers would be "younger and hungrier" than those in New York. "In Madison," he said, "people used to just come in off the street and we'd give them a shot."

But of *The Onion's* sixteen writers in New York, only five agreed to move to Chicago. *The Atlantic Wire* dubbed these eleven holdouts "refuseniks," one of whom said he had, "Nothing against Chicago. I think it's a great town. But we're here in the center of everything." *The Onion* itself parodied the hoopla over moving to the No Coast by having its fictitious publisher, T Herman Zweibel, pen a column titled, "I'm Moving This Miserable Periodical to the Yukon."

Chicago may be a comedic backwater to New Yorkers, but its famous improvisational group, The Second City, produced almost the entire original cast for *Saturday Night Live* along with later greats such as Madison-born Chris Farley, Pennsylvania-born Tina Fey, and *The Colbert Report's* South Carolina-born host, Stephen Colbert.

It's one of those ironies that a region thought of mostly for its modesty and soft-spoken nature can also exude such comedic confidence. Our great comedians don't

Bill Murray
Wilmette, Illinois

David Letterman
Indianapolis, Indiana

Craig Kilborn
born in Kansas City, Missouri, raised in Hastings, Minnesota

Chris Farley
Madison, Wisconsin

flinch. Compare New York's Jay Leno to David Letterman.

In 2009, when Leno gave *The Tonight Show* to Conan O'Brien and then took it back, he got some flack in the media and turned into a crybaby, complaining to Oprah that Jimmy Kimmel "sucker punched" him when Kimmel made a joke about it on Leno's show.

Later in 2009, Letterman faced his own scandal: he had been cheating on his wife with an intern at the show. A *48 Hours* producer tried to blackmail him with this information, setting off a weekend-long media firestorm about how many employees Letterman had slept with, the nature of the blackmail investigation, and the feelings of his wife. The following Monday, Dave started the show by pacing for a little bit, then slowly asking the audience: "Did your weekend just fly by?"

That's not to say that we can't be introspective. We can be downright philosophical. You don't think of the Midwest for philosophy. Europe keeps a few big hitters on deck: there's Prussia's Immanuel Kant, subject of many a boring Ivy League dissertation; there's Czech Sigmund Freud, who did enough cocaine to kill a small horse and speculated that all young men wanted to have sex with their mothers and hated their fathers because of jealousy (too true!); and the German Friedrich Nietzsche, whose musings on nihilism in the late 1800s inspired such productive minds as Adolf Hitler.

Ah, Hitler, who *wouldn't* want to have inspired him?

These guys cooked up some pretty bizarre ideas. They also took a reeeeaaaaaaaalllly long time to get to the point. Take Nietzsche: his frustration with society led him to try to describe nihilism in his work *Will to Power*. "A nihilist is a man who judges of the world as it is that it ought not to be, and of the world as it ought to be," blah blah blah, "Our existence — action, suffering, willing, feeling — has no meaning," yadda yadda yadda, "At the same time, as pathos," and on and on and on. You know the drill: Dad didn't like him, angry at the world, cue World War One, cue Hitler, cue a bunch of angry college kids reading *Beyond Good and Evil* because it's short and because being seen reading it will help them get other angry college kids in the sack.

Midwestern philosophy summarizes a dissatisfaction with life in a lot fewer words: "I love mankind; it's people I can't stand."

So spoke Charles Schulz, who created *Peanuts* and, along with *Calvin and Hobbes'* creator Bill Watterson and filmmaker John Hughes, is one of the Midwest's most famous philosophers.

Midwestern philosophy is short, witty, and more solution-oriented. In 1889, Nietzsche's dissatisfaction with life led him to try to save a horse that was being flogged in Turin, signaling his mental breakdown and pending death. Schulz, on the other hand, offered a solution to issues with the world: "I think I've discovered the secret of life — you just hang around until you get used to it."

Nietzsche could have used a little advice from Charlie Brown.

Like the distinguished philosophers before them, these three address a range of topics. Watterson takes on war in a short exchange between Calvin and Hobbes when they each don their army helmets and Hobbes inquires, "How come we play war and not peace?" Calvin replies, "Too few role models."

And in *Ferris Bueller's Day Off,* Hughes offers some of the best life advice ever to hit Hollywood: "Life moves pretty fast. If you don't stop and look around once in a while, you could miss it."

DON'T FEAR THE F WORD: Yet the reach of Midwestern humor is even wider than dry wit. It's hard to have anything funny in this country without having some Midwesterner at the root of it somewhere. Milwaukee-born Gene Wilder starred in such classics as *Blazing Saddles, The Producers,* and *Young Frankenstein* in the '60s and '70s before teaming up with fellow Midwesterner Richard Pryor (Peoria, Illinois) for the 1975 *Silver Streak.*

A pioneer in over-the-top humor who was born in 1940, Pryor influenced a wide range of American comedians, from Eddie Murphy and Chris Rock to Louis CK and Denis Leary. But Pryor wasn't an anomaly in Midwestern humor. He represented another strain that developed with St Louis-born Redd Foxx and Cleveland-born LaWanda Page, who spent the 1940s entertaining in nightclubs before starring together in the influential 1970s sitcom *Sanford and Son.* After Foxx, Page, and Pryor came Chicago's Bernie Mac and Robin Williams, and Detroit's Lily Tomlin and Gilda Radner.

PREVIOUS PAGE:
Oprah Winfrey
raised in Milwaukee, Wisconsin,
settled in Chicago, Illinois

THIS PAGE:
Charles Schulz
St Paul, Minnesota

Bill Watterson
Chagrin Falls, Ohio

John Hughes
born in Lansing, Michigan,
raised in
Grosse Pointe, Michigan,
and Northbrook, Illinois

Ferris Bueller's Day Off
was John Hughes' "Love Letter to
Chicago," he said

Alan Ruck
Ferris Bueller Costar
Dayton, Ohio

1.7 WHERE THE WOMEN ARE STRONG? YOU BET YOUR ASS IT IS. EVEN OUR FICTIONAL FOLK LEGENDS ARE STRONG.

You can tell a lot about people through their myths and folklore. In Greek mythology, Zeus is the papa bear. He was born into the dysfunctional family of all dysfunctional families: his father, Cronus, ate his children as soon as they were born, fearing a soothsayer's prediction that one of his kids would overthrow him. Though all powerful, Cronus apparently couldn't invent a condom, which could have drastically reduced the rate of euthanasia-by-ingestion in ancient Greece.

Zeus was saved by his mother, Rhea, who swaddled a stone and gave that to Cronus to swallow.

Like Nixon, Cronus found out that just because you're paranoid doesn't mean they're not after you: When Zeus reached manhood he challenged his father, forced him to disgorge the stone — *and* all of his siblings, who subsequently overthrew Cronus and his Titan buddies.

Once in charge, Zeus laid around (and I mean *laid* around) Olympus, fathering children with an estimated 23 women—goddesses, nymphs, even mortals. But this was no ancient *Big Love:* his wife, Hera, was a jealous broad with a temper. Once, Zeus had to enlist a nymph named Echo to distract Hera by talking incessantly while he shacked up with some side action. When Hera found out, she took away Echo's voice and forced her to spend eternity repeating others.

With role models like this, it's no wonder a few thousand years later, in 2010, the Greek people would borrow heavily and not pay taxes, leading to a downgrade of their bonds to junk status that helped bring financial panic to Europe. The Organization for Economic Cooperation and Development estimates that the Greek black market is over 25% of its GDP, and Transparency International found that almost 15% of Greeks had admitted to paying cash bribes, totaling 1.75% of the Greek GDP.

Maybe if Zeus had kept it in his pants and stuck to just controlling the weather and conducting board meetings with the other gods, things would have played out differently.

For the Midwest, our mythological figure is a reflection of the people:

"THE NAME'S ZEUS. I'VE BEEN KNOW TO SLAY A NYMPH OR TWO AND I OCCASIONALLY SLIDE ON MY TAXES. BUT IT'S FINE. I'M SURE GERMANY CAN BAIL MY BROKE ASS OUT."

WITH GODS LIKE THESE, DUDE ...

James MacGillivray
settled in Oscoda, Michigan

William Laughead
settled in Minneapolis, Minnesota

Paul Bunyan. This wholesome folk legend was born out of the logging communities in the upper Midwest and has Midwestern strength and work ethic in the place of Zeus's disconcerting sex addiction. This large-yet-modest man didn't kick it on top of a mountain eating grapes and letting his junk hang out. He wore blue jeans, a flannel shirt, and carried around an axe that he needed for his day job of logging — only a Midwestern semi-deity has a full-time job. He doesn't have a flashy steed like the Northeast's Headless Horseman or a souped-up Dodge Charger like the South's Dukes of Hazzard. Instead he has Babe the Blue Ox, a neutered bull used only for towing and hauling — like a superhero with a Ford F-350.

Unlike Zeus' rough childhood on the wrong side of Mount Olympus, the oversized baby Paul Bunyan was brought to his parents by five storks. When he was seven months old, the itch to be productive took hold of him, and he started using a saw — beginning with the legs of his parents' bed.

When he got older, he created the Grand Canyon by dragging his axe along the ground. The Great Lakes were Babe's watering hole; Minnesota's 10,000 lakes were the footprints of Paul and Babe wandering in a blizzard. Paul even created Mt Hood by stacking stones on top of a campfire he needed to extinguish — Smokey the Bear would have been so proud.

In 1910, Michigan writer James MacGillivray brought Bunyan to life in his story, "The Round River Drive." In 1914, William Laughead took Bunyan to a grand scale when Minneapolis' Red River Lumber Company hired him to create drawings and stories based on Bunyan's life for a public relations campaign.

Since then, Bunyan's image has popped up around the country, but most famously in the Midwest. Statues of him with Babe the Blue Ox in Bemidji, Minnesota, are on the National Register of Historic Places; Paul Bunyan Land is an amusement park near Brainerd, Minnesota; and August 10, 2006, was named "Paul Bunyan Day" in Michigan.

There is something to be said for a region that idolizes a man whose claim to fame is that he can work faster than others, and that he cruises around with his ox.

Then there are the hot summers and cold winters. Minnesota sees an annual range of about 130 degrees; the record was set by North Dakota in 1936, when the thermometer hit 120 degrees and minus 60 in the same year.

Almost all the Midwest falls under the Koppen-Geiger's "Humid Continental Dfa" climate classification — marked by year-round precipitation and summers with average temperatures above 71.6 degrees. The Midwest is the largest region of this kind in the world. Similar climates are found only in Pennsylvania, part of southern Russia, and parts of Japan. So while many areas complain about their harsh climates, we have scientific proof. If the humid summers don't get you, the ungodly cold winter will.

This kind of weather sorts the Midwesterners from everyone else. It leads to a heartier group of natives. Or, as Clint Eastwood's character remarks in the Detroit-based movie *Gran Torino:* "You'd think the cold would keep all the assholes away."

For the most part, it seems to. The New York-based band The Mamas and The Papas sang in "California Dreamin'" that "All the leaves are brown/and the sky is gray." That forces those Godless folksters into a church to get down on their knees and "pretend to pray." Boo-fucking-hoo. If autumn forced them into a church, a winter in International Falls, Minnesota, would have turned them into Southern Baptists.

But after living here, people form a strange bond with the weather. It changes so drastically that there's always something to complain about. Watching thunderstorms is as exciting for us as looking out over the ocean. And faced with one of the most mysterious of all natural disasters — the tornado — we've

WE ARE SURVIVORS, WE'RE NOT GONNA GIVE UP. *Our toughness doesn't run out after our folk heroes. It trickles allllll the way down.*

Survivor (Chicago, Illinois) Do we know a thing or two about survivin'? Please, we not only possess the "eye of the tiger," we wrote the gol-dang song on it. The Chicago-based band Survivor formed in 1978 and scored their first Top 40 single with "Poor Man's Song." When Sylvester Stallone heard that song, he contacted the band about writing one just like it for *Rocky III* (Stallone had wanted Queen's "Another One Bites the Dust," but was denied permission). Survivor whipped up "Eye of the Tiger," which has since moved two million vinyl copies, three million digital downloads, and been sung badly by at least six million breathless people after running up Philly's Art Museum steps.

Jeff Probst (Wichita, Kansas) The man who puts the survivor in *Survivor,* Probst has been hosting the reality show since it first aired on CBS in 2000.

John Wayne (Winterset, Iowa) The "Most Interesting Man in the World" is apparently not from the Midwest. He is Jonathan Goldsmith from New York. However, the guy who "shot" Goldsmith in the face for "seven painful takes" in *The Shootist* is John Wayne.

Dick Butkus (Chicago, Illinois) NFL Films ranked this Illinois-lifer first in *The NFL's 100 Toughest Players.* Though the 1969 Bears team he played for went 1-13, *Sports Illustrated* did call him "The Most Feared Man in the Game" in 1970. Unfortunately the rest of the team wasn't particularly intimidating.

Annie Oakley (North Star, Ohio) Born in 1860, Annie grew up in poverty, learning to trap and shoot in the wilds of Ohio as a girl. By 1885 her shooting skills were so well known that she joined Buffalo Bill's *Wild West Show,* touring the world and even shooting the ash from the cigarette of Germany's Kaiser Wilhelm. After the outbreak of the First World War, Oakley sent a letter to the Kaiser requesting a second shot. He declined.

Elliot Ness (Chicago, Illinois) In the late 1920s, Ness was tapped by the FBI to assemble a team to tackle Chicago's organized crime. Ness' team, "The Untouchables," eventually helped bring down Al Capone, and Ness survived numerous attempts on his life.

Neil Armstrong (Wapakoneta, Ohio) You don't get to the moon by being a crybaby, and once you've been there, you know how to keep yourself composed. In 1979, while working on his farm near Lebanon, Ohio, Armstrong lost the tip of his finger in an accident. He calmly collected the piece, packed it in ice, and drove himself to the hospital to have it reattached.

MIDWESTERN WEATHER:
AS USUAL,
IT'S JUST US,
JAPAN, AND KAZAKHSTAN

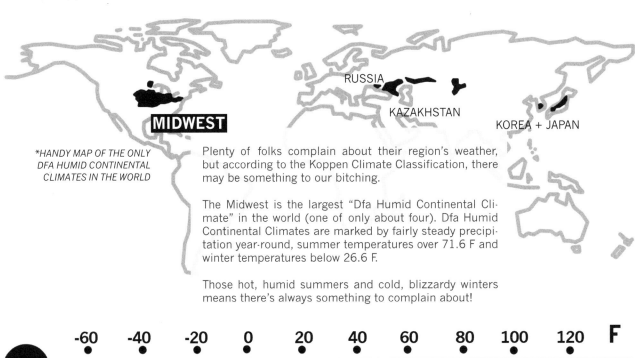

RUSSIA

KAZAKHSTAN

KOREA + JAPAN

MIDWEST

**HANDY MAP OF THE ONLY
DFA HUMID CONTINENTAL
CLIMATES IN THE WORLD*

Plenty of folks complain about their region's weather, but according to the Koppen Climate Classification, there may be something to our bitching.

The Midwest is the largest "Dfa Humid Continental Climate" in the world (one of only about four). Dfa Humid Continental Climates are marked by fairly steady precipitation year-round, summer temperatures over 71.6 F and winter temperatures below 26.6 F.

Those hot, humid summers and cold, blizzardy winters means there's always something to complain about!

| -60 | -40 | -20 | 0 | 20 | 40 | 60 | 80 | 100 | 120 | **F** |

"Cold! If the thermometer had been an inch longer we'd have all frozen to death!"

— **Mark Twain**

"You'd think the cold would keep the assholes away."

— **Clint Eastwood**
in Gran Torino

"Don't knock the weather; 9/10 of the people couldn't start a conversation if it didn't change once in a while.

— **Kin Hubbard**
cartoonist from Ohio

The heat in Indiana descends like a 300-pound fat lady onto a picnic bench in the middle of July. It can literally be sliced into chunks and stored ... Indiana heat is not a meteorological phenomenon — it is a solid element, something you can grab by the handles."

— **Jean Shepherd**
creator of A Chrimas Story

formed odd coping mechanisms.

For example, when my wife first moved to Iowa, there was a tornado warning for the Des Moines area. She wanted to go to the basement of our building, but I had an instinctive feel for what to do: I walked out onto our fifth-story balcony in my boxers to keep an eye out. My logic was that, due to the unpredictable nature of the tornado, it's better to keep an eye to the sky, and once I spotted one, I'd alert the little misses and head to the basement. It must come with the region, because as I looked out, I saw five other guys in my building on their balconies in their boxers.

"The traits that were said to be Middle Western," writes cultural geographer James Shortridge, "were the direct products of experiences, especially of a prolonged drought and economic depression that had gripped the central plains for a decade, beginning in the winter of 1887/88 and lasting until 1897 ... Weak-willed settlers left the region. Those who stayed and weathered the bad years were humbled, but at the same time gained confidence in themselves."

James Shortridge
settled in Lawrence, Kansas

Indeed, the states themselves emphasize the strength of the people. In Wisconsin, the mascot "Badger" dates to the winter of 1823. During the mining boom, many arrived to work, but as winter approached, a large number headed south for warmer weather. Those who stayed simply dug into the hillside to wait out the cold, earning the nickname Badgers.

On the other side of an independence born out of geographic hardship comes an independence born out of the fact that a lot of crazy folks settled the Midwest looking to be left alone.

After the Northeast, the Midwest attracted the most utopian or religious societies in the United States. One of the most famous was the New Harmony, Indiana, religious group headed by George Rapp and called Rappites (they probably found that a religious group called "Rapists" didn't do so well on the marketing side of things). Fallen away Shakers, the Rappites left Pennsylvania in 1815, drained and cleared 30,000 acres of land in southwestern Indiana and set up a commune called Harmonie. Discipline was harsh, celibacy was required, all possessions were collectively owned, and free time was divided between waiting for the coming of Jesus, chores, and waiting for the coming of Jesus.

About ten years went by with no appearance from the carpenter-in-the-sky, and I can only imagine the nocturnal emission rates were reaching dangerous levels. Members began to leave, and in 1825, the commune disbanded and was sold to a secular utopian, Robert Owen, who rechristened the development New Harmony.

Owen had failed to set up a socialist working community at his textile mill in New Lanark, Scotland, so he set off for America to create a knowledge-based community, with no inequity and with a balance of great minds from the creative, scientific, and cultural fields. One of the first groups of settlers was brought to New Harmony down the Ohio River on a flatboat dubbed the "Boatload of Knowledge."

In some ways, New Harmony was extremely successful. It attracted social reformers such as Frances Wright and scientists including Thomas Say and William Maclure — those two created the first accurate geological map of the U.S. in 1809.

New Harmony has been called one of the "world villages that have made history" because it pioneered education from infant school to kindergarten, encouraged equal opportunity for boys and girls, had a free library, and developed the concept for the Smithsonian Institution — a concept that Robert Owen's oldest son, then a U.S. Congressman, brought to life when he introduced the bill that established the Smithsonian in 1846.

But like *The Simpsons* episode in which Springfield's Mensa chapter takes over Springfield, New Harmony was plagued by constant quarreling, and dissolved in 1829 after only four years.

There were so many Utopian groups across the Midwest that by the mid-1800s they started to splinter, and like New Harmony, to swap sites. In 1839, Nauvoo, Illinois, was founded by Joseph Smith and his Mormon followers on the banks of the Mississippi River. By the early 1840s, Nauvoo was the largest city in Illinois, and in the politically divided state, Nauvoo had worked out a charter for home rule that allowed the city to have its own court system and laws. It was the second-largest military force in America after the federal military.

In 1844, Smith was murdered, and in 1846, Brigham Young headed for Utah while his rival, James Strang, set out for Beaver Island in Northern Lake Michigan.

Like Smith finding golden tablets that were additions to the Bible, Strang told his followers that he'd found *more* long-lost works that were additions to the additions to the Bible. He set up the Church of Jesus Christ of Latter Day Saints (then known as Strangites) and arrived on Beaver Island in 1848.

He promptly declared himself King of Beaver Island, started carrying a wooden scepter for regal effect, and decided that polygamy wasn't so bad after all. He married five women, including his "male" secretary who turned out to be a nineteen-year-old girl in disguise (her cover was blown when "he" became pregnant). Since passing off her pregnancy as the immaculate conception would have really taken their brand of Mormonism to strange, new heights, Strang just stuck with the marriage.

Strang was charged with, but acquitted for, mail fraud and forgery and won a seat in the Michigan legislature in 1852. But in 1856 he was assassinated by a group of four disgruntled followers. With no succession plans, his kingdom fell apart.

Meanwhile, back in Nauvoo, the Mormons had been replaced by an Icarian group of French Communists who moved up from Texas in 1849. After some unpopular regulations and internal lawsuits, the group in Nauvoo split. Cabet headed for St Louis in 1856, and the colony failed due to a financial collapse in 1860.

Today, the legacy of Utopian societal experiments remains evident throughout the Midwest. The Amana Colonies in eastern Iowa were founded in 1855 by 800 German settlers known as the Community of True Inspiration. They grew into a large company when Amanaite George Foerstner built a beverage cooler in 1930. Today, Amana is still a respected company, and the Amana colonies are a tourist attraction south of Cedar Rapids.

In the woods of northwestern Michigan, the Interlochen Center for the Arts is the premier music boarding school and summer camp that has grown out of Joseph Maddy's 1928 National High School Orchestra Camp on the same site.

And the southeastern Iowa town of Fairfield is home to the Maharishi University of Management, founded in 1973 by Maharishi Mahesh Yogi. It features consciousness-based education including the Transcendental Meditation technique. The school has attracted all sorts of folks who normally wouldn't be heading to southeast Iowa: film director David Lynch, who in 2005 began hosting an annual "David Lynch Weekend for World Peace and Meditation" at Maharishi University of Management; to Moby; Oprah, who went to get her head straight. "Seeking the fullest expression of self," Oprah explained on her website. "That's the story of my life in six words."

Oprah visited Fairfield in February of 2012 for a little TM during the filming of her new show, *Next Chapter.* "Fairfield, Iowa — population 9,500, smack in the middle of Midwestern farmland," she writes. "The last place you'd expect to get stuck in an evening traffic jam because so many people are headed off to practice transcendental meditation."

Tell me about it!

"It was a powerfully energizing yet calming experience," she concludes. "I didn't want it to end. When it did, I walked away fuller than when I'd come in. Full of hope, a sense of contentment, and deep joy."

Just another day in Iowa, Oprah.

Joseph Maddy
Wellington, Kansas

![CHIROPRACTORS](logo with winged figure holding banners reading "HEALTH" and "CHIROPRACTIC")

MIDWESTERN CRACK DEALERS

HOMEGROWN MEDICINE: Chiropractic medicine was founded by D.D. Palmer in Davenport, Iowa, around 1895. The Palmer College of Chiropractic is still in Davenport, and has a good rugby team (FYI). **YOU'VE GOT THE SPINE OF A 60-YEAR-OLD MAN!** The core of chiropractic is spinal manipulations. Some chiropractors have claimed manipulating the spine can cure just about anything, which has landed the profession in a little hot water now and then. **WHO NEEDS THERAPISTS?** Still, Midwesterners can't get enough. While people on the coasts make small talk about advice their therapist gave them, across the Midwest you can hear "Well, my chiropractor said" in an alarmingly wide range of conversations. **NOT OUR FIRST ALTERNATIVE MEDICINE RODEO:** One alternative medicine just isn't enough for us! In 1874, A.T. Still developed Osteopathic Medicine in Kirksville, Missouri. A more holistic approach to medicine, gaggles of doctors in the Midwest are "D.O.s" in addition to "M.D.s." And all of us here at RAYGUN lived to tell the tale.

1.8 POLITICS IN THE MIDWEST: IT'S RAINING MEN AND "GOD HATES FAGS" SIGNS

In early spring 2008, my wife let me know that we were going to have our first child later that fall. I was a little surprised. Well, even anatomy class in an American public school had taught me that what we'd been doing had consequences, but I guess in the early spring of 2008, I didn't put together that nine months meant we'd be having a child later *that* year.

"Not even another New Year's Eve without a child? But my 2008 New Year's Eve resolution was going to be to put off having children!"

My wife wisely took the lead on all baby-related planning and signed us up for an eight-week birthing class that was built around the Bradley Method of natural, anesthesia-free birth either in the hospital or at home.

I approach all things with an open mind born from a lack of desire to do much research on my own, so I was down with a natural, home birth. At the very least, I figured it would give me something to talk about with the folks from Portland who sell knit items at the clothing trade shows we visit for RAYGUN. The year before, one couple had their eighteen-month-old with them at a three-day show in Las Vegas, traveling in what appeared to be a hammock over his mom's shoulder, and breast-feeding when necessary.

I was fine with all of it, though at eighteen months, once the child can start undoing the buttons on his mom's shirt, breast feeding does reach a new level. Some of the other vendors and visitors were a little mystified, but you think: "Hey, they're from Portland, we should be happy they're not burning incense inside the convention center, foraging for food in the Dumpster outside, and explaining that they are 'definitely spiritual' but aren't really 'religious, how most people mean it' and have found a lot of stuff they 'can really relate to' in Buddhism."

When you think of natural home births, you don't really think of Iowa, or really anywhere in the Midwest. But the region that houses the Maharishi has also produced some out-of-the-box thinkers such as Malcolm X, Bob Dylan, Jesse "The Body" Ventura, and Ina May Gaskin, "the mother of authentic midwifery."

PREVIOUS PAGE:
Mike's Oldest Son
Des Moines, Iowa

Malcolm X
born in Omaha, Nebraska,
raised in Lansing, Michigan

Bob Dylan
born in Duluth, Minnesota,
raised in Hibbing, Minnesota

Jesse Ventura
Minneapolis, Minnesota

Ina May Gaskin
Marshall County, Iowa

All of the above have had outsized influence around the country. Gaskin grew up near Marshalltown, Iowa, and in 1971 set up The Farm Midwifery Center with her husband in Summertown, Tennessee — one of the first out-of-hospital birth centers in the United States. Her stature grew with the 1977 publication of her book, *Spiritual Midwifery*, which Carol Lorenete considers, "A seminal work, it presented pregnancy, childbirth and breast feeding from a fresh, natural and spiritual perspective." Across the U.S., Gaskin became a household name for midwives and natural-birth advocates.

So if she's not a household name to you, just ask yourself this one question: am I a midwife or natural birth advocate?

Indeed, the Portland MamaBaby Center defines "midwife" on their website using Gaskin's words and examples.

We have out-Portlanded Portland!

> " '**Whoever thought,**' commented Rachel Maddow, 'that gay couples would be able to get married in Sioux City before they could in New York?' "

One midwife aside, the Midwest took alternative lifestyle support in America to new heights in April of 2009, when Iowa's Supreme Court unanimously upheld a District Court ruling that held there was no important governmental interest in denying citizens marriage licenses based on their sexual orientation. This made Iowa only the third state — after Connecticut and Massachusetts — to legalize gay marriage. "Whoever thought," commented Rachel Maddow on MSNBC that day in April, "that gay couples would be able to get married in Sioux City before they could in New York?"

You could hear the coastal media pee their collective pants in surprise. Iowa? Gays? ... Iowa? Our great state was now as gay as Connecticut! Though we're not as gay as Massachusetts (they have Mitt Romney).

Mitt Romney
Detroit, Michigan

Some pointed out that this wasn't surprising, considering the progressive streak in Iowa's history: in 1851 it was one of the first to remove a ban on interracial marriage, in 1868 it ruled that no child could be barred from a school because of race, and in 1869 it became the first state to admit women to the bar.

Indeed, across the Midwest there is a solid progressive streak when it comes to education, politics, and social issues: the University of Michigan became the first state-operated university in America in 1813, then the first major university to admit women in 1837; Indiana became the first state to incorporate a graduated education system into its constitution in 1816; Ohio's Oberlin College became the first small college to admit women in 1833; and 1856 saw the first truly public high school open in Chicago and the first kindergarten open in Watertown, Wisconsin.

The country's only strong third parties grew out of the Midwest: The Populists across the Midwest and the Progressives in Wisconsin. Wisconsin's Governor Robert LaFollette started the "Wisconsin Idea" in 1904 — pensions for the blind, old-age assistance, and laws governing working conditions for children and unemployment compensation (a laundry list of all the things Glenn Beck loves!). LaFollette's Progressive Party spawned Teddy Roosevelt's third party run in 1912, and LaFollette himself ran on the Progressive ticket in 1924, winning more than five million votes.

Robert LaFollette
Primrose, Wisconsin

LaFollette's Wisconsin labor laws built on a movement that had been growing across the Midwest for decades. Michigan as a territory instituted a mechanic's lien law in 1813; the *Workingman's Shield,* founded in Cincinnati in 1833, was one of the oldest labor newspapers in the country; and in 1912 labor leader Eugene Debs received 6% of the total vote for President running for the Socialist Party of America.

Eugene Debs
Terre Haute, Indiana

The Midwest's pinko credentials are exemplified by our love of America's Communist mouthpiece of choice: National Public Radio. The Midwest took to NPR like Trotsky to collective farming. At its inception in 1971, as now, NPR depended on member stations around the country. The South had 19, the West had 17, the Northeast had 13. But the Midwest had 38 member stations.

Leon Trotsky
Eau Claire, Wisconsin ... JK!

It turns out our only gripe with NPR was that it wasn't *enough* of a lefty-elitist-refuge. In the late 1970s, Garrison Keillor's *A Prairie Home Companion* was burning up the charts on Minnesota Public Radio. Environmentally conscious folks with glasses and used Volvos had found their radio soulmate. When Keillor looked to take his show national, NPR's Beverly Hills-born president Frank Mankiewicz was the only one not laughing. Too folksy? Too down home? Too Midwestern? None of the above, apparently. According to NPR history, *This is NPR,* Mankiewicz found the show "too elitist," considering it a "put-down of small-town-life."

Nobody puts down the small-town Midwest like small-town Midwesterners.

Rebuffed by NPR's right-wing-authoritarian overlord, Keillor and NPR President William Kling organized a new distribution entity called Public Radio International that took *APHC* national in May of 1980. It quickly acquired the largest audience of any public radio program.

Minnesota-based PRI has gone on to pick up some of the shows that define public radio: *Bob Edwards Weekend*, *Michael Feldman's Whad'Ya Know?*, *Marketplace*, and *World Cafe*. In the 1990s, PRI picked up yet another program on which NPR passed. *This American Life* and its host, Ira Glass, were snubbed by the folks in DC, forcing them into the arms of Chicago's WBEZ and, as Ira puts it, "NPR's archrival, PRI."

But before you grab your hammer and sickle and start calling out, "Hey, Comrade," to anyone you see in Davenport, be warned that Iowa's move in 2009 wasn't a total surprise. After all, only a four-hour drive from the Iowa Supreme Court building is the headquarters of the Topeka, Kansas-based Westboro Baptist Church — which is best known for protesting veterans' funerals by holding (extremely flamboyant) signs reading: "God Hates Fags."

The Westboro Baptist Church has drummed up a lot of publicity in the last few years. They protested Iowa's gay marriage ruling in 2009, they protested a 2006 memorial service for miners who died in the Sago Mine collapse (it was God punishing America for tolerating gays), and they protested a Topeka appliance store for selling a Swedish vacuum (Sweden, of course, made it onto their shit list for prosecuting the anti-gay Swedish pastor, Ake Green).

A fringe group that almost everyone in Kansas hates, Westboro is the other extreme of Midwestern politics — as right wing as we can be left wing. Kansas today has one of the most conservative governors in the country, Sam Brownback, who has helped push the state so far to the right that *Harper's* contributor Thomas Frank referred to the state as "Brownbackistan." Brownback has done a few pointless things the right loves, such as signing a bill that bans Sharia Law in Kansas. But Brownback has also been serious in some significant moves to the right, such as slashing taxes on the richest residents with the Kansas Tax Act after the recession, thus charging headlong into massive debts in the future. This caused the KansasPrairie.net to call Kansas' tax policy "the most regressive in the nation" and announced that "Governor Brownback has gored your ox!"

Gored my ox? Must be a Kansas thing.

These certainly aren't the first conservative ideas out of the Midwest. Hillsboro, Ohio founded the Women's Christian Temperance Union in 1873, leading to Prohibition (Kansas was the last state to repeal Prohibition). Wisconsin produced Senator Joe McCarthy, whose paranoia about Communists in the United States exposed Hollywood for the Pinko-hotbed it was between 1947 and 1957. His work also led to confrontations with Midwestern labor leaders, and inspired Arthur Miller to write Salem witch trials-inspired *The Crucible*.

In 1995 the Federal Building in Oklahoma City was bombed by radical militants from Indiana and Michigan: Timothy McVeigh and Terry Nichols. The two brought attention to the "Michigan Militia" when it was erroneously speculated that they were involved in the group that had formed in 1994 out of fear that the Federal Government was encroaching on individual liberties and aiming to establish a tightly controlled New World Order.

The conversations over s'mores must be pretty uplifting!

Since 1952, the Midwest has voted as one bloc in only three elections (1952, 1964, 1972). It has divided in the other elections since then, while the Northeast has voted entirely Democratic in every election since 1992 (except Vermont voted for Bush in 2000), and the South has voted entirely Republican in both 2000 and 2004.

In 2011, the national battle over budget cuts was framed in Wisconsin when the state's governor, Scott Walker, proposed drastic changes to the budget and to union ability to collectively bargain. In protest, thousands filled the state capitol building in early February and refused to leave for days — making cleaning tricky. Democratic senators literally left the state to prevent a vote on the measure, and a recall campaign was launched against Walker. Wisconsin's actions also inspired the Occupy Wall Street movement in September 2011.

"*ALRIGHT, WE ISLAMIST RADICALS HAVE TAKEN OVER KANSAS, NOW WE CAN IMPOSE SHARIA LAW.*"

"*WAIT A MINUTE, IT LOOKS LIKE THEY BANNED SHARIA LAW IN THIS STATE. BETTER TAKE OVER IOWA INSTEAD.*"

BROWNBACK OUTSMARTS ISLAMIC EXTREMISTS AGAIN!

S'MORES AND FIGHTING THE NEW WORLD ORDER

"*FIRST IT'S TAXES, THEN THE U.N. THEN THE COMPUTER CHIPS IN OUR WIVES ... THEY'LL OWN US ALL!*"

"*I HEAR THAT ... CAN YOU PASS ANOTHER GRAHAM CRACKER?*"

Fittingly, the Occupy movement that grew out of Midwest progressivism was fighting a Midwestern nemesis: Wichita's Koch brothers. David and Charles Koch are industrialists at the head of petroleum-based Koch Industries, and have poured more than $100 million into the Heritage Foundation, the Cato Institute, Freedom-Works, and the Tea Party movement.

The Midwest's liberal side and conservative side exist simultaneously, and this political oddity may be more politically important than ever. In the 2012 presidential election, the Islamo-fascist-yet-at-the-same-time-socialist-wealth-spreader incumbent, Barack Obama, hailed from his adopted hometown of Chicago (and is married to a local). His challenger, the do-anything-for-money-and-say-anything-to-get-elected-so-I-can-build-an-oversight-free-vulture-capitalist-paradise, Mitt Romney, was born in Michigan (as was his wife, Ann). And not only were two Midwesterners facing off at the top of the ticket, but Romney picked Wisconsin's Paul Ryan as his running mate. If Obama had replaced his vice president, Joe Biden, with Chicagoan Hillary Clinton, then all sides of the 2012 ticket would have been Midwestern for the first time in American history. So heads the Midwest wins, tails the Midwest wins!

The only defining quality of Midwestern political thought is the independent and unpredictable spirit of it. Even on the smallest scale, it's tough to know where people are going to stand. On the first night of our birthing class, one couple arrived before us and was discussing homemade granola recipes with the instructor. My "oh shit, this place is going to be waaaaaay too liberal for me" alarm went off, but it faded once the rest of the group came in. There was an evangelical Christian couple, two young farmers who wanted to give birth the salt-of-the-Earth way, and a social worker and her real-estate-developing husband. Each was there for different reasons and had a range of opinions.

And check yourself when pigeon-holing the region. Hillsboro, Ohio, may still be still associated with the Women's Christian Temperance Union, but that didn't mean the whole town was on board. The group went from tavern to tavern, protesting outside until the owners agreed to stop selling booze. One drugstore not only refused to comply, but the owner sued the women for trespassing and disruption of business, winning a $5 judgment.

DRESS TO MIDWEST

The untrained eye may not think there is an emphasis on fashion in the Midwest, but what you're wearing can say a lot about you. Here are a couple of hints to help you send the right message.

BUTTON-DOWN SHIRT WITH UNDERSHIRT: I can be trusted in business or friendship relationships because I have a little decency and a Middle American upbringing.

BUTTON-DOWN SHIRT WITHOUT UNDERSHIRT: I am either from Europe, in which case you can offer me directions and a smile, or I am from New York, in which case I will try and sell you a mortgage-backed security or shoot you.

CUBS SHIRT: Baseball fan? No, I'm just here to party like my days at Sig Ep, bro.

YANKEES HAT: No.

COWBOYS SHIRT: I am either from Texas or, worse, I am not from Texas but like the Cowboys. Either way: avoid all conversation.

TAPOUT SHIRT: Not only am I violent, I'm also dumb.

1.9 IT'S HARD TO BE MODEST WHEN YOU'RE PERFECT IN EVERY WAY ... BUT WE MANAGE

" THE WAY WE
SERVE
ICED TEA
SAYS A LOT ABOUT US "

Iced tea swings some serious pipe in the Midwest. Its hold on the region goes all the way back to Estelle Woods Wilcox's 1870 *Buckeye Cookbook*, which contains one of the oldest recipes for iced tea. And the national popularity of iced tea exploded when Richard Blechynden introduced his version at the 1904 World's Fair in St Louis.

The way we serve iced tea, though, says a lot about us. From the nicest restaurants to McDonald's, you get unsweetened iced tea. Many places don't even have a pre-sweetened version. They bring you the iced tea, then they bring you the sweetener, then lemon — anything you need to accessorize your drink. It's our way of saying: only you know how sweet you like your tea.

Good luck getting unsweetened iced tea in the South. In fact, good luck getting iced tea that is just regular iced tea with sweetener mixed in. Those fascists add sugar to the boiling water before the tea even cools. Watching them then throw in more sugar at the table is like witnessing a Type-2 diabetic put *more* salt on his McDonald's fries.

And although no one can be 100% sure, I attribute the "passion fruit" iced tea movement to California. What started as a fringe iced tea blend at some point in the 1990s became just, "iced tea." Which means that if you sat down at a restaurant and ordered "iced tea," they'd bring you passion fruit iced tea.

"What's this?"

"That's your iced tea, sir."

"But there's fruit in it. Are you telling me that you got fruit-infused tea leaves from somewhere in India?"

Many have joined the movement against passion fruit iced tea. In 2011, after the death of Osama Bin Laden, Adam Carolla tweeted, "Now that Bin Laden's been put in the ground we can turn our full attention to hunting down the maniac who invented Passion Fruit Iced Tea."

Though so exceptional in almost every facet of life, Midwesterners are a modest people who keep things simple. We love open skies, America, and freedom to do what we like with our iced tea.

POP VS SODA

BECAUSE "SODA" IS FOR HEDGE FUND MANAGERS, ASSHOLES, AND PEOPLE FROM EASTERN WISCONSIN OR ST LOUIS

POP: When someone orders a carbonated beverage, you will instantly know whether they are a handsome, intelligent, and productive member of society, or if they're from the Northeast, California, or South. **SO ST LOUIS AND EASTERN WISCONSIN, WHAT'S THE DEAL?** The only hiccups are the greater St Louis area and Eastern Wisconsin, which use Soda. **THANKS, BRITISH POET LAUREATE:** Robert Southey first called carbonated beverages "pop" in 1812, explaining that "pop goes the cork" when it's drawn. Why the Midwest has taken to the term so fervently, though, is yet to be discovered. **GET OVER IT, NEW YORK:** Yes, I called that can of Pepsi "pop," figure it out. It's not like I ordered a slice of pizza and a beverage by saying, "Yeah, I'd like a slice of pizza and a wet hand job ... What!? That's what we call 'soda' in the Midwest!" **POP OF CHOICE:** We drink so much Mountain Dew here that if Yellow #5 really did cause you to go sterile, the Midwest would have ceased reproducing years ago.

We have a, "take it if you like it, and if you don't like it, don't worry, our feelings won't be hurt, we know you've probably seen a lot better things than what we have to offer" approach. Witness Michigan's state motto: "If you seek a pleasant peninsula, look around you."

It's not a brash threat like New Hampshire's "Live Free or Die." It's not a declaratory boast of discovery like California's, "Eureka!" In fact, it's not even much of a sales pitch like, "We're the largest inland peninsula in the world." It's just a, "So, you say that you're looking for a peninsula? Well you're in luck!" But say you'd like an isthmus instead, well, don't let us keep you.

Midwestern mothers, like all mothers, want to make sure you get plenty to eat. But they also don't want to hold you up. Southern moms will throw time right out the window and move from grits to fried chicken to dessert, although you told them you needed to be at a meeting by 2:00, it'll be 6:23 before you're out of there.

Midwestern mothers assume you have somewhere else to be. They'll keep an eye on the clock for you to make sure you're not late. If your meeting is a 2:00, they'll be getting your keys and coat by 1:33 and cautioning you about having enough time to park and walk to the building and wait for eighteen minutes in the lobby. You've probably got important things to do, and they don't want to be responsible for ruining those important things. After all, you'll most likely have more fun there anyway.

This is the reason that the Midwest leads the country in "gateways" to other places. Ohio is called the "Gateway State," because it was the first stop on your way to the West in the early 1800s. Kansas City took the mantle as the gateway to the West later in the 1800s as it started outfitting pioneers for the Oregon Trail. At the same time, Fargo, Sioux Falls, and Omaha all vied with Kansas City for a chance at being the best place to start to leave for some better place.

Rhinelander, Wisconsin, is the "Gateway to the World's Most Concentrated Lake Region;" Springfield, Missouri, is the "Gateway to the Ozarks;" and Indiana is the "Crossroads of America."

Hot damn, there's a major intersection in our state! People are going to come from miles around to drive through us!

Then in 1965, St Louis, "The Gateway City," completed the Gateway Arch. At 630 feet tall and with a price tag of $13 million at the time, it became America's tallest man-made monument and set everyone else in the Midwest straight as to which city was *really* the best city to pass through on the way to somewhere else.

Maybe no one here likes being the tallest nail. Maybe our agricultural tradition cautions us about being too sure of ourselves. Maybe we're just really good at being modest. In any case, modesty permeates life in the Midwest. We focus on accomplishments rather than acquisition — "To produce rather than to be conspicuous," as Miami University of Ohio puts it.

But our modesty means we're terrible at boasting. Even while tooting our horns, we're subjugating ourselves to another place. Des Moines calls itself "The Hartford of the West;" Lake Geneva, Wisconsin, is called "The Second Newport;" and the University of Michigan fight song declares them, "The Champions of the West." Come on, Wolverines! It's an inspirational fight song, it's fiction, you can be champions of the world or of the gol-dang universe!

Our state mottos are pretty subdued as well. New York declares, "Ever Upward;" Maine announces, "I lead;" North Carolina is, "To be, rather than to seem;" and in West Virginia, "Mountaineers are always free" (does "free" mean "poor" in West Virginian?).

We take a subtler approach: Nebraska just hopes for, "Equality before the law" (don't set your sites too high, Cornhuskers); North Dakota really sells itself short with, "One sows for the benefit of another age" (things aren't so hot now, but if we work really hard, our grandkids will love it here); and Wisconsin cryptically says, "Forward."

Missouri's nickname as "The Show Me State" seems a little brash for us. To fit in with the crowd, they may want to go with, "If you say so, I'll take your word for it. You know, wouldn't want to make a fuss."

Our cities are just as resistant. "We need to make sure we aren't so bashful, with Midwestern modesty," lamented Columbus, Ohio, Partnership director Alex Fisher in 2010. He went on to deliver this sales pitch: "Candidly, we believe we are one of the brightest stars in Ohio's future."

One of the brightest stars in Ohio's future? How many bright stars are there in Ohio's future, Alex? Columbus: We're pretty much in the top 25 best things in Ohio, probably.

Strangely, we let our modesty slide when it comes to the field of "World's Largest" roadside attractions. According to Wikipedia, the Northeast has eight official World's Largest roadside attractions, the West has 25, the South has 42, but the Midwest crushes all with 71.

World's Largest roadside attractions don't even originate in the Midwest. One of the first was a huge pop bottle built in 1924 near the city of The Bottle, Alabama. There's the World's Largest Catfish in Troy, Alabama; the World's Largest Cow Skull in Amado, Arizona; the World's Largest Spinach Can in Alma, Arkansas; the World's Largest Peanut in Ashburn, Georgia; and the World's Largest Clam Box in Ipswich, Massachusetts.

Booorrrring.

You wanna see how the big boys build roadside attractions? The Midwest comes out guns blazing, literally.

Ishpeming on Michigan's U.P. has the "World's Largest *Working* Rifle." Nick-named "Big Ernie," this rifle lives in Da Yoopers Tourist Trap, is permanently mounted to a pick-up truck, is 35 feet long, weighs more than 4,000 pounds, and can be fired using a 12-volt electrical igniter system. In July 2005, Big Ernie reached a new level of fame when it was featured in *Field & Stream.* It's the U.P.'s not-so-subtle way of saying: "Don't jerk us around, Lower Peninsula. And Canada, we don't need any shit from you, either."

There is the World's Largest Running Chainsaw, also in Ishpeming; the World's Largest Crucifix (hey, if Jesus does come back, we want to clearly mark our region) in Indian River, Michigan; the World's Largest Fake Nose and Glasses in Michigan City, Indiana; the World's Largest Laundromat in Berwyn, Illinois; and in case you still wondered which region was top dog in the "World's Largest" competition, Lucas,

SPEAK SOFTLY, BUT
CARRY THE
WORLD'S LARGEST RIFLE

*"DON'T JERK US AROUND,
LOWER PENINSULA! YOU TOO,
CANADA! WE DON'T NEED ANY
SHIT FROM YOU EITHER!"*

WORLD'S LARGEST ROADSIDE ATTRACTIONS!

God will forever keep the mystery of our secret love for "World's Largest" roadside attractions to himself. Below is just a portion of our World's Largest collection.

World's Largest Ketchup Bottle (Collinsville, Illinois)

World's Largest Laundromat (Berwyn, Illinois)

World's Largest Ball of Paint (Alexandria, Indiana)

World's Largest Sycamore Stump and World's Largest Preserved Steer (Kokomo, Indiana)
can you see everything Kokomo has in only 1 month?!

World's Largest Fake Nose and Glasses (Michigan City, Indiana)

World's Largest Frying Pan (Brandon, Iowa)

World's Largest Fake Popcorn Ball (Sac City, Iowa)

World's Largest Concrete Gnome (Ames, Iowa)
just when we thought we couldn't be prouder of our home state!

World's Largest Truck Stop (Walcott, Iowa)

World's Largest Ball of Twine (Cawker City, Kansas)

World's Largest Easel (Goodland, Kansas)

World's Largest Hairball (Garden City, Kansas)

World's Largest Hand-Dug Outdoor Concrete Pool (Garden City, Kansas)

World's Largest Hand-Dug Well (Greensburg, Kansas)
It's like they say in Kansas, if it's worth diggin', it's worth diggin' with your hands.

World's Largest Cherry Pie (Traverse City, Michigan)

World's Largest Picnic Table (Olive, Michigan)

World's Largest Working Rifle and Running Chainsaw (Ishpeming, Michigan)

World's Largest Crucifix (Indian River, Michigan)

World's Largest Indian (Ironwood, Michigan)
uhhh, what?

World's Largest Snowman (North St Paul, Minnesota)

World's Largest Pelican (Pelican Rapids, Minnesota)

World's Largest Loon (Vergas, Minnesota)

World's Largest Jolly Green Giant (Blue Earth, Minnesota)

World's Largest Ball of Twine by One Man (Darwin, Minnesota)

World's Largest Rocking Chair (Fanning, Missouri)

World's Largest Porch Swing (Hebron, Nebraska)
so many things things to sit on, so little time

World's Largest Railroad Yard (North Platte, Nebraska)

World's Largest Holstein Cow (New Salem, North Dakota)

World's Largest Scrap Tin Sculptures (Gladstone, North Dakota)

World's Largest Basket (Newark, Ohio)

World's Largest Cheese Wheel (Berlin, Ohio)

World's Largest Cuckoo Clock (Wilmot, Ohio)

World's Largest Drug Store (Wall, South Dakota)

World's Largest Muskie (Hayward, Wisconsin)

Kansas, closes the book with The World's Largest Collection of The World's Smallest Versions of The World's Largest Things Traveling Roadside Attraction and Museum.

We started sticking "World's Largest" on all sorts of stuff: World's Largest Hardwood Manufacturing Plant in Algoma, Wisconsin; World's Largest Cement Plant in Alpena, Michigan; World's Largest Bottle and Glass Container Plant in Alton, Illinois; World's Largest Broom Factory in Paris, Illinois; and the World's Largest Grain Elevator in Duluth, Minnesota.

Duluth here we come!

Perhaps our modesty covers braggadocio bubbling just below the surface. Like many repressed urges, this one manifests itself in strange ways. For some reason, as soon as this World's Largest thing arrived, the Midwest finally found an outlet for its pent-up urge to brag.

And this is only the surface of the showoff-ness that sometimes pops up in The Big Flyover.

America's circus culture has grown out of our modest region. Between 1847 and 1894, 28 circuses headquartered in Delavan, Wisconsin. In 1882, the McGregor, Iowa-born Ringling Brothers started what would become the world's largest circus in Baraboo, Wisconsin — now the home of the Circus World Museum.

Many associate the brothers with the showman and scam artist, Connecticut-born PT Barnum, who claimed, "There's a sucker born every minute." The Ringling Brothers took over PT Barnum's circus in 1907, eighteen years after Barnum's death.

Ringling Brothers
born in McGregor, Iowa, and raised in Baraboo, Wisconsin

In contrast, the Ringling Brothers were responsible Midwesterners. In 1884, when they began, John Ringling scouted locations. When he found one, he impressed the property owner by having a contract already drawn up and by guaranteeing to keep the property's trees safe from harm.

Peru, Indiana, calls itself "The Circus City of the World." In 1883, the Hagenbeck-Wallace Circus formed there. So did the American Circus Corporation, which coordinated wintering locations for many circuses. Detroit is home of the original Shrine Circus.

Colon, Michigan, calls itself "The Magic Capital of the World" because it

Harry Houdini
raised in Appleton, Wisconsin

manufactured so much equipment for magicians. Those involved the Appleton, Wisconsin-raised Harry Houdini, who started as a skilled trapeze artist in 1882 and became a famous escape artist before dying in Detroit in 1926. He promised his followers that after death, he would return to life on top of a bridge in Jackson Park, Chicago. Every year, followers keep a vigil at that site, but to no avail. Houdini is the Midwestern Jerry Garcia.

Buffalo Bill Cody
born in Le Clair, Iowa, raised in Fort Leavenworth, Kansas

Annie Oakley
North Star, Ohio

Meanwhile, in 1883, Le Clair, Iowa-born Buffalo Bill Cody put together "Buffalo Bill's Wild West Show." It toured the U.S. and Europe, earning Buffalo Bill a jeweled crest from Queen Victoria. His show featured buffaloes, Indians, and Annie Oakley, whose marksmanship was so skilled that she was able to shoot a cigarette from the lips of the German Kaiser. Although knowing what the Kaiser would pull a few years later, it might have been a little better if Oakley had been a worse shot.

But the Midwest would get another crack at the Kaiser a few years later when we pretty much single-handedly won the First World War.

SPEAKING OF POMPOUS MIDWESTERNERS

"*HEY GIRL FROM PENNSYLVANIA, I'MA LET YOU FINISH ... BUT, MY VIDEO COST A MILLION DOLLARS TO MAKE, IT DOESN'T WIN, THAT BRINGS THIS WHOLE SHOW DOWN.*"

"*YOU GOL-DANG MIDWESTERNERS CAN OCCASIONALLY BE SO BRASH.*"

> "Indiana is the first place in the United States of America where a white man was hanged for the murder of an Indian ... that's the kind of people for me" – Kurt Vonnegut

FT. WAYNE

★ INDIANAPOLIS

TERRE HAUTE

THE MIDWEST'S REDNECK COUSIN

CAPITAL: Indianapolis **SIZE:** 36,418 square miles **POPULATION:** 6,516,922 **ADMISSION TO THE UNION:** December 11, 1816 **RUBBIN'S RACIN':** Yes, indeed. When HBO wanted to check out dirt-track driving and honkies for their series, *Dirty Driving*, they headed to Anderson, Indiana. The southern part of the state is dangerously close to Kentucky, so close that they call pop "Coke," and have produced NASCAR greats including Tony Stewart and Jeff Gordon. **BUT DON'T FORGET BASKETBALL AND CATHOLICS:** Hoosiers made Indiana famous for basketball alongside Larry Bird, Chuck Taylor, Shawn Kemp, and John Wooden. As well, *Rudy* shined a light on one of Catholicism's bright spots: the God Quad and Touchdown Jesus of Notre Dame in South Bend. **IT'S NOT PARIS, FRANCE OR ROME:** But Gary, Indiana, did produce the Jackson Five. **SURPRISE! I'M FROM INDIANA:** Johnny Appleseed, Dan Quayle, Wendell Wilkie, James Dean, Greg Kinnear, David Lee Roth, Axl Rose, Don Mattingly, Bob Griese, Booth Tarkington.

PART TWO

MID-
WEST
SUPER
POWER

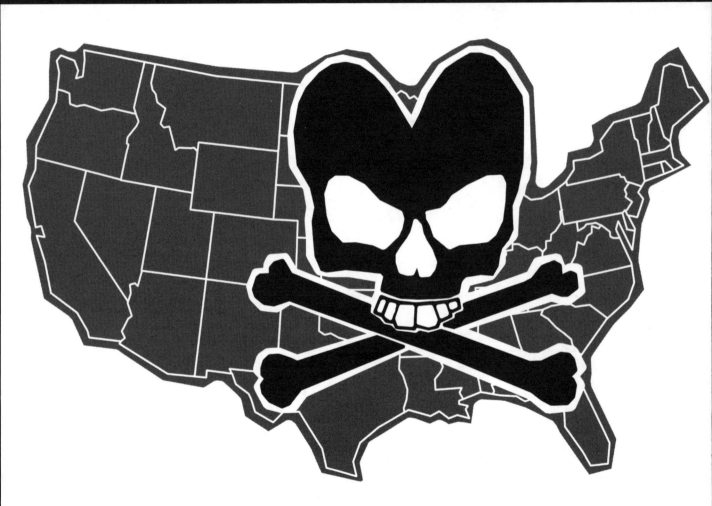

Nowadays, the term "Heartland" gives people a warm and fuzzy feeling. It sounds like it comes with Jell-O salad, a pleated quilt-patterned vest from JC Penney, and a pair of mom jeans. During the last 40 years, "Heartland" has become a synonym for "Midwest." The Heartland Institute is based in Chicago, Heartland Community College is in Normal, Illinois, and Heartland RVs has been selling its line of trusted transportation equipment out of Elkhart, Indiana, for years.

Heartland says, "We can be trusted," "We'll treat you right," "We still watch movies on VHS."

But Heartland originally meant "Area from which to execute totalitarian domination."

"The balance of power (between Oceania, Eastasia, and Eurasia)," warned George Orwell in *1984*, "always remains roughly even, and the territory which forms the *heartland* of each super-state always remains inviolate." Orwell uses "heartland" in its original sense, as it appeared in a 1904 paper by Britain's Sir Halford Mackinder. Mackinder told the Royal Geographical Society that the greatest threat to the British Empire was the vast north-central part of Eurasia. The area had produced several conquerors throughout history, and was unaffected by British sea power.

In the 1940s, Orwell built off of this idea that three super countries of the future would remain constantly at war on their borders, but the strings would be pulled from the vast, untouchable interiors. The heartland of Orwell's Oceania (dun, dun dun!) is the American Midwest.

I mentioned it earlier, but it bears repeating, partly because you're probably skimming this thing and partly for the fact that even if you're reading intently, your Internet-and-text-message-fried brain can't even remember how this sentence started, let alone what was mentioned dozens of pages ago.

If the Midwest were its own country, it would be one of the most powerful economies in the world. With a GDP of more than $3

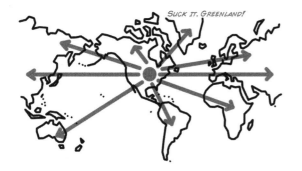

SUCK IT, GREENLAND!

**CENTRAL LOCATION
GOOD FOR
TAKING OVER THE WORLD**

PREVIOUS PAGE:
James Cash Penney
founder of JC Penney
Hamilton, Missouri

During World War II, Orwell's
good friend at the BBC was
TS Eliot
St Louis, Missouri

THIS PAGE:
Alan Freed
raised in Salem, Ohio

Chuck Berry
St Louis, Missouri

Ike Turner
settled in St Louis, Missouri

Smokey Robinson
Detroit, Michigan

Bo Diddley
raised in Chicago

Chester "Howlin' Wolf" Burnett
settled in Chicago

Tom Turpin
settled in St Louis, Missouri,
and Kansas City, Missouri

Scott Joplin
settled in Sedalia, Missouri

trillion, it would be the fourth-largest economy in the world. With a population of only 67 million, its GDP per person would be second among all economies, a little behind Japan.

Luckily for America, we have not *(yet)* seceded and ushered in an era of Orwellian totalitarianism and warfare. America as a whole gets credit for our accomplishments, but it is the Midwest that won the space race and the Second World War, and puts the "Kicks Some Ass" in Amer-kicks-some-ass-ica.

In 1975, the phrase, "As American as baseball, hot dogs, apple pie, and Chevrolet" (of course Chevrolet came up with this phrase) tries to put into words the mystery of American-ness. The problem: only one of those is 100% American. Baseball is an adaptation of similar English and French sports. Hot dogs come from the German frankfurter, and apple pie arrived with British settlers. But Chevrolet is 100% American (the cars run, the colors don't). Or, I should say, 100% Midwestern — founded in Detroit in 1911.

In fact, much of what is considered American is really Midwestern. Budweiser is from St Louis, McDonald's is from Illinois, our dialect is the traditional American accent, and rock and roll — the most American music — comes from the Midwest.

The term "rock and roll" was itself coined in the 1950s by Alan "Moondog" Freed, a DJ for Cleveland radio station WJW. At the time, he was playing R&B, blues, jazz, and combinations of those that were still emerging.

This new style was epitomized by St Louis' Chuck Berry, whose guitar solos and showmanship combined with lyrics like, "Hail, hail rock and roll/deliver me from the days of old" in 1957's "School Days." Berry was flanked by a host of other Midwestern rock pioneers such as Ike Turner, Smokey Robinson, Bo Diddley and Howlin' Wolf, all of whom were drawing from origins in Kansas City's ragtime of the 1890s.

Following the Civil War, waves of Southerners headed to St Louis, Kansas City, Chicago, and Detroit. Their styles started to combine with local music. This fusion first produced ragtime. This was the first style of music that spread over a wide area, largely due to sheet music sales and live performances by Kansas City's Tom Turpin and Scott Joplin — whose "Maple Leaf Rag" became a national hit in 1899.

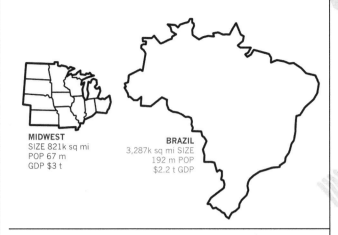

MIDWEST
SIZE 821k sq mi
POP 67 m
GDP $3 t

BRAZIL
3,287k sq mi SIZE
192 m POP
$2.2 t GDP

MIDWEST
SIZE 821k sq mi
POP 67 m
GDP $3 t

AUSTRALIA
2,900k sq mi SIZE
22 m POP
$1.5 t GDP

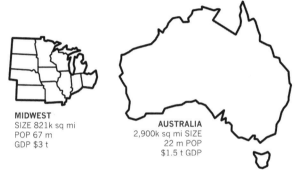

MIDWEST
SIZE 821k sq mi
POP 67 m
GDP $3 t

MEXICO
758k sq mi SIZE
112 m POP
$1.5 t GDP

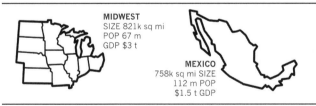

MIDWEST
SIZE 821k sq mi
POP 67 m
GDP $3 t

FRANCE
260k sq mi SIZE
65 m POP
$2.8 t GDP

MIDWEST
SIZE 821k sq mi
POP 67 m
GDP $3 t

UNITED KINGDOM
240k sq mi SIZE
63 m POP
$2.4 t GDP

UNITED
STATES OF
MIDWEST
BY THE NUMBERS

We may be just a couple of t-shirt printers, but we don't throw the term "superpower" around willy-nilly.

We talk the talk, and we walk the walk. From good-looking people to a formidable nuclear arsenal, from modesty to massive economy, the numbers below don't lie, they've just been rounded.

Our gross economy would be ranked fourth in the world. But among the top economies, only the Japanese have a higher GDP per person, but they also make terrible movies.

And if your mind only operates when things are compared to Brazil, Australia, Mexico, France, and the United Kingdom, we've taken care of that for you too.

	GDP	POP	GDP pr pop
China:	$6.9 t	1,340 m	$5,149
Japan:	$5.8 t	127 m	$45,669
Germany:	$3.6 t	81 m	$44,444
Midwest:	**$3.0 t**	**67 m**	**$44,776**
France:	$2.8 t	65 m	$43,076
Brazil:	$2.5 t	192 m	$13,020
UK:	$2.4 t	62 m	$38,709
Italy:	$2.2 t	60 m	$36,666

In the decades that followed, Midwestern music splintered from ragtime to jazz or blues, to R&B, to funk, to rock and roll. Cities developed their own playing styles and sound. There was Chicago style, Detroit style, Kansas City style, Chicago Blues, Kansas City Blues, and St Louis Blues. The latter was cemented in history when W.C. "Father of Blues" Handy recorded "St Louis Blues" in 1917, during years of traveling throughout the Midwest after he'd left the South in the 1890s.

"We always played the blues in St Louis," commented St Louis native Miles Davis. Davis grew up surrounded by a mix of music in St Louis, and rose to prominence in the 1940s, becoming one of the nation's seminal jazz musicians alongside Midwesterners Charlie Parker, Bix Beiderbecke, Art Tatum, Benny "King of Swing" Goodman, Count Basie, and Joe Oliver.

At the same time, blues grew and morphed alongside jazz. In 1950, Poland-born Leonard Chess founded Chess Records in Chicago, which helped cultivate local talent and also brought new talent into the city, such as Howlin' Wolf, Bo Diddley, Muddy Waters, and Etta James.

Detroit took blues in a different direction when Berry Gordy founded Motown Records in 1959. Gordy developed a unique style through Midwestern natives including The Jackson Five, Stevie Wonder, and Diana Ross, and out-of-towners such as Marvin Gaye who came to Detroit to record.

From the mid-Twentieth century through today, music in the Midwest has headed in so many directions that it is almost impossible to track. Chicago's Curtis Mayfield pioneered funk in the early 1950s that turned into Chicago's Earth Wind & Fire in 1969, Michigan's Grand Funk Railroad in 1969, and Minneapolis' Prince in 1974. Detroit's MC5 and Iggy Pop established themselves as one of hardcore punk's progenitors in 1963, northern Minnesota's Bob Dylan pioneered counter-culture folk music in the 1960s, Chicago musicians invented house music in the 1980s, Detroit musicians invented techno music in the 1980s, and a host of Midwestern cities launched hip-hop artists such as Common, Eminem, and Kanye West in the 1990s.

But rock and f'ing roll has always been king in the Midwest. Like niceness and wit, it is at the core of our being. In *Beyond the Lighted Stage,* a documentary about the Canadian band Rush, the band discusses how their big break came when Cleveland DJ

Miles Davis
born in Alton, Illinois,
raised in East St Louis, Illinois

Charlie Parker
Kansas City, Kansas

Bix Beiderbecke
Davenport, Iowa

Art Tatum
Toledo, Ohio

Benny Goodman
raised in Chicago, Illinois

Joe Oliver
traveled up to
Richmond, Indiana, in 1923 to
make some of the very first jazz
recordings

Leonard Chess
raised in Chicago, Illinois

Berry Gordy
Detroit, Michigan

The Jackson Five
Gary, Indiana

Stevie Wonder
born in Saginaw, Michigan,
raised in Detroit, Michigan

Diana Ross
Detroit, Michigan

Curtis Mayfield
Chicago, Illinois

Grand Funk Railroad
Flint, Michigan

Iggy Pop
Muskegon, Michigan

Donna Halper first started playing their single, "Working Man" across northern Ohio in 1974. Their Zeppelinesque sound took off, and later that year, London-based Uriah Heep took them as an opener for a Midwestern tour. "We found," said Uriah frontman Mick Box, "the best rock audience was the Midwest … They loved their rock music."

In 1984, Spinal Tap's American tour took them through Middle America. "We're heading next to … um … Dez Moynz," David St Hubbins tells his girlfriend over the phone. "What? (pause) I don't know, it's in Indiana or something."

Even before Chuck Berry, and before Alan Freed, "rock and roll" had been used occasionally, mainly to describe the style of Sister Rosetta Tharpe, who moved from the South to Chicago in the 1920s and started playing a mix of gospel, blues, and jazz. Though not well known today, she has been called "The Godmother of Rock and Roll" because her style of play and showmanship influenced Elvis Presley, Jerry Lee Lewis, Little Richard, and Robert Plant. Johnny Cash cited Tharpe as his favorite musician and Bob Dylan called her "sublime and splendid." In 1951, Tharpe had her third wedding in front of 25,000 fans in Washington, recording the whole thing for later release as an album.

From Tharpe to Berry, the Midwest has taken planet Earth on a wild ride, with classic rockers like Styx, REO Speedwagon, Kansas, Boston's Tom Scholz, and The Eagles, to edgier classic rockers like Alice Cooper and Ted Nugent. From the 1990s "industrial rock" of Chicago's Ministry to Ohio's Brian Warner of Marilyn Manson to Cleveland's Nine Inch Nails, we reached new heights of loud screaminess with Des Moines' *nine-member* band Slipknot in 1995. That is about four more people than you really need for a rock band, but without those extra dudes hanging around, who is going to pound on barrels and empty kegs with hammers while the first five grind through power chords and kick double-bass drums?

The Midwest knows when to tone things down, too. Just as rock was getting slightly overblown, along came Detroit's White Stripes in 1997 and Akron's Black Keys in 2001. Both were two-member outfits who stripped their sound waaaaay down. The White Stripes famously recorded their 2003 platinum-certified album *Elephant* in two weeks on a tape machine that was older than The Beatles.

There is not a challenge we have not met in our quest to bring all people the greatest music ever created. And so it's only fitting that when three Midwest states combined their powers, they forged the greatest rock band of all time: Tool.

Now, I've been pushing this "Tool is the greatest band of all time" thing since high school. Plenty have disagreed. When a roommate of mine at Penn asked what type of music I was into, I played him one of Tool's tracks. He waited for the song to end before commenting, "I can't imagine you get a lot of converts to your type of music."

It's not easy being a pioneering band. The Beatles, Led Zeppelin, Rush, and Radiohead — they all had their detractors. Tool has melded a musical style many call "art metal" by taking a guy from Ohio who runs an Arizona winery when not playing, a guy from Illinois who makes claymation videos in his free time, a guy from Kansas, and combining them with odd time signatures, hard guitar riffs, alto-pitch vocals, often-ironic lyrics, Afro-beats-meets-jazz drumming, psychedelic album artwork, live laser shows, and song titles like "Rosetta Stoned," "Jerk-Off," or "Hooker with a Penis." They headlined some of the biggest festivals in the world, and inspired dozens of bands and artists since forming in Los Angeles in the early 1990s.

For whatever reason, I have formed a deep, personal bond with this music. I look to Tool's lyrics and interviews as general life advice, quoting their opinions like English majors quote Shakespeare and Michiganders quote Bo Schembechler. When music magazines didn't include Tool in their "Greatest Bands" or "Greatest Albums" lists, I'd say: "I'm never reading this bullshit magazine again." But after about the sixth time that happened, I realized I was running out of music magazine options.

When people tell me that they don't like Tool, my knee-jerk response is not, "Oh, well, that's fine, to each his own," but rather, "You obviously haven't listened to *enough* Tool."

So like the Asian Christians who tried to convert me to Jesus at Penn, I'm carrying the torch for Tool. Even today, plenty take issue with their greatness. But this is a book that I have total control over and can write about any fucking band I want to.

Since I don't go to church or believe that all of the animals were on the Ark, a Tool concert is about the closest thing I get to a religious experience (and not too far off from happy-clappy Evangelical churches with their guitars and flat-screen TVs).

In June 2010, I drove from Des Moines to Colorado to see Tool play at Redrocks. It was warm and sunny, and I had time to take in the scenery along the

Bo Schembechler
according to my curfew-setting
mom, Bo said, "Nothing good
happens after midnight"
Barberton, Ohio

way: the largest railroad classification yard in North Platte, Nebraska, and the massive feed lots in eastern Colorado. Somewhere along the way I saw a billboard that read, "Meth doesn't help you hook up." I thought, "It's a good thing I'm married — kids must be trying some crazy shit to get together these days."

At Redrocks, I had another moment of thanks for my own marriage (rare for me to have two in one day) standing in the parking lot. Because, not to knock my own people, but if you were looking to reproduce, the parking lot of a Tool concert should not be at the top of your list for mate selection. There are the standard hard-rock kids with black shirts, guts, facial hair, always a little sweaty, who are wearing what can be classified as either really baggy black long shorts or really baggy black capris. There are the older guys who have followed Tool since the 1990s. There are the hippies who like Phish and The Dead but wish they just rocked a little harder, and as I walked past a group of them, they were literally playing hackie sack and debating what a Tool fan should look like: "I mean, dude, what does a Tool fan *look* like? You know? Do they have to wear the shirts? I don't have the shirts."

"Yeah, you do, dude."

"Okay, I have *one* Tool shirt, but I don't wear it a lot, you know? It's about the music, dude. You know? ... Are you hungry?"

Once the concert started, Tool rocked everyone's socks off, as you could imagine, I was overcome enough to high five the strangers standing next to me, and as the moon rose in the background over Denver,

AND ON THE EIGHTH DAY, GOD CREATED TOOL *The three core members of this life-changing prog-rock-meets-hard-rock band are Midwestern lifers.*

Maynard James Keenan (Ravenna, Ohio) Tool's vocalist was born in Ohio, moved to Michigan with his father, and said that he was inspired to join the Army because of Bill Murray's (Wilmette, Illinois) performance in *Stripes*. The Army later paid for Keenan's schooling at the Kendall College of Art and Design in Grand Rapids, Michigan, where he studied before moving to Los Angeles.

Adam Jones (Park Ridge, Illinois) Tool's guitarist met Keenan in Los Angeles around 1990. Jones had been out in LA, working on stop animation for films. Though born in Park Ridge, he had been raised in Libertyville, attending high school and playing in a band with Tom Morello (Libertyville, Illinois), who went on to found Rage Against the Machine in LA.

Danny Carey (Lawrence, Kansas) Tool's drummer lived next door to Jones and would practice with Jones and Keenan when other drummers didn't show up. Carey had moved out to LA as a studio drummer for Carole King, having played in high school in Paola, then studied jazz at the University of Missouri-Kansas City while playing with drumming greats such as Ben Kelso in Kansas City.

TOOL WISDOM *Tool is the perfect blend of Midwestern work ethic, genius, modesty, and philosophy. They are a wellspring of advice.*

On the importance of staying true to the art: "All you know about me is what I sold you ... I sold out long before you ever even heard my name, I sold my soul to make a record ... All you read and wear and see on TV is a product waiting for your fat-ass dirty dollar. So shut up and buy my new record."

On death: "This body holding me reminds me of my own mortality. Embrace this moment, remember, we are eternal, all this pain is an illusion."

On politics and yoga: "Foot in mouth and head up asshole what ya talkin 'bout? Difficult to dance 'round this one 'till you pull it out."

On L Ron Hubbard: "Fuck L Ron Hubbard."

On planning ahead: "Feed my will to feel this moment. Urging me to cross the line. Reaching out to embrace the random, reaching out to embrace whatever may come."

One lovemaking: "Travel a mile six inches at a time on Maynard's dick."

On the importance of television: "Vicariously I live while the whole world dies."

BANDS THAT SOUND LIKE THEY'RE FROM THE MIDWEST BUT AREN'T ACTUALLY FROM THE MIDWEST

Your product's gotta have a good name. With such musical dominance, it is only logical for bands in other regions (or countries) to c'mon and ride our train, and ride it.

Quad City DJs (Jacksonville, Florida) This group's single, "C'mon N' Ride It (The Train)" took America by storm in 1996. As a young Iowan, when I heard the name Quad City DJs, I thought there was no way they were from the Quad Cities. And they weren't. They're from Florida. Why the name? Who knows. There aren't even four people from four different cities in the group. They probably just co-opted their name to establish some street cred from a connection to Eastern Iowa and Western Illinois. The country saw through this sham, and the train seemed to stop after 1996.

Bay City Rollers (Edinburgh, Scotland) Sorry Bay City in Michigan, Bay City in Illinois, Bay City in Wisconsin, and San Francisco, these rollers are from the U.K. However, the band did actually name themselves after Bay City, Michigan. Originally called The Saxons, the band decided to change its name by throwing a dart at a map of the United States. The dart apparently landed right in between Michigan's thumb and index finger. Bay City itself, though, is no backwater. It is the birthplace of Madonna, Warren Avis (the founder of Avis Rent A Car), and Annie Edson Taylor (the first person to go over Niagara Falls in a barrel and live).

The Des Moines Riot (Edinburgh, Scotland) WTF Scotland?! You're stealing Midwestern city names again? This four-piece band isn't particularly good or popular, but we bumped into them on MySpace years ago during some Des Moines-related searching. Apparently our region must play well in Braveheart-land.

Enon (New York, New York) This indie rock band formed in 1999 and though it splits its time between Philadelphia and New York, it is named after the village Enon, Ohio (near one member's hometown in Dayton).

Great Lakes (Athens, Georgia) Is a psych/pop/rock band connected to other Southern bands under the Elephant 6 Recording Company. Another Athens band in the group also adopts a northern locale for its name: Of Montreal.

I thought, "I can see why people move to Colorado." Dry air, cool nights, mountains.

The next day, I drove with the windows down out of Colorado into Nebraska. I put on a little Rush Limbaugh so that the next time I saw my grandparents I'd know what they want to talk about and what issues I should avoid — starting with "You know what I just *love* about Ted Kennedy" is a bad way to go.

After seven short hours I was reaching eastern Nebraska, El Rushbo was still talking about the formation of a socialist haven under Barack Obama, and it struck me how green everything was. After three days of a brown, western landscape, the Midwest looks almost like a lush jungle with white wind turbines dotting the horizon. It was really jarring how prosperous it appeared.

And it has always looked this way. "The Garden of Eden," wrote a New York correspondent to Nebraska in the early Twentieth century, "was not more purely pastoral." The land was productive, the people started to prosper, and we started putting the *Real* in Real America.

"The ascendancy of the term 'Middle West,' after about 1912," writes professor James Shortridge, "corresponds to an expansion of the perceived importance of that region to American society ... The Middle West had become the standard by which to judge the rest of the nation."

In the early Twentieth century, the idea of the Midwest as a Utopian land of farmers championing true democracy led to a near idolization of the region by the rest of the country. New York journalist Stephen Dale remarked that in the Midwest, "Every man who approaches a stranger is taken to be honest until he proves himself otherwise." Another East Coast correspondent in Nebraska wrote that the settlers were, "worthy specimens of a worthy type — plain, sensible, honest men, who have never begged any odds in the game

MIDWEST MUSIC

It's not every day that you see a list ranging from Miles Davis to Marilyn Manson or from Liberace to Insane Clown Posse.

But the Big Flyover can do it all, from jazz greats to the creation of modern Rock and Roll, Techno, and House. Take a minute to really drink in a couple of highlights from the last century or so of musical accomplishments.

NORTH DAKOTA
Lawrence Welk (1920s)

DULUTH
Bob Dylan (1961)
Low (1993)

TWIN CITIES
Bernie Leadon of
The Eagles (1961)
Prince (1974)
The Suicide
Commandos (1975)
Husker Du (1979)
Atmosphere (1990s)
Pitchfork Media (1995)

DES MOINES
Slipknot (1995)
The Nadas (1995)
The Envy Corps (2001)
**80/35 Music
Festival (2008)**

OMAHA
311 (1988)
Bright Eyes (1995)
The Faint (1995)
Cursive (1995)
Rilo Kiley (1998)
Tilly and The Wall (2001)

SHENANDOAH
*The Every Brothers
(1940s)*

TOPEKA
Kansas (1973)

WICHITA
Joe Walsh (1960s)

KANSAS CITY area
Scott Joplin (1894)
Tom Turpin (1897)
Count Basie (1929)
Charlie Parker (1934)
Tech N9ne (1985)
Danny Carey of
Tool (1990s)
Puddle of Mudd (1992)
The Get Up Kids (1995)

EAU CLAIRE
Bon Iver (2006)

MILWAUKEE area
Les Paul (1928)
Liberace (1936)
Violent Femmes
(1980)

DAVENPORT area
Bix Beiderbecke
(1920s)

GARY
The Jackson
Five (1964)

CHICAGO area
Benny "King of Swing"
Goodman (1920s)
Louis Armstrong (1920s)
Earl Hines (1930s)
Sister Rosetta Tharpe
(1930s)
Chess Records (1950)
Curtis Mayfield (1950s)
Howlin' Wolf (1951)
Bo Diddley (1951)
Muddy Waters (1953)
Etta James (1960)
Styx (1961)
REO Speedwagon (1966)
Chicago (1967)
Earth, Wind & Fire (1969)
Patti Smith (1971)
Cheap Trick (1973)
Ministry (1980s)
Big Black (1981)
"Invention of House" (1980s)
Farm Aid (1985)
Local H (1987)
Smashing Pumpkins (1988)
Twista (1990)
Adam Jones of Tool (1990s)
Tom Morello of RATM (1990s)
Tortoise (1990)
Common (1991)
Kuk Harrell (1992)
Liz Phair (1991)
Tricky Stewart (1994)
Disturbed (1994)
Chevelle (1995)
Kanye West (1996)
Lupe Fiasco (1999)
Fall Out Boy (2001)
Lollapalooza Festival (2005)
Pitchfork Music Festival (2006)

ST LOUIS area
*WC "Father of Blues"
Handy (1917)*
Shorty Baker (1930s)
Miles Davis (1940s)
Chuck Berry (1941)
Ike Turner (1956)
Tina Turner (1958)

CENTRAL INDIANA
Joe Oliver (1923)
David Lee Roth (1969)
John Cougar (1976)
Axl Rose of
GNR (1980s)
Izzy Stradlin of
GNR (1980s)

**COLUMBUS
area**
RJD2 (1993)
John Legend
(2001)

DETROIT area
McKinney's Cotton
Pickers (1920s)
Doc Cook (1930s)
Dorsey Brothers (1930s)
John Lee Hooker (1948)
Smokey Robinson (1950s)
Motown Records (1959)
Stevie Wonder (1961)
Bob Seger (1961)
Marvin Gaye (1960s)
Diana Ross (1963)
MC5 (1963)
Alice Cooper (1964)
The Up (1965)
Glenn Frey of
The Eagles (1966)
Rodriguez (1967)

Iggy Pop (1967)
*Parliament-Funkadelic
(1968)*
Grand Funk Railroad
(1969)
Ted Nugent (1975)
Madonna (1979)
**"Invention of Techno"
(1980s)**
Kid Rock (1988)
Insane Clown Posse (1990)
Xzibit (1994)
The Detroit Cobras (1994)
Eminem (1996)
The White Stripes (1997)
Electric 6 (1999)
Sufjan Stevens (1999)

TOLEDO
Art Tatum (1925)
Tom Scholz
of Boston (1969)

CLEVELAND
Freddie Webster (1920s)
**"Rock and Roll" coined
(1951)**
Steven Adler of GNR
(1980s)
**Rock and Roll Hall
of Fame (1983)**
Tracy Chapman (1986)
Nine Inch Nails (1988)
Bone Thugs (1991)
Kid Cudi (2003)

AKRON area
Dean Martin (1939)
Devo (1972)
Macy Gray (1990)
Marilyn Manson (1990s)
Maynard James
Keenan of Tool (1990s)
The Black Keys (2001)

KEY: ***regular font (year)** are artists from that city, who either stayed or moved elsewhere to play.
*italic font (year) did a large part of their work in that city.

of life, and whose strongest wish seems to be to stand square with their fellows."

By 1920, Midwestern commentator Charles Hunger noted that the people and the land added up to "a kingdom of plenty ... It is in the sturdy, healthy, full-blooded heyday of its strength."

At the start of the First World War, the Midwest produced the highest enlistment quotas in the country. Illinois and Indiana, for example, filled two-thirds of their quotas by May, 1917. The highest rate in the northeast was Pennsylvania's one-third. Kansas' William Allen White observed, "We who are really doing our part in furnishing soldiers and sailors might well consider the puzzle of the East and the flabbiness of New England."

Suck on that, Rhode Island!

By the 1940s and 1950s, the Midwest was an engine of mass production — of cars, trains, tanks, and planes.

The Midwest is the beating heart of America, projecting power, strength, and rock and roll from inside its kingdom and recognizing that things could have been a lot different if we had decided to split long ago.

"I love Ohio." – Dave Chappelle

CLEVELAND

COLUMBUS
★

CINCINNATI

THE *ACTUAL* BIRTHPLACE OF AVIATION (SO CUT THE BULLSHIT NORTH CAROLINA!)

CAPITAL: Columbus **SIZE:** 44,825 square miles **POPULATION:** 11,544,951 **ADMISSION TO THE UNION:** March 1, 1803. Not only the first state in the Midwest, but the first state outside the original 13 colonies. **STATE BEVERAGE:** Tomato Juice **STATE SYMBOL:** The Buckeye. **WHAT IS A BUCKEYE?** It's a tree that produces a fruit that is poisonous for animals and slightly for humans. **AND THAT'S THEIR STATE SYMBOL?** Yup. **PRESIDENTS:** If you count William Henry Harrison (and why the hell wouldn't you?), Ohio has produced a whopping eight presidents, more than any other state. **THANKS FOR ALL THE HELP, GEORGE WASHINGTON, NOW CLAIM YOUR PRIZE:** 70,000 acres in Ohio. This was Washington's official payment for his Revolutionary War service. But really, what's better than a spread of land in the Buckeye State? **SURPRISE! I'M FROM OHIO:** Toni Morrison, Charles Manson, Nine Inch Nails, Halle Berry, Clark Gable, Paul Newman, The Black Keys, Dean Martin, Neil Armstrong, Don King, Ken Griffey Jr, and The Naked Cowboy.

2.2 YOU KNOW, REST OF AMERICA, IF WE DON'T START GETTING SOME RESPECT, WE'RE GONNA SECEDE FROM YOUR ASS.

"IF THE MIDWEST, RATHER THAN THE SOUTH, HAD SECEDED, THE CIVIL WAR WOULD HAVE TURNED OUT DIFFERENTLY"

We should be getting an annual "thank you" card from the rest of the country for not seceding. We've often considered the notion.

The Upper Peninsula Independence Association (UPIA) advocates that the Upper Peninsula should break the Lower Peninsula's yoke of domination, take a few counties in Wisconsin with it for good measure, and form the state of "Superior."

Kurdistan never got its own country. Instead, it was split between Iraq, Turkey, and Syria. So it has been with the U.P. Thomas Jefferson had once apparently penned their territory to be the state of "Sylvania." But in 1835, when Michigan was ready for statehood, it was locked in the "Toledo War" with Ohio, a dispute over how far south Michigan's border would go. To resolve the conflict, the federal government promised Michigan that if it moved its border claim a little to the north, giving Toledo back to Ohio, Michigan could take the entire Upper Peninsula.

For the next 130 years, the U.P. lived in a state of oppression until the UPIA's formation in 1962. That year, the UPIA collected 20,000 signatures on a ballot for independence, but fell short of the 36,000 needed by law (or so the Lower Peninsula would have us believe!). The Lower Peninsula didn't seem to grasp the gravity of the situation, and started jokingly referring to U.P. residents as "Yoopers" and their Canadianesque dialect as "Yoopanse" in the early 1970s.

In 2009, the Michigan Economic Development Corporation (run by Lower Peninsula puppets in Lansing) kicked the U.P. straight in the balls by producing state maps that didn't include the Upper Peninsula.

Damn you, tyrannical Lower Peninsula! Can't break away, but can't get included in state maps?!

U.P. State Representative Mike Lahti introduced a resolution requiring that all official maps show the entire state of Michigan. The bill passed and the Lower Peninsula dodged another bullet. Remember, the World's Largest working rifle is housed in Ishpeming on the U.P. (see *Part One* if your short-term memory has been fried by the Internet and texting).

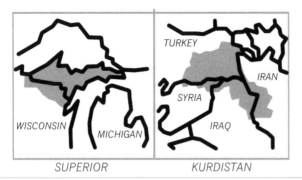

SUPERIOR   KURDISTAN

IS THIS PLACE KURDISTAN?

**PEOPLE FROM MISSOURI
BE CUTTIN'
DOWN TREES**

"MISTER, I BELIEVE YOU JUST CUT DOWN ONE OF MY PRIZE-WINNIN' BEE TREES!"

"OH NO I DI'INT... THAT WAS MOST DEFINITELY NOT ME. NOPE."

In smaller-scale acts of departure, St Louis explored the idea of home rule in 1875. Throughout the 1800s, western Nebraska discussed seceding from eastern Nebraska, possibly to join with Wyoming (things must get pretty bad when you're talking about merging with Wyoming).

Western Nebraska had always felt pushed around by the powers in Omaha, and they had a point. When the state was forming in the late 1850s, many thought the state capitol should be in Lancaster, just west of Omaha. But Omaha engineered to change the name of Lancaster to Lincoln to play on anti-Abraham Lincoln sentiments and play up pro-Douglas sentiment (Omaha is located in Douglas County).

Travel considerations prevailed and the newly named Lincoln became the capitol. Omaha refused to give up the state seal until a band of Lincolnites took it by force and carried it back to Lincoln across the frozen Platte River.

The Lincoln/Omaha brush-up of the 1860s is just one of many. The 1835 "Toledo War" gets the most play, but later there was the 1839 "Bee War" and the 1846 "Honey War" that pitted Iowa against Missouri, following a border dispute that led Missourians to claim part of southern Iowa in 1839 and cut down three prized bee trees. Because sugar was in short supply on the frontier (and because high-fructose corn syrup was a century away), honey was the Ranch dressing of the 1830s. Cutting down bee trees was cause to raise a militia and throw down.

The 1839 matter was resolved, but things flared up again in 1846. One Iowa captain showed up with men and six wagonloads of supplies. Luckily, only one wagon was filled with weapons — mostly pitchforks and shovels. The other five were filled with liquor.

These wars never escalated to shooting, and like good Americans, Iowa and Missouri sued each other, settling in 1850 at the US Supreme

Court, which awarded Iowa a large stretch of land along its southern border (and we've been trying to give that southern line of counties back to Missouri ever since zing!).

In the 1930s, the "Cow War" broke out between the Dakotas and Minnesota when Dakota ranchers attempted to drive cattle across the border to escape drought. Minnesota Governor Floyd Olson called out the National Guard to restore order.

There were countless disputes over state capitals and county seats. Minnesota census takers were kidnapped to prevent town populations from being properly counted in the 1800s. In 1852, St Paul residents feared the state capital would move to the city of St. Peter, which inspired Joseph Rolette to steal the bill proposing the move and hide with it in a hotel room until the constitutional time limit passed and St Peter lost its bid. The 1852 equivalent of "hiking the Appalachian Trail," maybe.

In 1868 a wagonload of men from Naperville, Illinois, "invaded" Wheaton, trying to steal county records and take them back to Naperville — apparently whoever had possession of county records had the county seat? Seems precarious.

The most serious case of Midwest-on-Midwest violence was the "Bleeding Kansas" conflict from 1854 to 1859. It took place between Kansas and Missouri, within Kansas itself, and was a free-for-all to determine whether Kansas would be a slave state. Fifty-six people died. John Brown led an anti-slavery gang, and South Carolina Senator Preston Brooks bludgeoned Massachusetts Senator Charles Sumner on the Senate floor along the way.

On January 29, 1861, the anti-slavery forces won, and Kansas was admitted to the union as a free state, a fact that they've lorded over Missouri for the last 150 years. Our Lawrence, Kansas-born RAYGUNer, Blake, assures us that Missouri will, "Never live it down. Never."

The closest any of the Midwest came to *actually* leaving the country wasn't very close. In the early 1800s, Germans were leaving Pennsylvania to settle the Midwest and were attracting liberal Germans fleeing political oppression in Europe. Together they dreamed of creating the country of New Germany. That idea gained steam after the unsuccessful European revolutions of 1848. Those brought a wave of

"Forty-eighters" to the Midwest who pushed for a German society that would break away from America, setting up their country in Wisconsin Territory. But in 1861, the Civil War broke out, and something about the 600,000 or so lives lost in that really dampened further secession ideas. Still, German culture continued to expand across the Midwest, with German schools, German newspapers and, by 1890, enough beer gardens in Milwaukee to seat 105,000 people at once.

> **By 1890 [there were] enough beer gardens in Milwaukee to seat 105,000 people at once.**

The First World War led to the banning of the German language across the Midwest. Frankfurters became hot dogs, hamburgers became Salisbury steak, and a German-led secession was bound to go over like a hydrogen-filled blimp trying to park in New Jersey.

The rest of the country is lucky the Midwest never pulled any serious secession plans. If the Midwest, rather than the South, had seceded, the Civil War would have turned out differently.

I'll give you a hint about who wins: it starts with an M.

As the Civil War dragged on, the South was outmatched in population, agriculture, and industry.

The Midwest and the North were more evenly divided: the Northeast had about 13.3 million inhabitants in 1870, the Midwest had 13 million; the country's timber production from 1839 to 1889 shifted from New York and Maine to Michigan and Wisconsin; almost all the wheat, corn, and hogs America produced in 1880 came from the Midwest; of the 22 blast furnaces in the iron-steel industry in 1890, half were in the Midwest and half were in the Northeast; and in 1880, America's manufacturing centers with more than 20,000 workers were Boston, Providence, Hartford, Buffalo, New York City, and Pittsburgh in the Northeast; Chicago, Milwaukee, Cincinnati, Detroit, and Cleveland in the Midwest; and none in the South.

The Midwest was also playing with a full deck when it came to military leadership. Ulysses S Grant oversaw Robert E Lee's surrender at Appomattox; William Tecumseh Sherman led the march to the sea; Ambrose Burnside's unique facial hair inspired the "sideburns;" George Armstrong Custer was one of the war's most suc-

Ulysses S Grant
Point Pleasant, Ohio

William Tecumseh Sherman
Lancaster, Ohio

Ambrose Burnside
LIberty, Indiana

George Custer
New Rumley, Ohio

William Cushing
Delafield, Wisconsin

cessful cavalry officers, and William Cushing sank the confederate ironclad *Albermarle* and was known as the "hero of the Civil War."

The North put up a few bumblers such as Philadelphia-born George McClellan. When this first head of the Army of the Potomac wasn't wasting time continuously training his troops, he was leading the disastrous 1862 Peninsula Campaign against an army led by Robert E Lee that McClellan vastly outnumbered. Lincoln removed McClellan remarking, "If he himself can't fight, he excels in making others ready to fight him." After his removal, crybaby McClellan ran against Lincoln in the 1864 election on the antiwar campaign, and lost. Meanwhile, the Midwestern triumvirate of Lincoln, Grant, and Sherman took care of business.

Supporting those Midwestern generals were a people who were fearless and ready for action. In 1862, when it looked like Cincinnati might be invaded, Ohio Governor David Tod called for volunteers under the command of 25-year-old Lew Wallace. An astounding 15,766 men responded in such a hurry that their casual dress made them look like squirrel hunters (while fox hunting required more formal attire, apparently just a t-shirt and jeans got one ready to shoot squirrels). The Ohio legislature adopted a resolution honoring "the patriotic men of the state ... who will be known in history as the Squirrel Hunters." Today they should continue the honor by scrapping the Bearcats in favor of the University of Cincinnati Squirrel Hunters.

THE POWER OF BEN HUR COMPELS YOU! Lew Wallace (Brookville, Indiana) is one of those really bizarre guys in history. After the Civil War he was appointed governor of the New Mexico Territory. By 1881 he was made Military Minister to the Ottoman Empire. Along the way he wrote *Ben Hur: A Tale of the Christ* in 1880, which became the best-selling American novel of the Nineteenth century, passing Harriet Beecher Stowe's *Uncle Tom's Cabin*. It remains one of the best-selling American novels of all time, and in 1959, was made into a film starring Charlton Heston (Evanston, Illinois).

David Tod
Youngstown, Ohio

Republican Party
possibly fathered in Ripon, Wisconsin, and officially founded in Jackson, Michigan

Iowa sent a higher percentage of its population to war than any other state. Its "Greybeard Regiment" featured men who were over the legal army age of 45, many were over the age of 70, and two were killed in combat.

More importantly, the Midwest had right on its side. While New Hampshire-born President Franklin Pierce and Pennsylvania-born President James Buchanan were Southern sympathizers who attempted to admit Kansas as a slave state, the Midwest put its abolitionist money where its mouth was: forming the antislavery Republican Party in Jackson, Michigan, in 1854 and successfully running Abraham Lincoln in 1860.

And if there's any doubt about the Midwest winning the Civil War, know that the only bald eagle used as a military mascot was "Old Abe," who was found in the wilds of the Flambeau River in Wisconsin. He went into 42 battles with Wisconsin's Eighth Battery, and was unscathed. At a parade in Madison, Old Abe flew from his perch, grabbed an American flag, and carried it high in the air over the parade route, to the cheers of the crowds below. You don't see Northeastern or Southern bald eagles doing that. I mean, the Southern bald eagle would have had a tough time flying with its white hood on.

So in the game of battle-ready bald eagles, we have the Midwest beating the Northeast and South 1 to 0 to 0.

Case closed.

RANCH: NECTAR OF THE MIDWESTERN GODS

CREATION: Most likely, God himself mixed up this delectable blend of buttermilk, mayonnaise, salt, garlic, onion, herbs and spices himself, after creating chicken fingers, french fries, wings, and celery. **BUT:** There is a story that it was created in 1954 on a dude ranch in California. **STILL:** We can't get enough of this stuff in the Big Flyover. It's more than a condiment. "I'd like some french fries with Ranch …. What? You don't have Ranch? Then I'll starve!" **CONDIMENT ETIQUETTE:** Don't worry, other regions, you can use Ranch like any condiment. So if you're from the Southwest, use it like Tabasco. If you're from Manhattan's Financial District, just use Ranch on your chicken wings in place of cocaine. However, you do want to make sure to get the hooker's permission before snorting Ranch off her ass.

MEDIO OCCIDENTEM CALCIBUS ASINUM

2.3 THE UNITED STATES OF MIDWEST

By 2008, all was forgiven when it came to the South. American philosopher Sarah Palin, while running for Vice President, declared that the small towns of North Carolina were "the real America" and the "pro-America areas of this great nation."

Uh .... what?

How quickly we forget. One Hundred and Forty-Seven years later and it's as though the Civil War never happened. The South's secession led to a four-year conflict and longer recovery. A Midwest secession would have meant that Sarah Palin in 2008 would have been running for the Vice President of the United States of Who-Gives-A-Shit, hoping to get a little media attention from her country's more successful neighbor, the United States of the Midwest.

Because if the Midwest had seceded, it would be the greatest country in the universe.

The Midwest could have just left, but it also could have turned Manifest Destiny into Manifest Midwest Destiny: taking everything to the Pacific and taking over Canada (a region's gotta stretch out). Even without the West and Canada, we would have mopped up the Twentieth century's major accomplishments: manned flight, both World Wars, Super Bowls I and II, the space race, and the defeat of Communism.

Did the rest of America lend a hand in these? Not really. It was a supporting role, sure, but not one that I could really call "significant."

From the late 1800s, the Midwest built a massive industrial empire on a foundation of intelligent and attractive people. The human capital and vast space in America's middle played right into the Midwest's dominance of aviation. The Wright Brothers flew their planes outside in the summer, but built a wind tunnel at their workshop in Huffman Prairie, where they progressed in the long off-seasons, perfecting their design.

But the vast space of the Midwest does more than lend itself to quiet reflection. It also means it takes a long time to get anywhere. Out East, you bump into a major city every two hours or so. Even the slow train from Philly to New York (a city of 3 million to a city of 12 million) took only about two hours. Amtrak made it in less than two hours. But take Amtrak west from Chicago to the next city over one million people, Denver, and you'd better pack a toothbrush and an extra pair of undies, because it's going to be a while.

One of the first American aviation innovators was Chicago's Octave Chanute, who started experimenting with gliders in the late 1800s. By 1890, he was the country's leading authority on flying machines. In the late 1890s, when Wilbur Wright contacted the Smithsonian about information on airplanes, they directed him to Chanute.

For several years, Chanute helped the Wright Brothers with designs and ideas. In December 1903 at Kitty Hawk beach, the Wright Brothers succeeded in flight and ensured that North Carolina would forever use the major accomplishment of a couple of guys from Ohio as their license plate slogan.

The Wright Brothers went on to open a flight school in Dayton, Ohio, and Orville Wright estimated that he personally taught more than 100 pilots in the early Twentieth century, including almost all of the top pilots in the Army Air Service during the First World War.

Their flight inspired others, such as Glenn Martin, born in Macksburg, Iowa, and raised in Salina, Kansas, who put the "Martin" in Lockheed Martin. After reading about the Wright Brothers, he built his own plane in 1909, and in 1912 he traveled to California and broke the over-water flight record by flying 68 miles from Newport Bay to Catalina and back. Soon after, he established the Glenn Martin Company that later merged with the original Wright Company.

Later in 1912, stunt pilot Lincoln "Fool of the Skies" Beachy introduced the idea of airmail when he was invited by the Dubuque, Iowa, Post Office to demonstrate flying. Although he literally just dropped the mail from the sky near where the addresses were, airmail started to take off … so to speak.

One early airmail carrier was Redfield, South Dakota-born Billy Robinson, who moved to Grinnell, Iowa, at a young age. He built his own plane in 1911, and in 1914 was carrying mail from Des Moines to Chicago when he intentionally overshot, flew all the way to Kentland, Indiana, and set the nonstop flight record for the time.

By 1925, William Bushnell Stout inaugurated Stout Air Services, the first regularly scheduled airline in the U.S., running between Grand Rapids and Detroit.

THIS PAGE:
Octave Chanute
settled in Chicago, Illinois

Glenn Martin
born in Macksburg, Iowa, and raised in Salina, Kansas

Billy Robinson
born in Redfield, South Dakota, and raised in Grinnell, Iowa

NEXT PAGE:
William Stout
Quincy, Illinois

Charles Lindbergh
Little Falls, Minnesota

T Claude Ryan
whose San Diego company built the Spirit of St Louis Parsons, Kansas

Amelia Earhart
Atchison, Kansas

Hall Hibbard and Clarence Johnson
original designer of Lockheed's Electra, which Earhart was flying around the world Fredonia, Kansas, and Ishpeming, Michigan

One of the most famous aviators was another airmail pilot who started flying at the Nebraska Aircraft Corporation's flight school in 1922: Charles Lindbergh. In May 1927, Lindbergh became world famous after he flew nonstop across the Atlantic at the age of 25 to win the Raymond Orteig prize — $25,000 for the first person to fly solo from New York to Paris. The prize had started in 1919 and had been taken up by many of the world's most famous pilots. Six died trying to win.

Lindbergh was a latecomer to the competition. His "partner," the *Spirit of St Louis*, was custom built with money from investors and $2,000 of Lindbergh's savings from flying mail. He took off at 7:52 AM on May 20, and arrived in Paris 33.5 hours later. Onlookers stormed the airfield and carried him on their shoulders for nearly an hour.

A year later, in 1928, Lindbergh's feat was matched by Amelia Earhart, who became the first woman to fly across the Atlantic. She was awarded the Distinguished Flying Cross by the U.S. Government and went on to teach aviation at Purdue University. In 1937 she disappeared over the Pacific while attempting to circumnavigate the globe.

Midwest aviation combined a pioneering spirit with industrial capacity. In the early Twentieth century, for instance, Stout's air service grew out of his partnership with Henry Ford, who invested in the Stout Metal Airplane Company in the early 1920s, then partnered with Stout on the construction and engineering of craft.

The letter that initially drew Ford and almost two dozen other Midwest investors into Stout's project, was one Stout sent asking for $1,000 from each, noting that, "For your one thousand dollars you will get one definite promise: You will never get your money back."

That letter perfectly captures the spirit of the time: innovation above all. There seemed to be no limit to progress.

Ford himself was a product of this innovative culture. In 1891, at the age of 28, the Detroit-area native went to work for Thomas

---

A SHORT LIST OF AMERICA'S TWENTIETH-CENTURY ACCOMPLISHMENTS THAT WERE MORE OR LESS SINGLE-HANDEDLY ACHIEVED BY MIDWESTERNERS *Good God. Both World Wars and Super Bowls I and II? How do we do it? Can we bottle this magic for the other regions? It's just not fair.*

Manned Flight The **Wright Brothers** (Dayton, Ohio) invented and flew the first successful airplane in 1903. 99 years later, Connecticut-born George W Bush established the TSA and made the miracle of flight a pain in the ass.

First World War The Midwest's **John J Pershing** (Laclede, Missouri) was the commander of American forces and the only man besides George Washington to hold the rank of "General of the Armies."

Second World War Not only did **Dwight Eisenhower** (Abilene, Kansas) ascend to Supreme Commander of Allied Forces, but **Omar Bradley** (Clark, Missouri) was one of his generals who led the largest American field force in history.

Space Race Three of the seven Project Mercury astronauts were Midwesterners (more than any other region). One of them, **John Glenn** (Cambridge, Ohio) became the first American to orbit the Earth. But we didn't just sit on our hands after that. Instead we sent **Neil Armstrong** (Wapakoneta, Ohio) to become the first man to walk on the moon. And when America needed a hero to rescue the endangered *Apollo 13*, they turned to **Jim Lovell** (Cleveland, Ohio).

First Super Bowl Green Bay, Wisconsin, Packers.

Second Super Bowl (just for good measure) Green Bay, Wisconsin, Packers.

Defeating Communism When it comes to ideological warfare, only one region will do. **Ronald Reagan** (Tampico, Illinois) was no longer president when the Eastern Bloc and the USSR fell, but it was his steely Midwestern resolve that scared the living shit out of the Russians, causing them to throw in the towel on all their Commie bunk.

Edison's Edison Illuminating Company, where he became chief engineer in 1893 and started experimenting with gasoline engines, culminating in his "Ford Quadricycle" in 1896 — his first self-propelled vehicle. Later, he met Thomas Edison, who encouraged Ford's experimentation, leading him to resign from the Edison Illuminating Company and found the Detroit Automobile Company in 1899.

Ford joined a host of entrepreneurs in the region who were competing, swapping ideas, and failing — Ford's first company folded in two years, and it was almost ten years before the Model T came to life. Many others worked on cars and on the idea of mass production that Ford later made famous. Elwood Haynes made cars profitably in 1893. Ransom Olds founded Oldsmobile and built the first assembly line in 1901, leading to the first mass-produced, low-priced American car. Des Moines' luxury Duesenberg Company survived only twenty years, but left us with the phrase, "What a Doozie" to describe something remarkable.

Just before the turn of the Twentieth century, there were so many car companies in the Midwest that Illinois alone had almost a dozen. Moline's Deere and Company had started 60 years earlier to sell the cast-steel plow to early settlers. It grew into a massive industrialized farm implement company, and experimented with bicycles and introduced one version of the automobile.

John Deere's rise from steel plows to machinery mirrored the rise of the industrialization of the Midwest, with companies including Ford Motor in Detroit, Edison's General Electric in Cleveland, John Rockefeller's Standard Oil in Cleveland, Charles Hall's Alcoa in Oberlin, and Goodyear and Firestone in Akron. In 1896, when the Dow Jones Industrial Average formed, almost half of the original twelve companies were in the Midwest.

In 1906, the United States Steel Corporation founded Gary, Indiana, as a company town. It was the largest city founded in the U.S. in the Twentieth century. Its docks were more than a mile long, taking in shipments of iron ore from Lake Superior and smelting it in massive factories, making it the world's largest integrated steel mill.

In 1919, Hibbing, Minnesota, found itself on top of coal deposits, so it dismantled every building and moved to make way for a new mine.

In 1928, Henry Ford completed his River Rouge plant in southeastern Mich-

RANDOM LIST OF INVENTIONS FROM THE MIDWEST:

The Toaster: The alloy called chromel that made the modern toaster possible was created by Connor Neeson (Detroit, Michigan) and William Hoskins (Chicago, Illinois) in 1906. And in 1909, Cleveland's General Electric submitted a patent for the modern toaster.

The Pop-Up Toaster: Did you think we were too good for improving our inventions? Charles Strite (born in Iowa) created the first pop-up toaster in Stillwater, Minnesota, in 1919.

The Airplane: Developed by Orville and Wilbur Wright (Dayton, Ohio).

The Cash Register: Invented by James Ritty and distributed by John Patterson through the National Cash Company (Dayton, Ohio) in 1883 and 1884.

Post-It Note: Created for 3M (Minneapolis, Minnesota) by Arthur Fry (born in Minnesota and raised in Iowa and Kansas City) in 1974. Beyond Post-Its, 3M has brought the world **Bondo, Scotch Tape, Scotchgard,** and **Hockey Grip Tape.**

Shopping Bag: This is a little hyperbole, but the "handled paper shopping bag" apparently didn't come around until Walter Deubener (St Paul, Minnesota) created them in 1912 for his grocery store, S.S.

Kresge. But the shopping bag was another notch on our retail-invention belt. Marshall Field (settled in Chicago, Illinois) made retail history when his eponymous department store opened in 1852 and made history by **putting prices on products.** That same year, Potter Palmer's (settled in Chicago, Illinois) Potter Palmer & Co instituted the first **"no questions asked"** return policy and allowed customers to **inspect goods** before purchasing them. Just goes to show that we not only reach for the stars with the airplane and toaster, but we take the low-hanging fruit of the invention world.

Zipper: The "zipper scene" in *There's Something About Mary* would never have been possible without Whitcomb Judson (Chicago, Illinois), who invented the zipper in 1890. Called "a clasp-locker" in his day, Judson's product met with little commercial success. In 1923, Akron's BF Goodrich took Judson's invention and put it in a line of rubber galoshes that they called "Zippers."

Strobe Light: Midwest inventions like Techno and House Music in the 1980s may not have been possible without Harold Edgerton (Fremont, Nebraska) who developed the "stroboscope" in the 1930s. The strobe light went on to commercial success, and Edgerton became a professor at MIT, where today he is memorialized with the Edgerton Center for undergraduate research.

INVENTIONS!

It would be hard to have anything in this world without the Midwest -the typewriter, Kleenex, kitty litter, Lincoln Logs, disposable diapers, processed cheese, or the traffic signal to name a few. Even more impressive when you compare our inventions to a few randomly selected inventions from other regions.

RANDOM LIST OF INVENTIONS *NOT* FROM THE MIDWEST:

The Backup: Appropriately nicknamed "Your Bedside Gun Rack," this invention from Newark, Delaware, is literally a gun rack that slides between your mattress and box spring, allowing you to reach down from a resting state and grab your firearm. As its infomercial appropriately explains, The Backup, "eliminates the wasted time of searching for a handgun (or other forms of protection) stored away in your nightstand or closet." Finally! "We as Americans have the right to bear arms," they go on, "but our arms need to be readily accessible in time of need." Thanks, Delaware, you've seen us the airplane and raised us The Backup.

Truck Nuts: These are why the world hates America. A fake scrotum filled with testicles that you hang from the back of your pick-up truck to pretend that the truck you are driving is really something that has a

ballsack. Though associated with "Middle America," the "original nutz on the 'net" are sold by Your Nutz Inc out of San Diego. They are, as they say, a "purveyor of premium novelty testicles since 1996." For only $48, you can order a 16" fake ballsack for your truck. But really, why limit yourself?! Everything you operate should have a set of balls. So put them on your dining room chair, your couch, your lawn mower, or your kid's stroller.

The Shake Weight: For those who always wondered what jerking off a dumbell looks like comes FitnessIQ's (Vista, California) Shake Weight. Its uncomfortably erotic commercial was parodied on *Saturday Night Live* who advertised a way to buy just the infomercial. "I like the slow-mo parts," *SNL* explains, "which technically slow it down for 'science' but really it just gives you more time to ... imagine stuff."

igan. The facility had its own harbor, its own steel processing and, at its peak, employed nearly 100,000 workers in 93 buildings. The man who started tinkering 30 years earlier was now in charge of the largest factory in the world.

With such power amassing throughout the decades, it's little wonder that so many associations have established headquarters in the American Midwest, including the American Cemetery Society in Columbus and the National Funeral Directors Association in Milwaukee. So if you're looking to go quietly into the next life, it would be wise to stay on our good side. You may have already visited the National Macaroni Manufacturers Association and the National Association of Coin Laundry Operators in Chicago, and if it's not on your list, be sure to include Cleveland's National Flexible Packaging Association.

Those of you who like breathing will be happy to know that the International Oxygen Manufacturers Association is headquartered in Cleveland. All those people working to save trees should really just be working to keep northern Ohio safe.

Association headquarters' placement is a kill-or-be-killed industry, and the Midwest has to hold its own. In 2007, disaster struck when the Society for the Preservation and Encouragement of Barber Shop Quartet Singing in America, Inc (or as you probably know it, the SPEBSQSA) moved from Kenosha, Wisconsin — its home since 1957 — to Nashville. This may seem like a minor incident, but the SPEBSQSA maintains the Old Songs Library, which holds more than 100,000 titles (750,000 sheets!), a collection of sheet music second only to the Library of Congress. Was foul play involved? We may never know. But probably. I mean, it's Tennessee.

THE UNITED STATES OF MIDWEST

OUR MAIN INDUSTRY IS KICKING ASS AND OUR SECONDARY INDUSTRY IS TAKING NAMES!

CAPITAL: Chicago **SIZE:** 821,034 square miles **POPULATION:** 67,010,688 **NATIONAL MOTTO:** Medio Occidentem Calcibus Asinum (Latin for "Midwest Kicks Ass") **NATIONAL SEAL:** A Red-Tailed Hawk outline with the USMW's 13 states inside, a pitchfork in one talon and a wrench in the other. **EXPORTS:** Agriculture, heavy manufacturing, and attractive people. **IMPORTS:** Men and women from around the globe seeking a higher level of happiness as well as spiritual and sexual fulfillment. **FOUNDED:** The USMW broke away from the United States on July 13, 1787. **BACK THEN:** It was known as "The Northwest Territory," was composed of Ohio, Michigan, Indiana, Illinois, and Wisconsin, and its capital was Marietta, Ohio, where settlers first arrived. The capital moved to Oxford, Ohio in 1810, then finally to the newly incorporated city of Chicago in 1833.

2.4 HEY, REST OF AMERICA: UHHHH YOU'RE WELCOME

> "WE CAN EVEN DO REDNECK BETTER THAN REDNECKS"

On February 18, 1861, the inauguration of Jefferson Davis was accompanied with the de facto Confederate anthem, a song called "Dixie" that had been written a few years before. Confederate Henry Hotze remarked that, "It is marvelous with what wild-fire rapidity this tune 'Dixie' has spread over the whole South." Indeed, the Southern U.S. became known as Dixie or Dixieland.

But without Ohio, the South would have had no catchy tune to hum while enslaving other humans. Songwriter Dan Emmett composed the original lyrics and melody in the 1850s, and performed it with Bryant's Minstrels at Mechanics Hall in New York City in April of 1859. With Midwestern wit, the song mocked the pro-slavery South, with the lyrics meant to be sung from the point of view of a free black in the North who looks Southward and longs for slavery.

Confederates changed a few of the lyrics and adopted it as their own. Emmett remarked that, "If I had known to what use [the South was] going to put my song, I will be damned if I'd written it."

Dixie wasn't all we did for the South. Missouri-born George Washington Carver studied and taught at Iowa State University. He developed crop rotation and new agricultural products for the South — such as sweet potatoes, and peanuts to turn into peanut butter — that improved agriculture in the South and the health of its citizens. In 1921, Carver actually testified before Congress in favor of a tariff to aid southern peanut farmers.

Without Carver, we may not have had Jimmy Carter. Win some, lose some.

A century or so went by without so much as a friendly call from south of the Mason-Dixon, but the Midwest took it upon itself to carry all three legs of the Southern-identity stool in the 1980s: *Dallas, Miami Vice,* and *The Dukes of Hazzard.* Without these TV shows, America might not have seen that the region that lost the Civil War had grown into a bunch of cowboy hat-wearing drama queens, white blazer-wearing crime fighters, and good-ol' rednecks who cruised around in an orange '69 Dodge

Charger emblazoned on top with the Stars and Bars and called "The General Lee."

Without the Midwest, those shows may never have happened. *Dallas* aired in 1979, directed by Irving Moore and starring Jim Davis, who played Jock Ewing. *Miami Vice* was produced by Michael Mann and followed the Miami detective duo of Sonny Crocket and Rico Tubbs –played by Don Johnson and Philip Michael Thomas.

When *The Dukes of Hazzard* aired on TV in 1979 it introduced America to dead-end rednecks and gave a name to cut-off jean shorts. It featured outlaw brothers Bo and Luke Duke, who drove "The General Lee," and their attractive cousin Daisy Duke. But the South may not know that Daisy was played by Cleveland native Catherine Bach, and Luke was played by Lodi, Wisconsin-born Tom Wopat.

We can even do redneck better than rednecks.

But the South isn't the only region to which the Midwest has lent a hand. Two of Yale University's fight songs, "Bulldog, Bulldog" and "Bingo Eli Yale" were written by Indiana native Cole Porter, during his time there from 1909 to 1913. Porter went on

"UHH, YOU'RE WELCOME, CALIFORNIA"

1848: WT Sherman administers California just before it becomes a state.

1902: HJ Whitley (Chicago, Illinois) becomes the "Father of Hollywood" when he opens the Hollywood Hotel.

1909: The first production company, Selig Polyscope, moves from Chicago to Hollywood.

1917: The Warner Brothers (raised in Youngstown, Ohio) open a studio in Hollywood.

1937: The Joseph Strauss (Cincinnati, Ohio) designed Golden Gate Bridge opens.

1951: Stanford Engineering School Dean, Frederick Terman (English, Indiana), becomes the "Father of Silicon Valley" when he starts the Stanford Industrial Park.

1955: Walt Disney's (born in Chicago and raised in Marceline, Missouri) Disneyland opens.

1961: Dow Corning (Midland, Michigan) develops silicone breast implants.

1968: Robert Noyce (born in Burlington, Iowa, and raised in Grinnell, Iowa) founds Intel and gets the nickname "The Mayor of Silicon Valley."

1970: *Sports Illustrated*'s Swimsuit Issue goes for the "California Look" with Cheryl Rae Tiegs (Breckenridge, Minnesota).

1972: Johnny Carson moves *The Tonight Show* to Burbank.

1976: The Eagles release "Hotel California," co-written by Glenn Frey (Detroit, Michigan).

1977: Eli Lilly (Indianapolis, Indiana) invents Prozac.

1985: Axl Rose (Lafayette, Indiana) co-founds Guns N' Roses.

1998: The Coen Brothers (St Louis Park, Minnesota) make *The Big Lebowski.*

2003: Larry Flynt (who founded *Hustler* in Dayton, Ohio) runs for governor of California during the Gray Davis recall election.

to write the music for *Anything Goes* and hit songs "I Get a Kick Out of You" and "I've Got You Under My Skin."

New York Magazine was founded in 1968 by Missouri's Clay Felker. In 1995 the *New York Times* gushed that, "Few journalists have left a more enduring imprint on late Twentieth century journalism - an imprint that was unabashedly mimicked."

The New Yorker declared that it was "not edited for the old lady in Dubuque" in 1925. But it was co-founded by Jane Grant, and its humorous style was developed by James Thurber — considered the greatest American humorist after Mark Twain. Thurber was *The New Yorker's* main writer until the 1950s and drew many of its cartoons.

Time **magazine once wrote that,** "California is the flashy blonde you like to take out once or twice. Minnesota is the girl you want to marry." But that flashy blonde in California may actually *be* from Minnesota. In 1970, *Sports Illustrated* wanted someone with a "California look" to spice up their Swimsuit Issue. They chose Cheryl Rae Tiegs of Breckenridge, Minnesota.

That is just one of a long line of good deeds the Midwest has done for California. To start with, William Tecumseh Sherman administered California until its civilian organization in 1848. He oversaw the renaming of the town of Yerba Buena to San Francisco (though we unfortunately missed out on *Real World: Yerba Buena* 150 years later), surveyed the city of Sacramento, and officially confirmed the discovery of gold, inaugurating the California Gold Rush.

In 1955, Walt Disney's Disneyland opened in Los Angeles. In 1961, Dow Corning developed the first silicone breast implants that paved the way for the 1989 hit show about Los Angeles County lifeguards, *Baywatch.* But as things started to heat up for California through these times of fame and stardom, the Midwest stepped in to help calm everyone down as Eli Lilly and Company released a drug in 1977 called Fluoxetine, better known as Prozac.

THIS PAGE:
Catherine Bach
Cleveland, Ohio

Tom Wopat
Lodi, Wisconsin

Cole Porter
Peru, Indiana

Clay Felker
Webster Groves, Missouri

Jane Grant
Joplin, Missouri

James Thurber
Columbus, Ohio

Cheryl Rae Tiegs
Breckenridge, Minnesota

William Tecumseh Sherman
Lancaster, Ohio

Walt Disney
born in Chicago,
raised in Marceline, Missouri

Dow Corning
Midland, Michigan

Eli Lilly and Co
Indianapolis, Indiana

PART THREE

IS IT JUST ME, OR DO THE OTHER REGIONS KEEP TRYING TO KILL US?

3.1 IF YOU CAN'T BEAT 'EM, ASSASSINATE 'EM.

President William McKinley was shot in the abdomen by Leon Czolgosz on June 13, 1901 in Buffalo while attending the Pan-American Exposition. Over the summer, McKinley developed gangrene and by September 13, it was clear he was not going to live. Like any strong Midwesterner, he took the news like a champ, telling the doctors, "It is useless gentlemen. I think we ought to have a prayer." And when his friends and family gathered, he told them not to worry, because, "We are all going."

On September 14, McKinley died.

What had he done to deserve this fate? Was it his support of the gold standard? Was it because he was a Methodist? Was it because Leon Czolgosz was a mentally ill anarchist inspired by assassinations in Europe? Or was this part of a larger plot by the other regions of the United States to undercut the Midwest wherever possible — be it by assassinating our presidents, or invading us and poisoning our region's great minds with loose women, hard booze, and salt-filled bodies of water?

For just a moment, I'm going to need to put aside my Heartland modesty and say this: The rest of the country is a jealous bitch.

William McKinley was only one victim. There have been four assassinations of U.S. presidents. Three of those presidents have been Midwestern: Lincoln, Garfield, and McKinley. All were succeeded by non-Midwestern vice presidents. There have been eight serious assassination attempts against sitting presidents. Six were aimed at Midwesterners: Lincoln, Hoover, Truman, Ford, Ford (again?!), and Reagan. Two of the four presidents who died in office, Warren G Harding and William Henry Harrison, were Midwesterners.

If you're a president from the Midwest, the good news is that you are now the leader of the free world; the bad news is that you have a 70% chance of being shot, being shot at, or dying early.

Now, does a string of unrelated events that seemingly form a loose pattern *actually* prove a massive conspiracy in which men are gunned down merely because of the state that they are associated with?

Yes.

PREVIOUS PAGE:
William McKinley
Niles, Ohio

Abraham Lincoln
*raised in Perry County, Indiana,
and Coles County, Illinois*

James Garfield
Moreland Hills, Ohio

Herbert Hoover
West Branch, Iowa

Harry Truman
Lamar, Missouri

Gerald Ford
*born in Omaha, Nebraska,
raised in Grand Rapids, Michigan*

Ronald Reagan
Tampico, Illinois

Warren G Harding
*the ORIGINAL regulator
Blooming Grove, Ohio*

William Henry Harrison
settled in North Bend, Ohio

THIS PAGE:
Leon Czolgosz
*raised in Detroit, Michigan,
and Warrensville, Ohio*

After being shot, McKinley should have looked at his vice president, New York-born Teddy Roosevelt and said, "Et tu, Teddy?" I think Roosevelt was the man behind the scheme. McKinley's assassin, Leon Czolgosz, was originally from the Midwest. I can only imagine that little Leon was a sweet and charming guy in those early years. But trouble started when he moved to Natrona, Pennsylvania, in 1889. While there, the Northeast cabal came to him and said, "Leon, in twelve years, there will be a president from Ohio and a vice president from New York. Although we'd like our New York guy to get elected president, people in this country just love the Midwest too much. So the only way for us to get our man in is for you to kill the Midwestern president." Leon probably tried to resist, but he was brought over to the dark side by cocaine, LSD, and promises of getting in on a really hot tech stock's IPO.

McKinley didn't stand a chance.

Someone recognized this conspiracy and tried to take the law into his own hands: John Schrank.

On October 13, 1912, Schrank shot Teddy Roosevelt, which he explained to authorities was revenge for the assassination of William McKinley (possibly the only assassination-revenge-assassination-attempt in U.S. history). For months, Schrank had been having a dream in which he was approached by William McKinley, who told him, "Avenge my death." McKinley would point to a man dressed like a monk and explain, "This is my murderer."

And that man dressed like a monk was … Teddy Roosevelt!

That's all the evidence *I* need.

Although Midwesterners let the assassination of William McKinley slide (we are truly a forgiving people), New York-born John Schrank put these dream orders from McKinley into action and set out for ol' Teddy "Do Anything I Can to Undercut the Midwest" Roosevelt.

Most would agree that Schrank was mentally ill, but he may have been the first to recognize the national conspiracy against the No Coast.

In the fall of 1912, Roosevelt was campaigning against both William Howard Taft and Woodrow Wilson and headed to Wisconsin. Schrank followed him there, waiting in the lobby of Milwaukee's Hotel Gilpatrick, and at 8:00 PM, pulled out a gun as

Roosevelt was standing up in a car outside. But Schrank aimed for Roosevelt's head, and a spectator knocked his arm down as he fired (we are truly a brave and selfless people), causing the bullet to miss Roosevelt's head and instead hit him in the chest.

Luckily for Roosevelt, the bullet was slowed by his twice-folded 50-page speech. Roosevelt survived, drove to the Milwaukee Auditorium and gave a speech that night, where he explained that although he'd been shot, "it takes more than that to kill a bull moose!"

Cocky bastard.

Yet it wasn't TR's possible connection to McKinley's assassination that earned his title nickname of Teddy "Do Anything I Can to Undercut the Midwest" Roosevelt. It was that in 1883, at the age of 25, while hopelessly adrift due to a youth spent in the den of sin and iniquity that is New York City, TR moved to the Dakota Territory to try ranching. The Midwest isn't a place for the faint of heart, and this "Bull Moose" credited the rough and rigorous life as being integral to everything that followed. "I have always said," TR remarked, "I would not have been President had it not been for my experience in North Dakota."

And having one of your henchmen assassinate one of our own is how you repay us!?

The Midwestern life experience isn't all TR took from us. His Bull Moose Party made off with the Progressive platform of Wisconsin's Robert LaFollette.

In 1902, LaFollette became the governor of Wisconsin and started implementing the Progressive "Wisconsin Idea" of government — statewide primaries to select candidates, pensions for the blind, old-age assistance, and more.

CONGRATULATIONS, MR PRESIDENT FROM THE MIDWEST, NOW YOU – DUCK!

If you're a president from the Midwest, you're not only the leader of the free world, you also have an alarming 70% chance of being shot, being shot at, or dying early in office. Below are the presidents who have either been shot at or who have died in office. Notice the large number of highlighted names.

Andrew Jackson (Tennessee): attempted assassination 1835

William Henry Harrison (settled in Ohio): died in office 1841

Zachary Taylor (Virginia): died in office 1850

Abraham Lincoln (settled in Illinois): assassinated 1865

James A Garfield (Ohio): assassinated 1881

William McKinley (Ohio): assassinated 1901

Teddy Roosevelt (New York): attempted assassination 1912

Warren G Harding (Ohio): died in office 1923

Herbert Hoover (Iowa): attempted assassination 1928

Franklin Roosevelt (New York): "attempted assassination" actually killed Chicago Mayor Anton Cermak 1933

Franklin Roosevelt (New York): died in office 1945

John F Kennedy (Massachusetts): assassinated 1963

Gerald Ford (Michigan): attempted assassination 1975

Ronald Reagan (Illinois): attempted assassination 1981

Why rest of country no like us? Probably because we are so gol dang successful! Below is how the regions do in producing presidents.

Midwest: 15 presidents
South: 14 presidents
Northeast: 13 presidents
West: 1 president (and it was Richard Nixon!)

And consider this: Ohio (our first state) wasn't admitted to the Union until 1803, meaning that the U.S. was already eight presidents in before our first leader of the free world (William Henry Harrison) ascended to power in 1841. After 1861, the Midwest racked up a remarkable fourteen presidents, compared to seven for the Northeast, six for the South, and one for the West.

Robert LaFollette
Primrose, Wisconsin

By 1908, LaFollette was a contender for U.S. President, narrowly losing the Republican nomination to Taft. By 1909, Lafollette had formed the National Progressive Republican League and started exploring a third party run at President. But in 1912, just as his star was rising, his health mysteriously failed, and TR swooped in to adopt many of LaFollette's ideas for his Bull Moose Party. Not only did LaFollette never forgive Roosevelt for this, but even after having been shot later in 1912, Roosevelt was heckled by LaFollette supporters in Milwaukee (we are truly a kind people, though have been known to heckle a bitch).

William Howard Taft
Cincinnati, Ohio

The party schism meant that the presidency slipped from Ohioan Taft to the Princeton elitist Woodrow Wilson.

Is it likely that Teddy Roosevelt secretly got LaFollette sick so that he could steal his ideas and then move on to another East Coast presidency? Yes, extremely likely.

Sadly, McKinley was not the only Midwestern president to meet this fate.

The first American President to be killed, Abraham Lincoln, was shot at Ford's Theater on April 14, 1865 by John Wilkes Booth. History has taught us that the Virginia-born Booth was exacting revenge for the South's defeat in the Civil War. But perhaps Booth was in cahoots with Lincoln's North Carolina-born Vice President Andrew Johnson. There is no evidence, but anything is possible.

The second president in U.S. history to be assassinated was James A Garfield, who was shot July 2, 1881 by Charles Geuiteau. Although Geuiteau was born and raised in the Midwest, things started to turn south when he joined a Utopian religious sect in Oneida, New York. It was most likely in New York that Geuiteau was brainwashed into killing Garfield so that Garfield's Vermont-born Vice President Chester A Arthur could move into office.

The only non-Midwestern president assassinated was JFK. But when you have ties to the Mafia, enemies overseas, and have been humping one-third of Hollywood, it's easier to see how you'll be shot 27 times from 24 different angles by 19 gunmen.

While one of the two non-Midwestern assassination attempts was merely vigilante justice, the only other was in 1835 against Andrew Jackson — who was an asshole.

There was a third non-Midwestern "assassination attempt," against Franklin Roosevelt in Miami in February 1933. But in this plot — supposedly against FDR and carried out by Giuseppe Zangara — only Anton Cermak, then the mayor of Chicago, was killed. It was difficult to tell if the attempt was even aimed at FDR. Zangara may have been sent to Miami by Al Capone to kill Cermak, with FDR an innocent bystander. God knows the New York-born FDR probably milked it for all the attention he could get. "I'm in a wheelchair and people are shooting at me? Woe is me! I should be allowed to cheat on my wife scot-free."

So pretty much every assassination attempt has really been against a Midwestern president or someone who deserved it. And the only people who can save Midwestern presidents are Midwesterners.

On September 5, 1975, President Gerald Ford was on the northern grounds of the California State Capitol when California-born Lynette Fromme, a follower of Cincinnati-born Charles Manson, pulled out a Colt M1911 as Ford went to shake her hand. The firing cartridge was empty when the trigger was pulled, and before a bullet could enter the chamber, Secret Service Agent Larry Buendorf restrained Fromme. Where did Buendorf learn this kind of strength and self-sacrifice? From his Midwestern roots in Minnesota, naturally.

Only seventeen days later, Ford foolishly went back to California. In San Francisco, West Virginia-born radical Sara Jane Moore pulled out a revolver. She fired from 40 feet, but luckily for Ford, there was a fellow Midwesterner in the crowd next to Moore. So while the

San Francisco natives probably stood around going, "Whoa, man!" or "Far out!" or "Hey, shooting the President is totally not groovy!" Oliver Sipple grabbed Moore's arm as she fired, causing the bullet to miss Ford.

What had Ford done so wrong to warrant two assassination attempts? We may never know, but it wouldn't hurt to ask his vice president, the Northeastern-born Nelson Rockefeller.

Like Ford, Ronald Reagan also had to deal with non-Midwestern crazies trying to impress non-Midwestern actresses, with only his wits and fellow Midwesterners to help. On March 30, 1981, the Oklahoma-born wacko John Hinckley, in an attempt to impress Los Angeles-born Jodie Foster, shot Reagan outside the Hilton Washington. Secret Service agent Tim McCarthy was wounded protecting Reagan, and Press Secretary James Brady was also wounded by an errant shot. But with these two Midwesterners to help, Reagan survived, even keeping his Midwestern humor and charm throughout, remarking to doctors helping him recover, "I hope you're all Republicans."

We can only guess what his Massachusetts-born Vice President, George H W Bush was thinking. Perhaps it was "I hope it doesn't look suspicious that yet another presidential assassination attempt has been carried out by a non-Midwesterner while a non-Midwesterner occupies the vice presidency, because if it does, our entire plan at repressing the Midwest may get out."

But karma gave George H W Bush his son, George W Bush.

Two other Midwestern presidents died under suspicious circumstances. William Henry Harrison, although born in Virginia, spent most of his time in Ohio. That proved to be his biggest mistake. Well, that and reading a nearly two hour inauguration speech in a cold rain that led to pneumonia and death. The nation mourned, but something tells me that Virginian Vice President John Tyler was secretly smiling as he ascended to power.

Warren G Harding, the original regulator, died early to make way for the Northeastern Calvin "Do Anything I

LONG ON WORDS, SHORT ON LIFE: William Henry Harrison was only part Midwestern, having been born in Virginia, so our wit and sparse use of words didn't come naturally to him. For example, the day Lincoln gave his *Gettysburg Address*, the main speaker was Edward Everett of Massachusetts. Considered the greatest orator of his day, Everett, like Harrison, spoke for two straight hours. After Everett's yawn-fest, the Midwestern Lincoln stepped up to the plate, killed it in about three minutes, and sailed into the history books.

Need To Do To Be President" Coolidge.

The Midwest has produced fifteen U.S. presidents. Three were killed, four others survived serious assassination attempts, and two died early. Our current Midwestern president, Barack Obama, may be in a dire situation. After all, just being a Midwestern president gives him a 70% chance of being killed, being shot at, or dying early. And he is standing in the way of Northeastern Vice President Joe Biden. Look out, Barack!

Heavy is the head that wears the crown. And if that head is a Midwestern one, it is probably going to be shot at, too.

Barack Obama
*born at a terrorist training camp in Kenya
settled in Chicago, Illinois*

3.2 AND IF YOU CAN'T ASSASSINATE 'EM, SEND IN FEDERAL FORCES.

"THE STRIKE WAS ONLY BROKEN AFTER GARY, INDIANA, WAS OCCUPIED BY THOUSANDS OF TROOPS FOR SEVERAL MONTHS"

Being a Midwestern president is risky, but being a Midwestern labor leader is worse. In 1938, after decades of work by Midwestern-led unions, the Fair Labor Standards Act finally passed Congress, giving workers an eight-hour day, a weekend, and overtime. Apparently no other region wanted to take the lead, since the whole process got us invaded by the federal military a handful of times.

The first major confrontation was in 1894, during the Pullman Car Strike. It was led by the American Railway Union's (ARU) chief, Eugene Debs.

Debs founded the ARU in 1893, and in early 1894 won a decisive strike against the Great Northern Railroad. In May of 1894 the ARU membership numbered more than 150,000 nationwide when 80% of Pullman's 3,300 employees walked off the job in Chicago.

The owner of the Pullman Car Co., George Pullman, was originally from New York City. Like most people from New York, he was an asshole. During the depression of 1893, Pullman laid off workers and hired them back only after they agreed to wage reductions and longer hours. Worker resentment compounded when none of the executives took pay cuts, investors still collected their 8% returns, and rents in the "model" company town of Pullman were 25% higher than those in Chicago.

Pullman refused to talk to labor leaders, so Debs' ARU boycotted work on all trains carrying Pullman cars, essentially bringing traffic out of Chicago to a halt. Within four days, the ARU's 150,000 workers on 29 railroads had quit rather than handle Pullman cars.

The railroad-owned attorney general and the New Jersey-born President Grover Cleveland — a Godless man who had children out of wedlock and whose state would produce Snooki and the rest of *The Jersey Shore* cast — issued an injunction to halt all strike activity and sent in 14,000 federal troops to enforce the injunction. The strike was broken. thirteen strikers were killed, 57 were wounded, and Grover "The Situation" Cleveland was probably high-fiving George Pullman while enjoying Cuban cigars as Debs was sentenced to six months in prison for violating the injunction.

PREVIOUS PAGE:
Eugene Debs
Terre Haute, Indiana

Victor Berger
settled in Milwaukee, Wisconsin

However, as Carnegie-Melon Professor Jason Martinek explains, Debs "left prison a celebrity — for some, the embodiment of demagoguery, for others, a hero of mythic proportions." Like Li'l Wayne, Debs' stretch in the can gave him the street cred he needed to found the People's Party in the late 1800s before joining forces with Milwaukee Socialist Victor Berger to found the Social Democratic Party in 1898 and the Socialist Party of America in 1901. He ran for president as a socialist in 1904, 1908, and 1912 — that last year receiving almost one million votes, or 6% of the entire vote.

In 1920, he ran for president as Prisoner #9653 while on a three-year stretch for a 1918 antiwar speech in Canton, Ohio. In 1920, even more Americans voted for him than in 1912, although prison had destroyed his health.

But to the end he kept trying to kick some ass, uttering the line that would later inspire John Steinbeck's Tom Joad in *Grapes of Wrath:* "While there is a lower class, I am in it; while there is a criminal element, I am of it; while there is a soul in prison, I am not free."

Considering that the percentage of Americans in prison has doubled since 1980 and the minimum wage has been essentially stagnant since 1950, Debs would be a busy dude nowadays!

WHEN YOU NEED TO PUT SOCIALIST SYMPATHIES TO MUSIC OR ON SCREEN, LOOK NO FURTHER! Tom Morello (Libertyville, Illinois) played "The Ghost of Tom Joad" live at the Rock and Roll Hall of Fame with Bruce Springsteen. And Henry Fonda (Grand Island, Nebraska) played Tom Joad in the film remmake of *Grapes of Wrath*.

AFL
founded in Columbus, Ohio

UAW
founded in Detroit, Michigan

AFSCME
founded in Wisconsin

SEIU
founded in Chicago

From the late 1800s to mid-1900s, the Midwest was the epicenter of labor unrest and left-wing radicalism. The region produced political parties such as the socialist Labor Party in 1876, the anarchist International Working People's Association in 1883, the Populist Party in 1892, the Minnesota Democratic-Farmer-Labor Party in 1918, and the American Communist movement in 1919. It saw the founding of almost every major American union, from the American Federation of Labor (AFL) and the Congress of Industrial Organization (CIO) to the United Auto Workers (UAW), American Federation of State, County, and Municipal Employees (AFSCME), and Service Employees International Union (SEIU).

In 1911, 75% of Socialist office-holders came from ten Midwestern states.

The fight for the eight-hour workday and a weekend started in the later 1800s, culminating in the Federation of Organized Trades and Labor Unions calling for a general strike in 1886, leading to a massive demonstration in Chicago's

Haymarket Square. Police arrived, a bomb was thrown, and the chaotic Haymarket Affair led to a repression of unions until Debs' arrival.

During his second imprisonment in 1918, Chicago-based Communist William Zoster started to organize the steel workers along southern Lake Michigan. On September 22, 1919, Zoster's organization initiated the Great Steel Strike, which was not only bigger than the Pullman Strike, but is the largest American labor conflict to date. For months, more than 250,000 workers from Pittsburgh to Chicago struck.

This time, the Virginia-born and Princeton-educated Woodrow "I Hate Productive Regions of America" Wilson once more sent federal forces to the Midwest. This time, the strike was only broken after Gary, Indiana, was occupied by thousands of troops for several months.

William Zoster
settled in Chicago, Illinois

3.3 **AND IF YOU CAN'T ASSASSINATE 'EM OR SUBDUE 'EM WITH THE FEDERAL MILITARY, THEN TAKE SOME OF THEIR BRIGHTEST MINDS AND POISON THEM WITH LOOSE WOMEN, HARD BOOZE, AND SALT-FILLED BODIES OF WATER.**

St Paul-born writer F Scott Fitzgerald wrote some American classics such as *This Side of Paradise* and *The Great Gatsby* during the 1920s. But in 1940, at the age of 44, he died of a heart attack in Hollywood, where he was living with little money, writing the occasional screenplay, and working on *The Love of the Last Tycoon.* His is a tragic story of the fast-living Jazz Age running headlong into the Depression and a new era in America.

His is also the story of a great Midwestern mind being dragged down by some floozie from another region: Zelda Sayre from Montgomery, Alabama.

When Fitzgerald first met Zelda in 1919, he was writing short stories in the evening and advertising copy by day. He fell in love and proposed, but Zelda said that she couldn't marry him because he wasn't successful enough. Or to put it another way: "I've been sent to drag the Midwest down, so I need to land someone really famous and then help destroy him."

Shortly after, in 1919, Fitzgerald won a deal to publish *This Side of Paradise* with Scribners. His star rose higher with *The Great Gatsby* in 1925. He became a symbol of Jazz Age extravagance in the 1920s, and coined the term "Jazz Age" in 1925. In *The Great Gatsby,* Fitzgerald uses two Midwestern characters, Jay Gatsby of North Dakota and Nick Carraway of Minnesota, to comment on the decadence of East Coast life. Carraway observes, after Gatsby's death, that socialites Tom and Daisy were careless people who "smashed up things and creatures and let other people clean up the mess they had made."

Little did he know, Fitzgerald was a target of those "careless" non-Midwesterners. What might have sealed his fate was "The Ice Palace," a short story he wrote for the *Saturday Evening Post* in 1920.

In it, a popular young man from St Paul invites his girlfriend, Sally Carrol Happer, up from her home in Georgia for a winter vacation in the Midwest. At first, Sally loves the refreshing cold, the nice people, and is taken in by the region that produces, Fitzgerald writes, "the best athletes in the world ... This is a man's country, I tell you."

Things take a turn for the worse when Sally finds that her Southern culture doesn't mesh well with many Midwesterners. Her insecurities blossom when she finds herself lost in the Ice Palace, a giant house of ice blocks made for St Paul's Winter Festival. She leaves her boyfriend and returns to Georgia.

The year it came out, the South must have felt the sting of Fitzgerald's perceived arrogance, for that was the year that Zelda discovered she "loved" Fitzgerald and married him. At the time, Fitzgerald's biographer Matthew Bruccoli explains, "Zelda was a Montgomery celebrity and Fitzgerald was one of a crowd of suitors. In New York, Fitzgerald was the famous one." *This Side of Paradise* was tearing through printings, selling only slightly fewer than fellow Minnesotan Sinclair Lewis' *Main Street*.

After that, Zelda wore Fitzgerald down. He drank heavily with her. His favorite beverage was gin, because he thought that people wouldn't be able to smell the alcohol on his breath if he stuck only with one that smells like a Christmas tree. He was wrong, but dammit if you don't admire his out-of-the box Midwestern thinking.

The Stock Market crash of 1929 was bad, but it took Fitzgerald nine years to follow *The Great Gatsby* with the 1934 *Tender is the Night,* mainly because Zelda was in and out of clinics for her health problems (AKA: Phase I of Operation Bring Down Another Great Midwestern Mind).

By the second half of the 1930s, Fitzgerald was in financial trouble, working in Hollywood to make ends meet. Though he found the work degrading, his Midwestern ethic pushed him to continue. Meanwhile, Zelda's Southern ethic led her to schizophrenia.

There were warnings for Fitzgerald. Mark Twain had met a similar fate almost half a century earlier. Like Fitzgerald, Twain literally defined his generation, coining the phrase "Gilded Age" to describe the heady period of American excess from the late 1860s through 1896. He was a keen observer of his time.

Also like Fitzgerald, Twain's early success was through books that focused on Midwestern characters — *The Adventures of Tom Sawyer* and *The Adventures of Huckleberry Finn.* But Twain also unwisely married a non-Midwesterner, New York-born Olivia Langdon, and left the Midwest for the East. There, Twain became a victim of the age that he lampooned, involving himself in risky get-rich-quick schemes, and relying on his Midwestern wit-based speaking tours to recoup his losses.

Fitzgerald also had contemporary warnings: Ernest Hemingway told Fitzgerald he thought Zelda was "insane" (we can be direct when necessary).

Hemingway wisely avoided the non-Midwestern-woman pitfall and played close to home, making sure that all *four* of his wives were Midwestern — Hadley Richardson, Pauline Pfeiffer, Martha Gellhorn, and Mary Welsh. And he kept his Midwestern buddies close — Fitzgerald heavily edited his 1926 novel, *The Sun Also Rises.*

But by the 1940s, Hemingway had spent a dangerous amount of time near saltwater between the Florida Keys and Cuba. In 1960, Hemingway left Cuba, although the damage was already done. The Mayo Clinic in Minnesota did what they could, but in 1961 he was, "released in ruins" and shot himself a few months later in Idaho.

PREVIOUS PAGES:
F Scott Fitzgerald
St Paul, Minnesota

Tom Buchanan
Chicago, Illinois

Daisy Fay Buchanan
Louisville, Kentucky

Sinclair Lewis
*the first American writer to win
the Nobel Prize for literature
Sauk Centre, Minnesota*

*Ernest Hemingway
Oak Park, Illinois*

Hadley Richardson
*St Louis, Missouri,
married Hemingway
in Horton Bay, Michigan*

Pauline Pfeiffer
*born in Parkersburg, Iowa,
raised in St Louis, Missouri*

Martha Gellhorn
St Louis, Missouri

Mary Welsh
Minnesota

3.4 **OR MAYBE JUST TRY TO HURT THEIR FEELINGS**

The term "flyover country" emerged in the 1970s when the Midwest was going through an atypical rough patch. Though true — we are kind of right in the way if you're heading from one coast to another — it's not particularly friendly.

"Jesus, why does the Midwest have be in the way of my flight from LA to New York? I sometimes appreciate the downtime to rest my fake boobs and watch the latest Jerry Bruckheimer flick, but other times I just want to get there faster."

One of our early shirts at RAYGUN was, "Des Moines: Let Us Exceed Your Already Low Expectations," because so many people would show up at the store and say, "We're in town from Boston for a wedding, and, you know, Des Moines isn't as bad as we thought it was going to be."

"Wooowwww, you sweet-talkin' Yankee-boys sure do know how to sweep a city off its feet!"

Then they ask if our store is a franchise from a city like Portland.

"No, we're based in Des Moines."

"Really? Wow. You guys should open up a store in Portland."

But on the national level, it's usually one backhanded comment after another. In the James Bond movie *Diamonds Are Forever,* the sinister Blofeld decides he needs to show off his death ray on a crowded coastal city, because, "As you see, Mr Bond, the satellite is, at present, over Kansas. But if we destroy Kansas, the world may not hear it for years."

Oh man, the first time we heard something that funny we laughed so hard we fell off our dinosaurs.

In the 1990s, NBC decided to set their show about aliens coming down to live on Earth — *3rd Rock from the Sun* — in Ohio, because it was normal, simple, and, as the NBC bigwigs agreed, "There are no trends being set in Ohio."

Keep it above the belt, please.

This catty simmer of insults and innuendo is pretty constant. But it really ramps up when the Midwest gets a little too much face time. That's when the skank bitches (AKA the other regions of America) pull out the claws.

In Iowa, we're used to this every four years when the first-in-the-nation Republican and Democratic caucuses roll around. "Why should Iowa be first?"

"The state is too small."

"Too white."

"Too backward."

"Our president should not be chosen by Iowa."

Well, first off, we're not "choosing" the president. We're just holding the first in one of more than 50 caucus or primary competitions that choose the candidates.

And this may be a good time to point out, since possibly only a simple Iowan has noticed — our country is governed by a massive bureaucratic machine that is a mix of elected officials, appointed government staffers, voters, PACs, and lobbyists working for special interests and corporations, which means that there will never be much difference in how the government operates from president to president anyway.

But just before the January 2012 Iowa caucus, New Jersey-born and California-raised (they're sending in a dual-coaster!) Journalism Professor Stephen Bloom went bat-shit crazy on us, penning, "Clinging to Guns and Religion: Observations from 20 Years of Iowa Life" for *The Atlantic*.

In more than 8,000 words, Bloom blends some Midwestern stereotypes with several things that he just made up, concluding, "The rural middle is where guns, unemployment, alcoholism, and machismo reign."

Ah yes, how could we forget our reigning overlord, Alcoholism? We were a little suspicious when he took power, but I think he's done a stand-up job.

"Those who stay in rural Iowa," Bloom continues, "are often the elderly waiting to die, those too timid (or lacking in education) to peer around the bend for better opportunities, an assortment of waste-oids and meth addicts with pale skin and rotted teeth, or those who quixotically believe, like Little Orphan Annie, that 'The sun'll come out tomorrow.'"

But without the meth, how would we be able to

> **Ah yes, how could we forget our reigning overlord, Alcoholism? Though we were a little suspicious when he took power, I think he's done a stand-up job.**

write this book in a long weekend *and* keep our jobs as over-the-road truckers?

Later, Bloom gets to his main gripe: "Whether a schizophrenic, economically depressed, and some say, culturally challenged state like Iowa should host the first grassroots referendum to determine who will be the next president isn't at issue ... In a perfect world, no way would Iowa ever be considered representative of America, or even a small part of it. Iowa's not representative of much."

Well, we're apparently representative of the gun-loving-unemployed-alcoholic-casual-speed-using constituency. And really, don't they need a voice most of all?

That article really shook my belief structure, made me reassess my state, and my Midwest. To dispel the accusations in Bloom's piece, I called my Iowa-born grandmother to get her comments, but she was too depressed and strung out on crank to respond.

PART FOUR

MIDWEST GIVETH, AND MIDWEST TAKETH AWAY

4.1 OUR PRIMARY MEANS OF RETALIATION: PASSIVE AGGRESSIVENESS

The Midwest giveth so much, from food to manufactured goods to good examples for the rest of the country to follow. But like disgruntled teenagers, the rest of the country can just throw it back in our face. "I wanted a *red* Porsche, not a blue Porsche, Dad! Jesus, can't you do anything right?!" We may seem like an easy target to pick on, because our primary power is passive aggressiveness.

It's not particularly menacing, and even in the arena of passive aggressiveness, ours is probably the least aggressive form of passive aggressiveness.

The Northeast Jewish mother takes the most direct approach to her passive aggressiveness: "Oh, you're going out tonight, even though you're only home for three nights from school? ... No, I understand, you're Mr Popular. So if you want to leave your poor mother, that's fine, that's fine. I like being home alone, slowly waiting to die. No, go on, go on, you have fun with your friends while your mother cries herself to death."

The Southern Baptist mother brings Jesus in for backup: "Going out tonight with those boys? Do you really think that's what an upstanding young Christian man should be seen doing? You can go, but I just want to help you pick between what's a good decision and Satan. Don't let Satan win."

A Midwestern mom plays it very passive: "Going out? You sure?"

Am I sure? I have my coat on and I'm holding the car keys. Am I sure I'm going out? Or am I sure I should be going out? Are you sure? Is there something else you want to talk about?

Our passive-aggressive nature reached judicial heights when Michigan-raised Supreme Court Justice Potter Stewart said that hard-core pornography was hard to define, but that, "I know it when I see it."

Oh, well that makes perfect sense. So all I need is access to your inner monologue when I'm creating what may be pornography.

A lot of what we say, though, can come across as passive aggressive, even when we don't mean it to. This is due to a use of words that is almost the opposite of the rest of the country. For instance, in a moment of grief or joy, where other regions may pour out their feelings, the Midwest clams up.

I was once riding in a car with two old timers up front. When we passed the Animal Rescue League, one of them said: "Was just there the other day."

"Oh?" the other chimed in.

"Yeah, had to put the dog down."

"That so?"

"Yup. Pretty sad."

"Always is."

It was less an emotional outpouring way and more of a sad-personal-moment-described-like-you're-telling-someone-how-your-morning-coffee-was way.

But speaking of coffee, where we're short on words for grief, we are waaaaaay long on words when it comes to interaction with members of the service industry. Though it's the barista's job to prepare coffee, if you're new in town or new in the coffee shop, you can't just go in and bark, "Black coffee, leave room for cream." An order like that gets you a one-way ticket to everyone-thinks-you're-an-asshole-ville.

To fit in here, you need to sprinkle in at least one, "How's it going?", "That's great," and "If it's not too much trouble." But those need to be coupled with no fewer than thirteen "Thanks!"

During a Midwestern dinner, you could hear well over 100 "Thanks," depending on how many people are at the table. Thanks for water being poured, for menus delivered, for orders taken, for orders delivered, etc, etc, etc. People in the Midwest are so deferential, that instead of hearing "Excuse me" from a person who happens to be in your way, you'll hear "Sorry." If your dog dies, you get a "Life's tough" or "That's a shame." A word like "Sorry" is only reserved for when you're accidentally in someone's line of sight in the freezer aisle.

Why does it all operate this way? Who knows. But to the uninitiated, it can be pretty confusing. The Internet is littered with blog posts like I Be Irate's "Passive-Aggressive Midwesterners" or Virago V's "The Midwest Passive-Aggressive Challenge."

Perfect! We make them guess what we're thinking until they're so mentally exhausted they give up.

SOUND LIKE A MIDWESTERNER!

What are we actually thinking? What do we think of you? You'll probably never find out! But you can blend in with the locals by developing a chipper personality even in the face of utter annoyance, and you should also keep an arsenal of cryptic words and phrases on hand like "fine" or "really" or "I see" or "hmm" or "you don't say" or "how about that" or "yeah, that'll happen." Just stringing those together at steady intervals allows for a half-hour Midwestern conversation.

SCENARIO:	POSSIBLE RESPONSES:	
You'd like to order coffee with room for cream.	**New York:** Yeah, hi, black coffee. Leave room this time.	**Midwest:** Hey there, how are you? (pause for reply) Yeah, I hear you there, with the humidity it sure feels hotter. Hey, could I just have a plain coffee? (pause for reply) Yup, just a regular old coffee, nothing fancy for me today. And would it be possible to leave a little room at the top of the cup for cream? Or I can pour some out on my own if it's too much trouble. Thanks!
Someone asks you how it's going moments after you found out your company is failing and you may have to file for personal bankruptcy.	**Los Angeles:** I'm a total wreck, a total fucking wreck! Things are ... hold on, someone's on the other line ... Hello? Oh, you're still there, I don't know who that was, I'm waiting for my mom to call. Everything is a total train wreck, my life is a disaster ... and on and on and on.	**Midwest:** Oh, could be worse.
Someone just told you the worst idea for a product you've ever heard.	**Boston:** That's fucking stupid.	**Midwest:** Huh, that's interesting.
You're a waitress and your table of twelve needs 24 separate bills (each person a bill for food and another for drinks).	**Philadelphia:** No.	**Midwest:** No problem, guys! I'll be back in just a minute with all these.
A conversation is winding down and you need to leave.	**Portland:** Good talk, man, I've gotta head out.	**Midwest:** Sooo.....

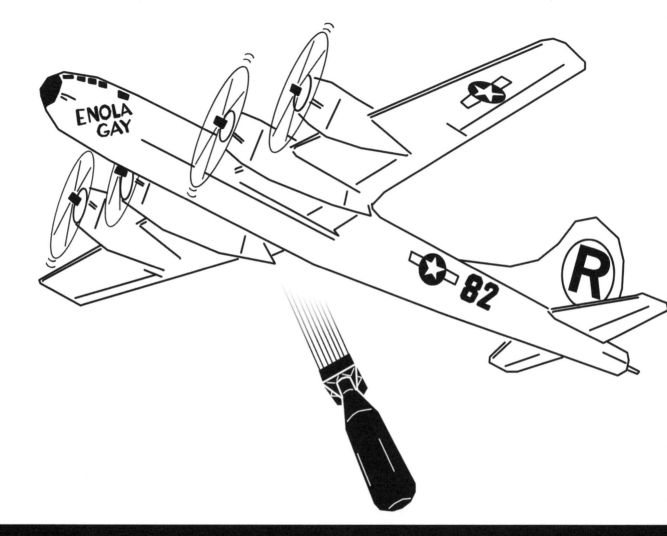

4.2 **OUR** *OTHER* **PRIMARY MEANS OF RETALIATION: KICKING MAXIMUM ASS**

Passive aggressiveness is usually just the primer to more forceful action.

I can attest to this after living with my grandparents in Northern Michigan. Around age twelve, I had a bad habit of forgetting to bring my towel from my room to the shower down the hall. I'd just take a new towel out of the cabinet in the bathroom. But by the end of the week I might have anywhere from five to thirteen towels in my room, depending on how many showers I took.

My grandmother ran a tight ship when it came to laundry, apparently worried that too much detergent would cut into their get-yet-another-Cadillac budget. I knew she wouldn't be happy with me using so many towels, so like any twelve-year-old in need of a foolproof concealment plan, I chose the only viable option: I hid them in the closet.

After about two weeks, the bath towels were almost gone and the closet floor was sagging under the weight of a towel supply accumulated over the years by an Irish Catholic family of seven. One day, my grandmother found my towel stockpile and brought it up with me in the car that afternoon, "I found some towels in the closet in your room."

"Oh really? That's strange," I said. Play it cool, Mike, play it cool.

"Do you know how those got there?" she asked.

"No," I replied. Smooooooooth.

"Oh, okay."

She dropped the subject, and I had figured I'd successfully defeated her passive assault.

But at dinner that night, my grandpa announced, "Mike, your grandmother tells me that you've been using too many towels and then lying about it."

Their tactic had changed from, "You wouldn't, by chance, happen to, maybe, know what happened to all the towels?" to "Stop taking so many goddamned towels!"

The direct frontal assault had begun.

One of the most famous direct assaults in history, D-Day in June of

1944 was run by a host of Midwesterners. At the very top was Dwight Eisenhower, the Supreme Allied Commander since December of 1943.

Under Eisenhower was Omar Bradley, America's last five-star general, and the man in charge of American ground forces preparing to invade France. On June 6, 1944, the 1st Infantry Division landed at France's Omaha Beach, commanded by Clarence Huebner, who had been hand-selected by Bradley to lead the 1st in 1943. Beside him was Maxwell Taylor who led the 101st Airborne — jumping with his men behind enemy lines — and George Taylor, who led the 16th Infantry.

Taylor arrived at Omaha Beach about an hour and half after it began and found his 16th pinned down. He famously told his men, "There are two kinds of people who are staying on this beach: those who are dead and those who are going to die. Now let's get the hell out of here." No passive aggression there.

When it comes to kicking ass, we think outside the box. In 1984, Manhattan was terrorized by the Stay Puft Marshmallow man. This massive menace was conjured up by the Sumerian god Gozer, and forced a showdown with New York-based outfit, the Ghostbusters.

This giant was only possible because of Illinois-born Alex Doumak's Doumak Company, which was founded outside of Chicago in 1961 and patented a way to mass-produce marshmallows. After 1961, Doumak's Campfire brand was being stuffed between chocolate and graham crackers across the country. By the early 1980s, this Midwestern confection had become a supernatural merchant of death, requiring the wits of all four Ghostbusters — Peter, Ray, Winston, and Egon — to stop its advances.

And we can even go *Lord of the Flies* on the world's ass — in a prehistoric way. The Manson Crater in northwestern Iowa is the site of one of the largest known impact events ever to hit the world — although it has since filled in with soil as the glaciers passed over. For years, it was believed that this impact wiped out the dinosaurs, though we now know that it was only a warning to the dinosaurs. A warning of what?

We can only imagine that a bunch of uppity brontosauruses out on the east coast of Pangaea — with seersucker suits, cigars, and croquet mallets at a garden party in the Hamptons — just kept poking fun at their hardworking, down-to-earth cousins in Pangaea's heartland. "Do you have running water in Middle Pangaea?" "We call it 'Flyover' Pangaea." "If you hit Central Pangaea with a meteor, would anyone even notice?"

After one too many PBRs, the brontosauruses of Middle Pangaea said, "'Would anyone notice if a meteor hit Central Pangaea?' they ask. Let's find out." And they called in the Manson meteor, which slammed into the earth and caused enough dust to black out the sky, nearly wiping out the whole dinosaur race.

But the dinosaurs got on with life for another few million years.

And then went extinct.

Several million years later, in 1969, the Midwest sent a firm "See what we're capable of?!" message when Ohio's Cuyahoga River caught fire, earning it the nickname "The River that Caught Fire."

Strangely, this wasn't the first time it had happened. There were 13 fires, the first in 1868. In 1952, a fire caused more than one million dollars worth of damage to boats and riverfront buildings. By 1968, the river was so polluted that it was devoid of marine life between Akron and Cleveland. A Kent State symposium held that year noted that the surface of the river was a "brown oily film" that was sometimes "several inches thick."

And when it comes to burning things, we don't just stop at rivers. Not only did the first chain reaction in nuclear fission occur at the University of Chicago in 1942, paving the way for the Atom Bomb, but when it came time to drop that bad boy on Japan, America used a Midwestern-made plane and a Midwestern-made pilot.

PREVIOUS PAGE:
Omar Bradley
Randolph County, Missouri

Clarence Huebner
Bushton, Kansas

Maxwell Taylor
Keytesville, Missouri

George Taylor
Flat Rock, Illinois

Alex Doumak
Illinois

Bill Murray
Wilmette, Illinois

Harold Ramis
Chicago, Illinois

Ernie Hudson
Benton Harbor, Michigan

Ray Parker, Jr
wrote the Ghostbusters
theme song
Detroit, Michigan

*North Dakota currently
has 1,140 nuclear weapons*

Enola Gay
built in Omaha, Nebraska

Paul Tibbits
Captain of the Enola Gay
Quincy, Illinois

"KEEP ROLLIN' AMERICA."

4.3 KILLING YOU SOFTLY WITH TYPE 2 DIABETES, CAR CULTURE, AND AGRICULTURAL BYPRODUCTS.

In the food expose, *Food, Inc,* the New York-born author of *The Omnivore's Dilemma,* Michael Pollan, says ominously, "What surprised me the most was that as I followed food back to its source, I kept ending up in the same place — and that's a cornfield in Iowa. So much of our food is clever rearrangements of corn."

That's right, Pollan. While you were sitting in your ivory tower out in Berkeley, the Midwest hatched its most diabolical campaign to bring the rest of the country to its knees. In today's P.C. society of whiners and maybe-massive-confrontations-that-cost-money-and-human-life-aren't-such-a-good-idea-ers, burning down the South Sherman-style, dropping an atom bomb on New Jersey, or calling in a meteor on California may be a little too forward.

But what you thought was a Corn Belt is actually a Corn Noose! Check your blood sugar levels. Seriously, put down this book and take a minute to check your blood sugar levels. If you live in America, there's a good chance that a lifetime of carbonated beverages and snack foods have resulted in Type 2 diabetes.

And when you look at all of that jiggling cellulite in the mirror, like a bag of cottage cheese stuck to your ass, what should you see?

The Midwest.

"All those snack calories," Pollan continues, "come from commodity crops. From wheat, corn, and soybeans."

Pollan's main culprit is not corn itself, but the massive corporations manipulating food. "You've got a small group of multinational corporations who control the entire food system," *Food Inc* explains, "from seed to the supermarket. They're gaining control of food."

And these evil corporations aren't on Wall Street, they're hiding right on Main Street, USA. There's Beef Products, Inc (maker of the ammonia-spritzed delicacy "pink slime"); there's ADM (the food-processing conglomerate whose massive 1993 price-fixing conspiracy was featured in *The Informant!* starring Matt Damon); Monsanto

PREVIOUS PAGE:
Beef Products, Inc
Dakota Dunes, South Dakota

Archer Daniels Midland
founded in
Minneapolis, Minnesota,
headquartered in
Decatur, Illinois

Matt Whitacre
ADM informant portrayed in
the film
Morrow, Ohio

Monsanto
St Louis, Missouri

THIS PAGE:
Pioneer Hi-Bred
Johnston, Iowa

Dekalb
Dekalb, Illinois

Lex Luthor
Smallville, Kansas

LexCorp
Metropolis, USA

High-Fructose Corn Syrup
born in Japan in 1966
∧

(A company the EPA estimates is responsible for no fewer than 56 extremely polluted — or "superfund" — sites); there's Pioneer Hi-Bred; Dekalb Genetics Corporation; and there's even businessman Lex Luthor, whose LexCorp dabbles in food genetics, among other things.

These companies have created spinoffs and subsidiaries including NutraSweet, Flavr Savr, and Celebrex. They also developed the almighty high-fructose corn syrup. Corn syrup took America by storm between 1975 and 1985, and now has a place in almost all sweet products. In 1984, both Pepsi and Coca-Cola switched from sugar to high-fructose corn syrup in all of their American products.

> "what you thought was a Corn Belt is actually a Corn Noose!"

By 2008, the average American was consuming almost 33 pounds of high-fructose corn syrup a year, and the Midwest was laughing all the way to the bank. Well, laughing almost all the way to the bank, since after that laughing fit the Midwest had to take a minute to catch its breath on the sidewalk, then continue onto the bank a little slower before taking another minute to catch its breath after opening the door to the bank, wiping the sweat from its forehead, and approaching the teller with a smile and a wheeze.

Corn also has some lesser-known cousins that it can be made into: maltodextrin, sorbitol, gluten, xanthan gum, or ascorbic acid. In fact, almost 90% of the products found in an average grocery store will have some derivative of corn or soy beans. Those products include Twinkies, batteries, Coke, syrup, Kool-Aid, charcoal, diapers, Motrin, and meat.

As Pollan laments: "Corn has conquered the world."

We don't stop at the make-up of your food — we take it all the way to your fat face, administering your corn syrup fix with a smile and a Happy Meal box containing a free toy.

The mother of all fast-food chains and star of the documentary *Supersize Me*, McDonald's, is a Midwestern staple. It was founded and headquartered in southern

McDonald's
Des Plaines, Illinois

HIGH FRUCTOSE CORN SYRUP

HIGH-FRUCTOSE CORN SYRUP: YOUR ASS WILL HATE YOU FOR IT, BUT HEAVILY SUBSIDIZED, INDUSTRIAL AGRICULTURE, AND THE COMPANIES MODIFYING THE FOODS THEY PRODUCE, WILL LOVE YOU FOR IT!

INVENTED: Japan in 1966 **MILESTONE:** In 1984, both Pepsi and Coke switched from sugar to Corn Syrup. **IS THAT A FOUR YEAR OLD STUCK TO MY ASS?** Nope, that's the 33 pounds of Corn Syrup that the average American sucks down every year. **YOUR BODY DOESN'T KNOW THE DIFFERENCE:** Let's face facts: Your body is fucking stupid. If you give it a naturally grown sugar or an artificially created sweetener taken from corn, it won't know the difference! **BUUUUUUT:** The FDA did reject the Corn Refiners Association's attempt to rename their product "Corn Sugar" as well as their attempts to label Corn Syrup "natural."

California in 1940, but purchased by Oak Park, Illinois, native Ray Kroc and moved to Des Plaines, Illinois in 1961. Today, McDonald's is the largest hamburger fast-food chain, serving more than 68 million people every day in 119 countries.

The company has become a symbol of what's wrong with America's diet, and the "Mc" that is used for McNuggets and McFlurry has been used as a stand-in for lots of shitty stuff on this planet. During the American invasion of Iraq in 2003, I was living in Europe and saw graffiti calling for an end to "McWar" and "McMurder." In Philly, Penn's expansion into the West Philadelphia neighborhood was called "McPennification." And in 2003, the term, "McJob" made it into Merriam-Webster's dictionary as, "A low-paying job that requires little skill and provides little opportunity for advancement."

Now if that doesn't say good ol'-fashioned Midwestern values, I don't know what does!

So now that you've dropped your Double Quarter Pounder in shock, your mind is probably racing for a way out of this mess. Drugs? Vegetables? Drugs? Exercise?

"Yes, exercise!" you exclaim to yourself. "I can burn off all of this processed food as I walk from my centrally located housing unit to work, or as I meet friends for a stroll to an outdoor-based recreation facility."

But then you realize: "Oh, shit. I'm eating in my car."

Did you think that we'd stop at just food? No way. We can't have you burning off those calories through lifestyle-based exercise! Couple poor food choices with car-culture-based lack of exercise, and you'll be eating out of our hand in no time — considering we're holding a pile of french fries and it's been 45 minutes since your last un-filling fast-food meal.

C'mon, who's a hungry America? Here comes the airplane!

The car culture took off in the U.S. in the last half of the Twentieth century, which led to an expansion of roads, an expansion of city size, an expansion of fast-food restaurant options, and an expansion of asses.

The Midwest produced almost 100% of U.S. cars in the mid-Twentieth century. The Midwest also recognized the need for roads for people to drive those cars on (we think of everything!). In 1912, automobile entre-

IF WE LOST COLUMBUS, WHERE WOULD OUR TEENAGERS WANDER AROUND UNCHAPERONED? Don't blame Minnesota for everything. When it comes to mall culture, Columbus, Ohio, has arguably been the biggest player in America. It is the home city of The Limited, a vehicle for Leslie Wexner (Dayton, Ohio) to buy and sell a stable of mall-based retailers: Victoria's Secret, Lane Bryant, Abercrombie & Fitch, Express, Bath and Body Works, White Barn Candle Company, New York and Company, Structure, Henri Bendel, La Senza, and CO Bigelow.

preneur Carl Fisher gathered a group of friends in Indianapolis to help fund a coast-to-coast road made out of rock. He was able to raise one million dollars with help from contributors like Thomas Edison, the Goodyears, Teddy Roosevelt, and then-president Woodrow Wilson. Henry Ford refused to contribute because he believed the government would step up and build roads across the country.

They originally thought of calling it, with poor Midwestern marketing, "The Coast-to-Coast Rock Highway," but "The Lincoln Highway" won out. In 1919, a military convoy was sent from Washington, DC to San Francisco across the entire Lincoln Highway. The road was so rough that it took four months to cross, nine vehicles were lost, and 21 men were injured along the route and could not complete the journey.

One young officer on that journey was Dwight Eisenhower. Decades later, his presidency gave car culture a massive boost by implementing the "System of Interstate and Defense Highways" in 1956 — under the direction of Iowan Thomas MacDonald, who had been the Iowa State Engineer at the time of the initial Lincoln Highway construction. The first states to start paving were Kansas and Missouri. I-70 became the first interstate highway built under the act.

Another symbol of suburban car culture also rose out of the Midwest: the mall.

Southdale Mall in Edina, Minnesota, opened in 1956, the world's first fully enclosed, climate-controlled mall. The architect was Austrian-born Victor Gruen, who developed the idea for Southdale after building the open-air Northland Mall near Detroit in 1954. For Southdale, he intended to build an actual enclosed city, with apartment buildings, schools, medical facilities, and parks, but the developers, Dayton Department stores, stopped at retail.

Soon after, malls were popping up all over America: Maryland's Harundale Mall in 1958, Des Moines' Merle Hay Mall in 1959, Phoenix's Chris-Town Mall in 1961, Illinois' Randhurst Center in 1962.

As the progenitor of the mall, writer Malcolm Gladwell called Gruen, "the most influential architect of the Twentieth Century," although by 1978, Gruen said that his ideas had been "bastardized" and that the American malls were nothing more than "land-wasting seas of parking" that sped suburban sprawl.

NOT JUST MAKING HIGH-FRUCTOSE CORN SYRUP, BUT TAKING IT STRAIGHT TO YOUR FAT FACE *We've done our best at "vertically integrating" our obesity delivery, by not only controlling food production in the U.S., but also providing many popular food distribution points.*

McDonald's (Des Plaines, Illinois) After starting in California in 1940, **Ray Kroc** (Oak Park, Illinois) moved the now massive fast-food giant to the Heartland.

White Castle (Wichita, Kansas) Before McDonald's, there was White Castle. Founded in 1921, White Castle used a "speedee" service system that defined fast food as we know it today.

Wendy's (Columbus, Ohio) The first fast food chain with a salad bar!

Culver's (Sauk City, Wisconsin)

Pizza Hut (founded in Wichita, Kansas) Wichita strikes again!

Arby's (Youngstown, Ohio)

Dairy Queen (headquartered in Joliet, Illinois)

Charley's (Columbus, Ohio)

Wimpy (Chicago, Illinois)

Domino's Pizza (headquartered in Ypsilanti, Michigan)

Little Caesar's (headquartered in Garden City, Michigan)

Hardee's (St Louis, Missouri) Carl Jr's Midwestern cousin.

Panera Bread (Kirkwood, Missouri)

Taco Tico (Wichita, Kansas) Wichita for the hat trick!

But in 1978, our land-wasting sea of parking kick was just getting warmed up! We kept on charging through to 1992, when Minnesota raised the bar once more by building the Mall of America (or Megamall) in Bloomington. At the time, it was the largest and most visited mall in the U.S., housing more than 500 stores, a roller coaster, and a theme park. Its gross area is more than four million square feet — almost 100 acres. If you measure space in terms of Yankee Stadium, that's enough room to fit seven Yankee Stadiums inside.

1992 was also the year 53% of all retail sales in the U.S. and Canada took place in malls. Mall culture was captured, naturally, in Minnesota: Kevin Smith released the movie *Mallrats* in 1995, filmed at the Eden Prairie Center in Minnesota.

But the ultimate symbol of American silliness, the suburban Death Star bent on blasting walkable downtowns like they were the planet Alderaan, has Midwestern roots as well: Disneyland.

There, you can cruise from Paris to an African Safari to a Midwestern Main Street to Splash Mountain — all without leaving your Rascal-brand mobility scooter. In his 1992 book about malls, *Variations on a Theme Park,* architect Michael Sorkin says that both malls and Disneyland grew out of the fantasy world provided in American theme parks. "Whether in its master incarnation at the ersatz Main Street of Disneyland," Sorkin wrote, "in the phony historic festivity of a Rouse marketplace, or the gentrified architecture of the 'reborn' Lower East Side, this elaborate apparatus is at pains to assert its ties to the kind of city life it is in the process of obliterating."

Now witness the firepower of the fully *armed* and *operational* battle station!

Once again, the hand at the helm of the "Obliteration Express" was a Midwestern one: Walt Disney. Born in Chicago in 1901 and raised in Missouri from age 5 onward, Disney studied at the Art Institute in Chicago and in the 1920s showed his first cartoons at Frank Newman's theater in Kansas City. Soon after, Disney moved his studios from the Midwest to Hollywood, marching his way up the fame ladder until he launched Disneyland in Anaheim in 1955.

The genesis of the idea behind Disneyland, though, may just be Midwestern. Disney was never specific about his inspiration, but some say his idea was nurtured by stories his father told him of Chicago's Columbian Exposition in 1893.

CHICAGO

★ SPRINGFIELD

MT VERNON

ONCE YOU LEAVE CHICAGO, YOU'RE IN ILLINOIS

CAPITAL: Springfield **SIZE:** 67,914 square miles **POPULATION:** 12,869,257 **ADMISSION TO THE UNION:** December 3, 1818 **STATE MINERAL:** Fluorite **STRANGEST INVENTION:** The diorama. In its modern form, the diorama is said to have originated in Chicago's Field Museum. **EGYPT?** The southern part of Illinois is called "Little Egypt," not because the enslaved Jews helped build pyramids, but because in the winter of 1830, the southern part of the state shipped food to the north, after the Biblical story of Joseph supplying grain to his brothers. **SPEAKING OF SODOMY:** In 1961, Illinois became the first state to repeal its law banning sodomy. **SURPRISE! I'M FROM ILLINOIS:** Elliot Ness, Al Capone, John Malkovich, Hugh Hefner, Cindy Crawford, John Cusack, John Wayne Gacy, Ernest Hemingway, Bill Murray, Richard Pryor, Kanye West, and Ted Kaczynski.

4.4 CONTROLLING YOUNG MINDS WITH COUNTERCULTURAL SMUT PEDDLERS, JERRY SPRINGER, AND OPRAH.

" IN 1968, LARRY FLYNT OPENED THE FIRST HUSTLER CLUB IN DAYTON, OHIO "

The rise of the shopping mall in the 1950s signaled the arrival of modern American consumer culture. Indiana State professor Richard Schneirov notes that the early Twentieth century labor movement in the Midwest led to "higher wages and job security in the 1930s and 1940s "that doubled take-home pay of the working class." Home ownership skyrocketed after 1948, suburbs proliferated — at the same time, the seeds of the counterculture were sown.

The hand that watered those seeds was Barney Rosset, who purchased the struggling Grove Press in 1951 and published countercultural writers such as Jack Kerouac, William S Burroughs, and Allen Ginsberg. After Rosset's death in 2012, NPR's Jon Kalish noted that, "A literary legend has died — not an author, but the publisher behind some of the greatest and most controversial writers of the Twentieth century."

In 1957, Rosset launched *The Evergreen Review,* arguably the most important 1960s counterculture magazine. Two years later, in 1959, Rosset fought the first of many legal battles regarding obscenity when he published DH Lawrence's provocative *Lady Chatterley's Lover.* The case went all the way to the Supreme Court, where Rosset won on First Amendment grounds.

Rosset found himself in court in 1961 for Henry Miller's *Tropic of Cancer,* in 1962 for St Louis-born William Burrough's *Naked Lunch,* and for the Swedish film *I Am Curious (Yellow).* He published *The Autobiography of Malcolm X, Waiting for Godot,* and works by Albert Camus.

Grove was at the center of much of the late Twentieth century upheaval in the 1960s that saw the assassination of JFK, the Civil Rights movement, the rise of communes and a proliferation of chicks' armpit hair. In the Midwest, there was the tumultuous 1968 Democratic Convention in Chicago; the arrest of University of Michigan-Flint professor John Sinclair (poet and founder of the "White Panther Party" ... seriously!) in 1969; and the Kent State shootings in 1970.

America's moral collapse wasn't just because the Midwest dabbled in

DAMN THE MAN! SAVE THE MIDWEST!

You think the Heartland is "too wholesome" for latter-Twentieth Century counterculture, radical thinking, and some good ol'-fashioned domestic terrorism and criminal activity? Think again, you phony square: the revolution will be televised from Middle America!

Society for Human Rights (Chicago, Illinois) Founded in 1924, this was the first recognized gay rights organization in America. It would later inspire California's pro-gay Mattachine Society in 1950.

La Leche League (Franklin Park, Illinois) Not really left wing, but definitely "out there" for the time, this pro-breast feeding group was founded in 1956. Now an international organization, it grew from some Illinois moms who just wanted to breast feed.

Students for a Democratic Society (Ann Arbor, Michigan) This symbol of "The New Left" started with a 1960 meeting at the University of Michigan and "The Port Huron Statement," written by **Tom Hayden** (Detroit, Michigan) and adopted in 1962. The SDS was at the core of 1960s political counterculture.

National Organization for Women Founded in 1966 by **Betty Friedman** (Peoria, Illinois), who became a leader of the women's movement after writing *The Feminine Mystique* in 1963.

The Weather Underground (Chicago, Illinois) A splinter group from the SDS, the Weathermen formed in 1969, and issued a "Declaration of State of War" against the U.S. government. One wonders who would actually believe some of the crazy shit these guys wrote, but not only did some people believe it, they even carried out several domestic bombings. These led to jail time for core members including **Bill Ayers** (Glen Ellyn, Illinois) and **Bernadine Dohrn** (Milwaukee, Wisconsin).

Symbionese Liberation Army This group was for those who thought the Weathermen were a little too mainstream. The most radical of all New Left groups, the SLA was founded by **Donald DeFreeze** (Cleveland, Ohio) after he escaped from prison in 1973. Not so much "political," the SLA was really just an arm for DeFreeze's criminal activities — from murder to bank robbery. In 1974, DeFreeze kidnapped Patty Hearst, who then assisted in a bank robbery that same year, later leading to DeFreeze's death in a police shootout in Los Angeles. In 1975, the last SLA member, **Kathleen Soliah** (Fargo, North Dakota) went into hiding in Minnesota under the alias Sara Jane Olson. She was caught in 1999, and served seven years in jail (not bad for murder!)

PREVIOUS PAGE:
Barney Rosset
Chicago, Illinois

William S Burroughs
St Louis, Missouri

John Sinclair
Flint, Michigan

THIS PAGE:
Hugh Hefner
Chicago, Illinois

Art Paul
Chicago, Illinois

Ray Bradbury
Waukegon, Illinois

Charles Beaumont
Chicago, Illinois

politically subversive material, we also weaved in a healthy dose of smut.

While Rosset was publishing cutting-edge literature, Hugh Hefner was launching *Playboy*. The first issue, in December 1953, featured nude pictures of Marilyn Monroe shot in 1949 — strangely, she and Hefner never met. Like Rosset, Hefner ran into a fair amount of trouble with the authorities. He was arrested and later acquitted for selling obscene literature in 1963. And through the 1970s, Hefner claimed that federal authorities harassed him and his staff because of his stance regarding the liberalization of drug laws.

Also like Rosset, Hefner had an artistic side. *Playboy* launched the career of its Chicago-born art director, Art Paul, whose creative magazine illustrations inaugurated what many designers call "The Illustration Liberation Movement" by emphasizing the role of design. After leaving *Playboy* in 1982, Paul went on to exhibit his work and serve on the board of the Chicago Museum of Contemporary Art and the Illinois Summer School of the Arts.

In 1954, during *Playboy's* first year, Hefner serialized the first novel by Ray Bradbury, *Farenheit 451*. In 1955, *Esquire* rejected a short story by Charles Beaumont, "The Crooked Man," because it dealt with a science fiction world where straight men were persecuted by gays. Hefner published it in *Playboy*. Beaumont published other stories in *Playboy* before writing, most famously, for *The Twilight Zone*.

In the world of smut, Chicago's *Playboy* couldn't hold a candle to Ohio, the home state of *Hustler*. The magazine's creator, Larry Flynt, grew up in Kentucky, but in 1965 took over a bar in Dayton. Tiring of breaking up white trash fights (the bar was called Hillbilly Haven, so he may have brought the rednecks on himself), Flynt wanted to rebrand his chain of bars into higher-class establishments, so in 1968 he opened the first Hustler Club in Dayton with nude hostess dancers (nothing says "higher class" like nipples).

Larry Flynt
settled in Dayton, Ohio

The model proved successful, and Ohio started growing Hustler Clubs alongside corn in the late 1960s. They popped up in Cincinnati, Columbus, Cleveland, Toledo, and Akron. Flynt later said he was taking multiple amphetamines to keep up with the 18-20 hour workdays. It's that Midwestern work ethic!

In 1974, the Hustler Clubs' newsletter became a full-fledged nudie magazine called *Hustler*. The idea for the magazine was born of desperation, because the 1973 oil crisis had caused such a drop in revenue for Flynt's clubs that he was verging on bankruptcy. In 1975, Flynt published photos of a naked Jacqueline Kennedy Onassis taken while she had been sunbathing in 1971, and the issue sold more than one million copies in just a few days.

Like Hefner and Rosset, Flynt was an obscenity law pioneer, facing lawsuits in 1973, 1976, and 1983. Even though in his 1983 appearance before the US Supreme Court he screamed, "Fuck this court! It's nothing but eight assholes and a token cunt," he went on to win that case against Jerry Falwell. Falwell had brought it for a cartoon in a 1982 *Hustler* that suggested Falwell's first sexual encounter was with his mother in an outhouse.

Bizarrely, Flynt commented that he considered Falwell a friend and "always appreciated his sincerity." In 1977 he converted to evangelical Christianity after meeting Ruth Carter Stapleton, the sister of Jimmy Carter. He vowed to "hustle for God." But in the 1980s he called himself an atheist — speed is a helluva drug.

Jerry Falwell
studied at the Baptist Bible College in Springfield, Missouri

In 1988, the same year as Flynt's victory over Falwell, the Midwestern invasion of American thoughts really started to take shape as Rush Hudson Limbaugh III debuted his national radio show just before the Republican National Convention.

While Limbaugh secured the mostly male Republican crowd that apparently has several hours free in the middle of the day, the Midwest opened up two other fronts: former mayor of Cincinnati Jerry Springer took on the high school/college crowd with the launch of *The Jerry Springer Show* out of Cincinnati in 1991; and in 1986, the Chicago-based *Oprah Winfrey Show* began the slow enslavement of middle-aged housewives' minds.

With three fronts on three different demographics, there was no way for your average American to come up with a thought not fed to them by a Midwesterner.

Rush Limbaugh
Cape Girardeau, Missouri

Jerry Springer
settled in Cincinnati

Oprah Winfrey
raised in Milwaukee, Wisconsin, settled in Chicago, Illinois

"Minnesota wouldn't be such a bad place to go back and die in." – Bob Dylan

MOORHEAD

DULUTH

ST PAUL

SNOWY WITH A CHANCE OF HEAVY SMUG

CAPITAL: St Paul **SIZE:** 86,939 square miles **POPULATION:** 5,344,861 **ADMISSION TO THE UNION:** May 11, 1858 **STATE BIRD:** Common Loon (but it should be the Mosquito, ya' mean?) **STATE CAR BRAND:** Subaru **I'M NOT FROM AROUND HERE, COULD YOU DESCRIBE THE STATE TO ME?** It's the agriculture of Iowa, the outdoorsy-ness of Oregon, the progressiveness of Scandinavia, the culture of Seattle, and the smugness of San Francisco. **WOULD THIS BE A GOOD PLACE TO USE ALL THOSE LUTHERAN JOKES I HAVE LYING AROUND:** It's the only place. **FINLAND WANTS THEIR SLOGAN BACK:** Minnesota has a lot to brag about, from F Scott Fitzgerald and Prince to the First Ave and Charles Lindbergh. But their "Land of 10,000 Lakes" is taken straight from Finland's national nickname, "Land of 1,000 Lakes." What's worse, Minnesota has only 11,842 lakes compared to Finland's 187,888 lakes. Watch your back, Minnesota.

4.5 IF YOU WANT AN ECONOMY DESTROYED, LET A MIDWESTERNER HANDLE IT

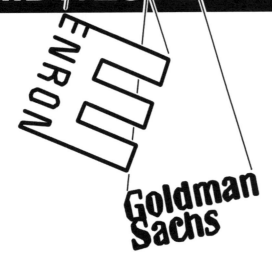

The Midwest is known for economic prudence. Our states are, for the most part, well run, and our most famous money manager is Warren Buffett, "Oracle of Omaha."

But if you want greed and irresponsibility done properly, let a Midwesterner do it.

In the Financial Collapse of 2008, Heartlanders were in the thick of things. From 2004 to 2007, John Thain was running the New York Stock Exchange before heading to Merrill Lynch in 2007, and from 1994 to 2006, Goldman Sachs was run by Hank Paulson and Jon Corzine.

"The first thing you need to know about Goldman Sachs," wrote *Rolling Stone*'s Matt Taibbi in April 2010, assessing the financial collapse of 2008, "is that it's everywhere. The world's most powerful investment bank is a great vampire squid wrapped around the face of humanity, relentlessly jamming its blood funnel into anything that smells like money."

And the Midwest is riding that vampire squid! Mid-west! Mid-west! Mid-west!

Indeed, Goldman went public in 1999, with Paulson taking the lead from Corzine that year, and the bank led a period of massive expansion in the "high risk financial products" that helped bring about the economic collapse about nine years later.

Looking back at Jon Corzine's career, a former partner told *Vanity Fair* in 2012 that, "There's an element of Machiavelli within Jon. He comes across as this simple guy from Illinois, but he kept *The Prince* on his bookshelf and he followed it." Once again, our wholesome Midwest facade provided the perfect cover for Corzine's free-for-all economics that was learned not out East, but with his 1973 MBA from the University of Chicago — "the bastion of free-market economics" *Bloomberg* called it in 2008. "The Chicago School" or "Freshwater School" of Economics had a patriarch in Milton Friedman, who won one of the ten Nobel Prizes Chicago would rack up. His laissez-faire thinking underpinned 1972's first financial futures contracts in foreign markets (approved by former Chicago dean and Treasury Secretary at the time, George Schultz), the

Reaganomics '80s, and the later derivatives market, whose complex math formulas came from Chicago economists.

This wasn't our first attempt to destroy America's economy with greed. In 1873, a massive financial panic swept through the country — The Panic of 1873. At the center of this panic was Ohio's Jay Cooke.

Like Paulson and Corzine, Cooke was a well-connected guy. His Jay Cooke and Company helped the government finance the Civil War, and in 1870 he tried to raise $100 million to finance the Northern Pacific Railroad. After reaching Bismarck, financing faltered, and in September 1873, Cooke and Company collapsed, setting off a chain reaction that led to the New York Stock Exchange closing for ten days. Eighty-nine of the country's 364 railroads went bankrupt, 18,000 businesses failed between 1873 and 1875, and unemployment reached 14% by 1876.

But Cooke was a wily one, and by 1880 he had invested in Utah silver mines and once again became a wealthy man.

Likewise, Paulson left Goldman in 2006 to become Secretary of the Treasury, where in 2008 he let Lehman Brothers collapse in what is still the largest bankruptcy in U.S. history, then organized the major banking bailout that made Goldman even more powerful than before.

Corzine left Goldman to become a Senator from, then Governor of New Jersey. In 2010, he became chairman of M.F. Global, which collapsed in 2011, becoming one of the ten biggest bankruptcies in U.S. history. But, more importantly, M.F. Global claimed that it could not account for $1.6 billion worth of customer accounts.

Roops!

Not to be outdone, John Thain collected more than $83 million in compensation in 2007, then jumped ship to oversee Merrill's takeover by Bank of America in 2008. In January 2009, federal disclosures showed that Thain had spent $1.22 million renovating two conference rooms, a reception area, and his office, with $131,000 for area rugs, $87,000 for guest chairs, and a $35,115 gold-plated toilet on legs.

We can even do total asshole better than the other regions.

When you look at the folks above, one home state really stands out: Illinois. The Midwest is certainly exceptional in worth ethic, strength, looks, and World's Largest Roadside Attractions. Corruption is not something we're going to cede to New Jersey.

"If Illinois isn't the most corrupt state in the United States," said the FBI's Chicago field office chief Robert Grant with a little Midwestern modesty, "it's certainly one hell of a competitor." Between 1953 and 2009, seven Illinois governors were charged with crimes related to corruption, and six of them were convicted. The most recent, Rod "Fucking Golden" Blagojevich, was born and raised in Chicago and convicted on seventeen felony counts (which, as Jon Stewart remarked, is called "a Chicago dozen") related to trying to sell Barack Obama's vacated Senate seat.

Rod Blagojevich
Chicago, Illinois

Almost more amazing, as Blagojevich started his federal sentence in 2011, is that he was doing so in a jail system that housed members from all three branches of Illinois' government, including the governor who served right before Blagojevich, George Ryan, who was convicted on eighteen felony counts including racketeering and tax fraud.

George Ryan
born in Maquoketa, Iowa, raised in Kankakee County, Illinois

Those last two convictions, racketeering and tax evasion, may bring Al Capone to mind. In fact, Capone was one of a long line in Chicago's history of organized crime, stretching back to the late Nineteenth century, when a gambling-house owner named Michael Cassius McDonald created the city's first political machine — Chicago had organized crime-based political machines before skyscrapers.

Michael Cassius McDonald is thought to have actually first used the phrase "There's a sucker born every minute," later credited to PT Barnum

In September 2006, the *Chicago Sun-Times* published a report that detailed corruption's persistence in the city and state of Illinois by noting that the list of elected officials with ties to organized corruption included (and this is before Blago): three governors, two state officials, fifteen legislators, two congressmen, one mayor, three other city officials, 27 aldermen, nineteen Cook County judges, and seven other Cook County officials.

Richard M Daley
Chicago, Illinois

It's all so common that Mayor Richard M Daley hired John Boyle — a man convicted of stealing four million dollars from the Illinois Toll Highway Authority — for a Department of Transportation job. When a reporter asked if being convicted of corruption disqualified him for a political office in Illinois, Daley replied: "No, I don't think so."

AND YOU SHOULD SEE WHAT MISSOURI CAN DESTROY! Before we all jump on that Illinois-is-so-corrupt bandwagon, we should point out that one of the biggest corporate scandals in American history was the Enron collapse. Behind it were: Ken Lay (Tyron, Missouri), Jeff Skilling (raised in Aurora, Illinois), Andrew Fastow (born in Washington, DC, but earned an MBA from Northwestern), and Rebecca Mark-Jusbasche (Kirksville, Missouri).

4.6 CANADA ATTACKS!

Let's face it, one day, Canada is going to get sick of America's shit — the "eh" jokes, the hockey jokes, the "America's attic" jokes, Nickelback (unfortunately, Nickelback is *real*) — and head south to try and go Charles Bronson on our ass. Imagine the terror and confusion our citizens will find themselves in if they see a group of what look like red-jacketed park rangers on horses firing AR-15s into the air.

"Why does that guy need a gun to warn me about forest fires?"

The question is not *if* Canada will try to invade America, but *where* the attack will come from. Maybe they'd go through the long, unguarded border on our Northwest. I imagine those trustafarians putting down their hackie sack and praising their Wiccan gods that a country with loose marijuana laws was to be their new overlord. "Finally, we don't have to live in America anymore, bro!"

Perhaps Canada would choose the rugged Northeastern border. And they might not encounter much of a fight there. Instead, Wall Street folks would just want to "make a deal" for tax incentives and lower rates on capital gains and deferred interest. Canada may win that war, but they'd slowly lose their soul as their universal health care and progressive social laws are chipped away, one loophole and lobbyist at a time.

Most likely, Canada will come straight through the Midwest. Why? Revenge.

In 1838, a group of Americans assembled in Michigan, bent on "liberating" Canada. They held a meeting in Detroit, stole arms and ammunition from the jail, and captured the schooner *Ann*. Michigan's "boy governor," Stevens T Mason (the youngest governor in American history), sympathized, and in December, the force landed just above Windsor, Ontario, where they were killed or captured in a matter of days.

Vermont must have sold us out.

This seemingly harmless incident wasn't the first time the Midwest pulled some business with Canada. In September 1813, during the War of 1812, Admiral Oliver Hazard Perry defeated the British fleet on

Lake Erie. This paved the way for pseudo-Ohioan General William Henry Harrison to invade Canada, winning decisively at the Battle of the Thames in October, 1813.

After the American capital in DC and the Canadian capital in York (now Toronto) were burned, both sides called it quits in 1814 with the Treaty of Ghent.

Tensions seem to have cooled — the Midwest and Canada have a cozy relationship with a busy border crossing from Detroit to Windsor, casino-exchanges in Sault Ste Marie, shared use of the Great Lakes, and even a division of Lake of the Woods in northern Minnesota. But those Canadians are up to something.

When the Canadians come at us, whether by land force over the Dakota border or by D-Day-style amphibious assault on the shores of Michigan, America will be glad that team Midwest is on the case.

We could unleash our aforementioned military cunning, but with Canada, we'd play it cooler. As they storm the beaches of the U.P., we'd send out just a couple of regular Joes in flannel shirts and Carhartts.

"Hey, Canada," we'd say, "let's just cool it for a minute. Come on, let's have a couple Labatt's."

They'd say, "What, you drink Labatt's here?"

"Of course we do! This is northern Michigan. Many of us have cottages in your land, we share lakes with you, and we celebrate all of your country's products from Labatt's to ... huh ... Canadian bacon? Okay, we can't think of anything else, but you get the point."

With tempers cooled, we would empathize with them on what it's like to be overlooked by major media markets, to be a land that can kick some serious ass, but is viewed as harmless Rockys and Bullwinkles.

THANKS FOR THE LIGHTBULB, SUCKERS! The invading Michiganders of 1838 were aiming to aid rebellious Canadians. After the rebellion's failure, one rebel, Samuel Edison, was forced to flee to America. He landed in Ohio and later fathered famed American inventor Thomas Edison.

The Midwest has a lot in common with Canada. Our demeanor is similar, the language is similar (Michigan's U.P. is pretty much Canada-lite). Their country's flagship beer, Molson, was bought by a foreign company (Miller-Coors), our country's flagship beer, St Louis' Budweiser, was bought by a foreign company (Belgium's InBev), and both foreign companies run patronizingly "patriotic" ads.

Our dry, wit-based humor is similar to Canada. And our humor has teamed up in the past, most famously for *Saturday Night Live,* created by Toronto's Lorne Michaels. Of the about seventeen members of the first *SNLs* in the 1970s, one was from the South (Garrett Morris), two were from the West (including LA's Laraine Newman), four were from the Northeast (including New York-born Chevy Chase), but ten were from the Midwest and Canada — from Canadians Peter Akroyd, Dan Akroyd, and Paul Schaffer to Midwesterners John Belushi, Bill Murray, and Gilda Radner.

The Midwest-Canada comedy connection came from Chicago's Second City improv group, which started turning out American comedians in the 1960s. In 1973 it opened its second theater in Toronto — helping launch 1975's *Saturday Night Live* on American TV and 1976's *Second City Television* on Canadian TV.

After a few beers and a few laughs, we'll lure them in with our secret weapon: ice hockey. Canada's national sport is bigger in the Midwest than in any part of America. America's Hockey Hall of Fame is in Eveleth, Minnesota, and the first professional hockey league, the I.P.H.L., was formed by a Canadian dentist (possibly to drive business for himself since the first goalies didn't wear masks) in Houghton, Michigan.

One of America's greatest sporting victories of all time came when the U.S. hockey team defeated the Soviets in the 1980 Olympics (the beginning of the end for those Commie no-good-nicks). This "Miracle on Ice" was coached by Minnesota's Herb Brooks and Detroit's Craig Patrick, and of the twenty players on the roster, seventeen were from the Midwest and three were from the Northeast.

Sorry South and West, we needed to do this one right.

John Belushi
Wheaton, Illinois

Bill Murray
Wilmette, Illinois

Gilda Radner
Detroit, Michigan

Herb Brooks
St Paul, Minnesota

Craig Patrick
Detroit, Michigan

PART FIVE

WE'RE #1 BY A WIDER MARGIN THAN USUAL!

"YOU ALL JUST HEAD FOR BRIGHTER PASTURES OUTSIDE OF MIDDLE AMERICA. I'LL CLEAN UP THE LAST OF THE STREET THUGS AND PUT OUT THE TIRE FIRE."

KEEP OUT!

5.1 WILL THE LAST ONE OUT OF THE MIDWEST JUST REMEMBER TO EXTINGUISH THE TIRE FIRE?

This whole book is well and good, but it's time to let you know the party's over. The invention of the car, the plane, the skyscraper — those were the glory days, when the Midwest was the country's handsome Homecoming King. Now we're the lonely guy at the bar who didn't pass computer skills class and lost his scholarship.

"The [Midwest's] nadir came about 1950," writes James Shortridge in 1989. After that, "the previous strong sense of local pride was gone. At best it was a region with mixed feelings about itself; at worst the nation's heartland had become a backwater."

Yessiree, it's been a long, slow slide to Who-gives-a-shit-ville. The Information Age came and we're here asking our grandkids how to text from our rotary phone. We're trying to upload photos to our computer by cramming film into the floppy disk drive. We're still using AOL.

Academia's end-of-the-Midwest bandwagon has been filling up over the last twenty years or so, most recently with books such as 2003's *The End of Detroit*, 2004's *What's the Matter with Kansas?*, 2008's *Caught in the Middle*, 2009's *Hollowing Out the Middle*, and 2009's *Methland*.

Each takes a hard look at the Midwest's last circle of the drain before heading to that big water treatment plant in the sky. Along the way, they reflect on the way things were in the glory days. In *Caught in the Middle*, Dick Longworth laments that in 1915, "Half of everything in America was made in the Midwest. It must have been an exhilarating time ... Midwestern innovation created the new world."

Now, as Longworth looks out over the 67 million desolate souls in Middle America who have nothing but an occasional night out at Perkins and memories of what could have been, he asks the question: "Where did it all go?"

"In a new, globalized age," Longworth summarizes, "the Midwest faces dire challenges to its economic viability ... [this book] surveys what's right and what's wrong in the Heartland, and offers a tough prescription for survival."

If that prescription is illegal amphetamines, Dick, we're way ahead of you.

In *Hollowing Out the Middle,* the Philadelphia-based duo Patrick Carr and Maria Kefalas "inspire and encourage readers struggling to defend their communities."

It's certainly a courageous act on their part. But what if we never learned how to read?!

Books aren't going to save us! Just send more guns and religion so that we can properly battle when we're finally living in the hellscape envisioned in 1987's *Robocop,* a film set in a "not-so-distant future" Detroit that is forced to bring a cyborg law enforcer to rein in rampant crime.

As far as 1980s cinematic depictions of the Midwest go, *Robocop* is one of the brighter visions. We were almost wiped off the map in 1983's *The Day After,* a TV movie that followed a group of Kansans around the Midwest after a nuclear attack. ABC, which aired the movie, had to set up a hotline with therapists for traumatized viewers. Forget not being in Kansas anymore — Kansas not *being* anymore. And in 1984's *Footloose,* Kevin Bacon was a city boy forced to live in what was billed as a "small, Midwestern" town that had banned dancing (though the movie setting looks a lot more like Utah than the Midwest).

Noooo!!!!! Nuclear attacks and crime are one thing, but banning dancing?!

We'll take *Robocop* any day of the week. That movie, oddly, does a great job of capturing the anxieties of both the late 1980s and today. In the movie, central Detroit is "Old Detroit." It is the area of town everyone has left for the suburbs, surrendering it to deserted factories, toxic waste, elderly holdouts, crime bosses, and street toughs. When police officer Alex Murphy starts his term in Old Detroit, his fellow officers tell him, "Welcome to hell."

Dun dun dun.

With less manufacturing to fund services, the city has contracted police protection to a multinational corporation called Omni Consumer Products, which sees growth for private industry in law enforcement as well as, "hospitals, prisons, and space exploration." OCP develops the technology for the Robocop, a bulletproof cyborg who is the only hope of taming the gangs roaming through Old Detroit.

Along the way, there is enough gratuitous violence for the whole family: a hand is shot off, acid is dumped on a face, a city council member holds the mayor hostage, a convenience store is robbed by thugs with automatic weapons, and South

Africa's white rulers obtain a nuclear weapon for use against the blacks. The movie was so violent it originally received an X rating.

In addition to mayhem, the hot new car is the 6000 SUX (with an advertised 8.2 MPG!), the OCP-controlled police are trying to organize a strike, and Robocop cruises around in a 1986 Ford Taurus (selected because in 1987, it apparently looked pretty futuristic).

Much of what is in *Robocop* (well, except for the Taurus, which was a great car) are projections of real concerns about the Midwest at the time: inner city crime, declining union strength in the face of multinational corporations, and the fall of manufacturing innovation (8.2 MPG).

These are the underpinnings, too, of a lot of modern books about the Midwest. They see half a century of decline, many using 1950 as the year just before the *SS Cornholed* plowed into an iceberg.

Most visible is the collapse of the Midwest's major cities. In 1950, Detroit was the fifth-largest city in America, with 1.85 million residents; Cleveland was the seventh-largest American city with 900,000 residents; and St Louis was the eighth-largest city with 857,000 residents. Fifty years later, all three had dropped by about 50%. Detroit's population had fallen to about 700,000, Cleveland's slipped to about 470,000, and St Louis was down to 357,000 — smaller than Omaha.

But back in 1950, those three cities seemed to be cruising along. In St Louis, city planners estimated that by 1960, St Louis would pass one million residents. With such projected growth, they looked to build denser

"*DON'T WORRY, ROSE! EVERYTHING'S GOING TO BE OKAY!*"

WELL, IT'S BEEN A NICE RIDE, BUT NOW THE MIDWEST IS TOTALLY FUCKED! ABANDON SHIP! ABANDON SHIP!

housing for low-income residents, which led to the construction of 1954's Pruitt-Igoe projects just northwest of downtown. Like Chicago's Cabrini-Green and other federally funded low-income-housing high-rises across the country, Pruitt-Igoe's 33 buildings were completed to great fanfare as a shining example of beautiful, dense, urban housing. By the late 1960s, it was world famous for rampant crime and poverty. It was demolished in 1972, and the photos of its demolition — buildings imploding on themselves — became symbols of America's failed attempt at government-sponsored housing.

Pruitt-Igoe was also a microcosm of racial strife across the Midwest in the 1960s, as citizens began to segregate, encouraged by subtle or overt government policy. In August 1964, there was the Dixmoor riot in Chicago, the 1966 Hughes riot in Cleveland, the 1966 Division Street riots in Chicago, the 1967 Twelfth Street riot in Detroit, the 1967 Milwaukee riots, and the 1967 North Side riots in Minneapolis.

In 1987, the year *Robocop* came out, *The New York Times* wrote that in Detroit, "where teenagers were killed over silk shirts and gym shoes and where newspapers publish a regular homicide toll, officials are trying to halt a wave of slayings unmatched since the mid-1970s." Among the nation's largest cities, Detroit topped the homicide-rate list and even contemplated holding a "No Crime Day" to "appeal to residents' sensibilities."

The environmental toll of the Midwest's staggering growth in the early 1900s started to show: Detroit's Lake St Clair was so polluted that humans often weren't allowed in it; the copper of the Masabi range and Upper Peninsula was depleted; in 1969 the polluted Cuyahoga River in Cleveland caught on fire (earning the city the nickname, "The Mistake on the Lake"); and in 1981, the Environmental Protection Agency ranked Treece, Kansas, as "the most contaminated site in the country."

In the 1920s, Treece was the top producer of zinc and lead in the country, supplying most of the Allied ammunition for both World Wars. The minerals were pulled from the land and the waste rock dumped into piles all around town. The piles today are small mountains, and the dust that blows off them makes the metal rates in local childrens' blood three times higher than normal.

In the late 1960s, the minerals started to run out, mining companies left and shut off power to the mines' pumps, leading to flooding, sinkholes, and streams so polluted that no life can survive in them. Kids swam in the reddish quarries and got out with chemical burns on their skin that locals mistook for sunburn.

By 1981, only a few hundred people remained, and a sign on the way into town announced: "Hell awaits." Today, the town is largely abandoned, with houses bulldozed to prevent them from being used as meth kitchens.

Global competition and tariff changes also undercut the massive car and steel industries. Innovation, corporations, and population shifted West. In the first half of the 1980s, although employment rose by 7% in America as a whole, employment fell in the Midwest. Union membership in the Midwest sank from 39% in 1964 to 19% in 2000.

Major Midwest companies started to suffer from a lack of foresight, best captured by Roger Smith ascending to the chairmanship of General Motors in 1981, a year after G.M. recorded its first annual loss since the early 1920s. Smith had worked his way up from the accounting department and was meant to reorganize the company. But instead of innovating products or making better cars, Smith started to carve up the expense side, reducing costs where he could, and from 1981 until his departure in 1990, G.M.'s market share steadily fell from 46% to 35%.

Roger Smith
Columbus, Ohio

Highlighting this drop was Smith's car, the GM10. Meant as a symbol of the new G.M., the company was losing $2,000 on every one it produced by 1989. In 1992, *Fortune* magazine called Smith's attempts to change G.M. "The biggest catastrophe in American Industrial history."

And in spite of Roger Smith's attempts at cost-cutting, in just nine years, G.M. moved from being the lowest-cost producer in Detroit to the highest.

In 1989's *Roger and Me,* director Michael Moore looks at G.M.'s decision to lay off 30,000 workers in Flint and the impact it had on the city. He comments that one challenge in the city was finding a U-Haul to drive out of town since so many were leaving and nobody was arriving. Another challenge was Flint's skyrocketing crime. In 1988, when *Nightline* came to do a story about the factory closures in Flint, their network van was stolen, abruptly ending the broadcast. Later, *Money* magazine called Flint, "The worst place to live in America."

Michael Moore
Flint, Michigan

At the end, Moore laments that, "This film cannot be showing within the city of Flint. All the movie theaters have closed." Feel-good film of the decade!

Mix industrial decline, urban decay, and pollution with the expansion of massive agri-corporations and dying small towns, and you either have the makings for what many think of as the modern Midwest, or the most depressing theme park of all time.

"Daddy, can we please ride the Lose-Your-High-Hourly-Wage-and-Benefits-Beef-Rendering-Job-When-a-New-and-Bigger-Company-Buys-Your-Plant-Driving-Your-Life-Into-Meth-Induced-Haze?"

"I don't know, son, the line for that one is so long. Why don't we just take a spin on the Another-Foreclosed-Family-Farmer-Arrives-in-the-City-to-Take-a-Minimum-Wage-Paying-Position? That one is supposed to be even more exciting than Six Flags' Batman ride."

Yes indeed, the only thing the Midwest produces today are memories and vague images of tranquil farm life. This is why so many people at Penn thought I must have been a farm kid.

Little did they know I had *survived* eighteen years in this post-industrial wasteland, fighting for every scrap of food or happiness, clinging to the faint hope that my future would involve a sheet metal shack roof over my head and the occasional hot bath.

> " Mix industrial decline, urban decay, and pollution with the expansion of massive agri-corporations and dying small towns, and you either have the makings for what many think of as the modern Midwest, or the most depressing theme park of all time "

FOOD PRODUCTS ON STICKS:
FINALLY YOU CAN KEEP HOLDING YOUR BIG GULP OF MOUNTAIN DEW IN ONE HAND WHILE ENJOYING A STICK OF FRIED BUTTER IN THE OTHER.

FRIED BUTTER ON A STICK? You heard right! Fried butter itself debuted at the State Fair of Texas in 2009, but in 2011, the Iowa State Fair put it on a stick. **WHY?** It's not clear when food first started appearing on sticks. **BUT:** One thing's for sure, it has hit the state fair circuit hard, and Midwesterners live for state fairs. **GOIN' TO THE FAIR:** The first official state fair was in Michigan in 1849, and the Iowa State Fair solidified its position near the top when the 1933 Iowa-based film *State Fair* came out. It starred Will Rogers as Abel Frake, a farmer whose "Blue Boy was the world's greatest hawg!" **I WENT TO THE FAIR AND ALL I GOT WAS TYPE-2 DIABETES:** And that's not all! Just reading a list of fatty food items at a Midwestern State Fair should require a prescription for Lipitor to control your cholesterol: Bacon-wrapped corn dog, chili cheese dog on a stick, cheese curds on a stick, deep fried cheesecake on a stick, Reuben sandwich on a stick, or cream cheese with bacon on a stick are just a few.

5.2 REPORTS OF OUR ECONOMIC DEMISE HAVE BEEN GREATLY EXAGGERATED

"THE STEEL WORKFORCE IN GARY, INDIANA, IS 10% OF WHAT IT WAS AT ITS PEAK ... BUT GARY PRODUCES MORE STEEL NOW THAN EVER"

History can be a crafty fox. It's misleading because it likes phases and doesn't often spend time looking back at how silly its old hairstyles once were. In the 1970s, history was wearing bell-bottoms and snorting coke at Studio 54. It opted for hammer pants and a boombox on its shoulder in the 1980s. Today it hasn't shaved for two months and sports a tank top and skinny jeans as if those hammer pants never happened.

The idea that the Midwest in the Twentieth century is divided into a rising phase before 1950 and a falling phase after is an easy arc to get your mind around. I went to a public high school and even I can understand it: "'Mer'ca used to make things, now we don't make nothin' and that's the problem. Give me a factory and a tractor and we'll make this region great again!"

The "rise and fall of the Midwest" arc isn't total bullshit, but it is a good 78% bullshit.

Today, the Midwest is tied with the South when it comes to most companies represented in the top 10 *Fortune 500* companies — Berkshire Hathaway out of Omaha, General Motors and Ford out of Detroit. The South has Wal-Mart, Exxon, and Conoco; the Northeast has General Electric; the West has Chevron and Hewlett-Packard.

The Midwest still has massive manufacturing companies and these are some of the biggest companies in the country — larger than Apple, larger than Google, larger than all of America's commercial banks.

In 2008, Congress handed billions of dollars to the banking industry at the start of the Great Recession, then hesitated to give a fraction of that to the auto industry. Jon Stewart may have best described the difference between bailing out a manufacturing industry and bailing out banks when he said of Congress: "You won't bail out the people who make cars, you only bail out the people who make car loans — wait — not even car loans! The people you bailed out make derivative paper transfers speculating on the future value of enormous groupings of said loans to China ... At least when Detroit loses money, we get cars!"

After the recession, some of the Midwest's biggest companies are more profitable and productive than at any point in their history. "We find," wrote Anthony Carnevale and Nicole Smith in their 2012 study of the Midwest for Georgetown's Center on Education and the Workforce, "that while agriculture and manufacturing employment continue to decline in the aggregate ... output in these industries will grow, mostly from increases in productivity."

The steel workforce in Gary, Indiana, is 10% of what it was at its peak in the early Twentieth century, leaving the city far from its population peak. But Gary produces more steel now than ever. Michigan's Global Engine Manufacturing Alliance in the 2000s was making more than 800,000 engines per year with a staff of 562, about a third of the staff needed for an older engine plant that produced fewer engines.

A writer like Dick Longworth, in *Caught in the Middle,* may see this as the Midwest hanging on to lost industries — even as they become more efficient, they are dying. The future is in services, in technology, and in alternative energy.

Perhaps. But the Midwest is not behind in any of these fields. For instance, in a developing sector like health care, San Francisco's McKesson Corporation is one of the largest in the field and the fourteenth-largest company on the *Fortune 500*. But Ohio's Cardinal Health, Minnesota's United Health, and Indianapolis' WellPoint are McKesson's main competitors, holding places 21, 22, and 45 on the *Fortune 500*.

Likewise, although Silicon Valley took the lead in technological headquarters, Midwestern minds have been at the forefront of digital ascendance. Google's cofounder, Larry Page, grew up in Lansing, Michigan, and went to college in Ann Arbor. Alongside Page are the founders of Twitter, the founders of Square, and the founder of Zynga. Before that came the founder of Netscape and the founder of Intel.

As the tech industry boomed, it expanded far beyond Silicon Valley — most notably in Chicago, with tech companies such as Groupon. Founded in 2008 by Andrew Mason, Eric Lefkofsky, and Brad Keywell, Groupon is just the tip of the tech iceberg in Chicago. Lefkofsky and Keywell have been working together since 1999, founding Starbelly, InnerWorkings, and Echo Global Logistics. They have since leveraged successful IPOs to become major investors in the Chicago tech world by cofounding the investment engine LightBank — which declares "you're not in the valley anymore" on its homepage. The two joined *Chicago Magazine's* list of "Most Powerful

Chicagoans" in 2012 as the 10th and 21st most powerful, respectively.

Others on that list point to Chicago's rise in general, growing for years, and capped with Barack Obama's election in 2008, sending a Midwesterner to the White House with Chicagoans like Rahm Emanuel and Hillary Rodham Clinton.

Dick Longworth authored *Caught in the Middle* from Chicago's Council on Global Affairs, and noted that many had left the city for dead in the 1980s. *The Economist* wrote in the mid '80s that the city's skyscrapers were "a facade" that hid the urban decay. But in 2006, *The Economist* wrote a special section called "A Success Story" about Chicago. "Chicago," it wrote, "is undoubtedly back ... the city is buzzing with life, humming with prosperity."

The city is the unofficial capital of the Midwest and has an identity distinct from other American centers like New York or Los Angeles. It was born at the nexus of agricultural commodities from the central Midwest and iron and copper from the northern Midwest. It cradled the industries those commodities spawned and sent goods outward in all directions.

Its grid pattern is like a big, Midwestern city. But it is also the home of the skyscraper. These towers rise above sandy beaches along Lake Michigan. Chicago is, as Frank Lloyd Wright said, "The greatest and most nearly perfect city."

And though it's fast-paced for most Midwesterners, compared to New York or LA, it still has that No Coast charm. When travel writer and New York native Stephanie Rosenbloom visited the city in 2012, she wrote that as she left the coffee shop Filter, "I headed for the door, which a man on his way in stopped to hold. I thanked him and a curious thing happened: He didn't grunt or mumble 'Welcome.' Instead, he looked at me and said, 'It's a pleasure.' ... That's my kind of town." Our Midwestern niceness mixed with a big city's culture kept Rosenbloom on her toes. While drinking in RockIt Bar and Grill on Hubbard Street, "A dark-haired stranger turned to me. 'I love your dress,' he said. Was it a come-on? Or just another friendly comment? In Chicago, you never know."

Chicago's sports teams reflect the mix of Midwest personality. On the one hand, the Midwest's blatant superiority is encapsulated in teams like the 1990s Bulls — possibly *the* greatest basketball dynasty in history — and the greatest football

" the greatest football team of all time — from playing to players to coaching to style — the 1985 Bears "

Phil Jackson
Bulls coach raised in
Williston, North Dakota

team of all time — from playing to players to coaching to style — the 1985 Bears. But Midwestern laid-back style and humility finds a home in the Chicago Cubs, a team that likes relaxed afternoon games, and hasn't won a championship in 103 years — the longest championship drought of any professional sports team. This piss-poor performance is taken in stride by fans such as famous Chicago humorist Mike Royko, who looked on the bright side of this streak in the 1970s: "Being a Cub fan prepares you for life. If anything bad can happen, it will happen to us."

As the city has risen, stars like Emmanuel have returned, and Lefkofsky and Keywell founded Chicago Ideas week in 2011 to showcase the city, national speakers like Bill Clinton, and some regional stars including Des Moines' Ben Milne, who runs our city's most prominent tech company, Dwolla.

Ben Milne
Cedar Falls, Iowa

Milne is an Iowa native and part of the tech world that is diffusing even further from major U.S. cities. I met Ben in 2008 when he was just starting out, and he explained the simple idea to me: build a network that allows money to be transferred for a flat fee, not a percentage like credit cards or PayPal. With smart phone technology, customers could pay for their items in RAYGUN using Dwolla, saving our company thousands a year in credit card fees. "We're building the next Visa," Milne explained, "not the next PayPal."

Along the way, Milne has demonstrated the advantages that Midwest tech can have. He started cheaply and built a network of local businesses first. Dwolla not only secured initial funding from the John Deere-backed Veridian Credit Union, but Veridian also used its clout as a regional banker to implement Dwolla's products.

Ashton Kutcher
Cedar Rapids, Iowa

Norwest Corp
bank bought Wells Fargo (but
kept the name) in 1998
Minneapolis, Minnesota

Jon Gaskell
SmartyPig cofounder
Des Moines, Iowa

Mike Ferrari
SmartyPig cofounder
Bowling Green and Dayton, Ohio

By 2011, Dwolla was projecting $350 million worth of transactions in the following year, and in 2012, Milne landed a spot on *Inc* Magazine's "30 Under 30" list and got $5 million in funding, some from the high-profile actor and investor, Ashton Kutcher. Kutcher explained that in Iowa there is a level of honesty and integrity that will make a financial company successful. "Dwolla can only be built here," he said at a press conference in April of 2012.

In Des Moines, Dwolla is growing among giants such as Wells Fargo Financial and among smaller outfits such as the savings-based SmartyPig.

For Dwolla, local connections both built a solid foundation and attracted attention from outside of Iowa. This may be the example for others to follow.

The "hollowing" of the Midwest is not as simple as it sounds. Populations are shifting, but this is not leading to a dead rural community and an active urban community across the board. Instead, hotbeds are forming. They can be in cities like Chicago, Indianapolis, or Columbus, but sometimes these hotbeds are in the rural Midwest.

While the region is known as the forefront of America's industrial agriculture — biological crop experiments, massive hog confinements, cattle feedlots — it is also at the center of America's organic food movement.

Pork you buy from the California-based Niman Ranch, one of the largest organic food brands in the country, comes from a collection of Midwestern farms that are organized by Paul Willis, a farmer in Thornton, Iowa.

Willis and his wife, Phyllis, and daughter, Sarah, teamed up with Bill Niman in the mid-90s. Paul had spent his post-college years in the Peace Corps in Africa before making up his mind to move back to Iowa and take over his family farm. As Nicolette Niman writes in *Righteous Porkchop,* "Paul has always marched to his own drumbeat." When hog confinements started to grow in the 1970s, he decided to raise his pigs the traditional way.

Today, Willis organizes more than 600 farms. These farms work together as a cooperative under the Niman Ranch label to leverage scale and distribution. His organization is at the forefront of the local, naturally raised meat movement, and is starting to change the industrialized side of the industry. "Everyone from Smithfield to Tyson/IBP," Nicolette Niman continues, "is now trying to imitate (at least in a superficial way) their success. The farmers of Niman Ranch give me great hope for the future of pig farming."

I was lucky enough to tour Willis's farms in northwest Iowa, one of which he has restored to natural prairie. He liked walking through the restored prairie to connect with and remember the land's past.

This hope for connection led Polish-born Marcin Jakubowski to buy a farm in northwest Missouri after graduating from Princeton and receiving a PhD in Physics from the University of Wisconsin. As NPR reported in 2012, Jakubowski was disillu-

Paul Willis
Thornton, Iowa

Phyllis Willis
Ventura, Iowa

Sarah Willis
Thornton, Iowa

sioned with academia. So he packed up for his farm in Missouri where he raised goats and tended a fruit orchard. Things changed one day when his tractor broke, and he realized he didn't know how to fix it.

"I came from an institution of higher learning," he said, "so I had no practical skills."

He picked up a welder and ended up not only building a tractor from scratch, but starting the Open Source Ecology Project. It encourages others to share stories about building their own machinery.

In 2011, Jakubowski was named a TED fellow for his work in decentralizing knowledge, encouraging people to reharness the power of production, and bringing people from all over the world to his farm to work and experiment in producing machinery, circuit boards, and even bricks. Twenty-year-old San Diego-native Briana Kufa had been studying architectural engineering when she went to the farm to build a compressed-earth brick press. That press churns out bricks made from dirt. And the process was posted online for free.

> "While it is true that for decades, the inner cities of Detroit, Cleveland, and St Louis lost population, that is no longer the case."

While it is true that for decades, the inner cities of Detroit, Cleveland and St Louis lost population, that is no longer the case. In the last ten years, Detroit's downtown population has grown to almost 7,000 residents, Cleveland's downtown has grown by more than 20%, and St Louis' downtown has added residents for the first time in almost 50 years — growing at a faster rate than the city suburbs, according to a study from The Transport Politic.

As downtowns fill again, the shuttered factories that were to be the backdrop for *Robocop*-style anarchy are actually providing canvases for downtown housing and also experimental companies. In a twist on the Midwest's agricultural heritage, the Milwaukee-based Growing Power has taken an empty warehouse just south of downtown and turned it into the largest aquaponics operation in a cold-weather climate — growing fresh produce for local restaurants while leading tours and classes to educate

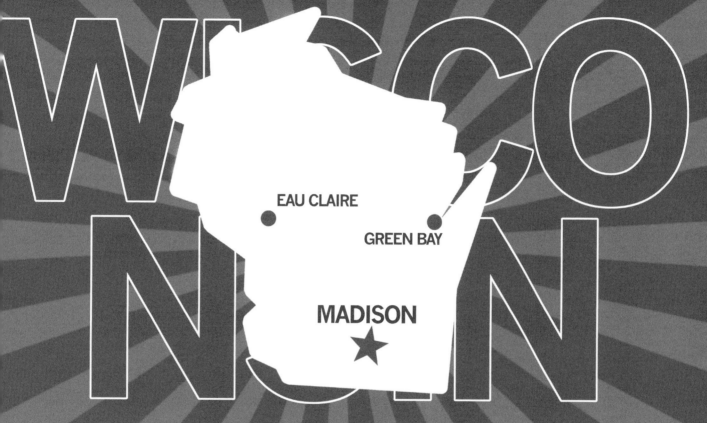

I BET SHE GIVES GREAT CHEESEHEAD

CAPITAL: Madison **SIZE:** 65,497 square miles **POPULATION:** 5,711,767 **ADMISSION TO THE UNION:** May 29, 1848 **STATE FISH:** Muskie **AND SO YOU DON'T FORGET IT:** The World's Largest Muskie is a statue in Hayward, Wisconsin. **HAPPY COWS MY ASS:** Wisconsin produces almost 14% of American milk, which is second to only California (21%). California's dairy ads claim the state has happy cows, but if you were one of those California cows, so pumped full of Botox, Prozac, and silicone implants, you'd probably be more numb than happy. **STILL:** Ralph Bruno helped Wisconsin stay one step ahead in the dairy wars when he hand made the first "Cheesehead" in 1987.
SURPRISE! I'M FROM WISCONSIN: Liberace, Les Paul, Houdini, Jeffrey Dahmer, Frank Lloyd Wright, Frederick Pabst, Joseph Schlitz, Chris Farley, Orson Welles, and Danica Patrick.

the public on eating and agriculture.

In February 2012, I took a weekend in Milwaukee to tour Growing Power, and learned about Will Allen, the CEO who is a former professional basketball player and corporate sales leader. Since running Growing Power, Allen has won a John D and Katherine T MacArthur Foundation Genius Grant. In May 2010, he was named to *Time's* list of the world's 100 most influential people.

About a half-hour after the tour ended, my wife and I ate what Growing Power produces a few blocks north at Braise Restaurant. It prepares locally sourced food, runs a culinary school, and helps deliver farmers' products directly to customers. On a snowy night, the restaurant was packed, one sign of downtown Milwaukee's resurgence. Throughout the city's center, buildings that had sat vacant for years were coming back to life as offices, apartments, and hotels such as the one we stayed in, the Iron Horse. Just like Chicago, Milwaukee has life everywhere you look. There are beautifully preserved historic buildings, phenomenal new architecture such as their art center, and new parks along Lake Michigan. The city is regenerating — slightly different from what it used to be, but better in a lot of ways.

This is true across the Midwest. In Fargo, the rehabbed Hotel Donaldson is an anchor of Broadway, serving locally raised produce and even bison meat. In Rapid City, South Dakota, the rehabbed Alex Johnson Hotel connects the modern city with its past, as does the rehabbed Grand Plaza Hotel in downtown Grand Rapids, Michigan. In Detroit, the idea of the city as a kind of outlier is embraced in Chrysler's "Imported from Detroit" slogan. They are also planning to build a *Robocop* statue.

There is a blend of innovation and reconnection. It's wrapped up in the tall, white wind turbines scattered across the upper Midwest. This old form of power has been updated, and is making the region a leader in alternative energy.

That field may never employ as many people as the car industry, but if we were cut off from the rest of the world, we could survive with what we have and produce here. Indeed, of the top seven states in the country that get a percentage of their power from wind, Midwestern states take up five spots: South Dakota (first with 22.3% from wind), Iowa (second with 18.8%), North Dakota (third with 14.7%), then Minnesota and Kansas.

Will Allen
settled in Milwaukee, Wisconsin

MacArthur Foundation
Chicago, Illinois

Ironically or not, some of the complaints against wind energy are similar to those made against cars in the early Twentieth century — the new technology is inferior to the old, and there is no distribution system. Cars were prone to breakdowns in the early days, and there was no maintained road network to drive them on. Technology improved and roads expanded, and we can expect wind technology and power distribution to improve as well.

This brings me to my other issue with the "rise and fall of the Midwest" arc: it wasn't even clear to everyone before 1950 that the Midwest was really rising.

Thomas Edison grew up in Ohio and founded General Electric, but he made Menlo Park, New Jersey, famous in the late 1800s by building his inventions laboratory there. His General Electric moved from Cleveland to New York City. Mark Twain, Ernest Hemingway, and F Scott Fitzgerald all moved out East. Johnny Carson, Walt Disney, and Charles Eames moved out West.

The Midwest was producing great minds and great companies, but it was also losing great minds and great companies. "The Midwest," as Garrison Keillor says, "is a great exporter of people."

5.3 FROM RAGS TO T-SHIRTS: THE HEARTWARMING MIKE DRAPER STORY

(FRIDAY 9/8C, ONLY ON LIFETIME)

> "T-SHIRTS HOLD A SPECIAL PLACE IN AMERICA ... IN 2010, *VANITY FAIR* REPORTED THAT, 'PRESIDENT OBAMA AND RAHM EMANUEL WOULD JOKE THAT, WHEN [THE PRESIDENCY] WAS ALL OVER, THEY WERE GOING TO OPEN A T-SHIRT STAND ON A BEACH IN HAWAII.'"

It hadn't been my life's dream to sell t-shirts. Until about two months before I started selling t-shirts in 2004, I was one of the Midwest's many human exports and I planned to stay that way. I was a senior at Penn planning on getting a Masters Degree in International Relations from St Andrews University in Scotland. I thought maybe I'd move to the United Kingdom permanently, or maybe stay out East. I hadn't really thought much past that Masters degree.

My intentions weren't particularly noble. I had spent my junior year at St Andrews on a scholarship and had met a girl there. To procrastinate joining the real world, I figured I would apply for another scholarship, called the Thouron, and go back to St Andrews to spend the year with her — and maybe along the way figure out what "international relations" are.

Confidence is one thing I've never lacked. Realistic planning is another matter. By January of my senior year, I had made no other plans outside of attending St Andrews — which was only feasible if I was one of the maybe four out of 150 or so people awarded the Thouron.

Things were moving in my direction: I was selected as one of the 24 finalists, and figured I had it made. I mean, I may not have been the best, or even second or third best, but I was *definitely* in the top four.

But everyone faces tragedy in their lives — death, poverty, lack of vaccines to stave off disease — mine was rejection for the Thouron.

Please, hold your tears until the end of the book.

It was the hardest thing I had dealt with since getting a B in Russian Politics. More depressing, I didn't take this as a signal to reassess my future. Instead, I went to the St Andrews Society of Philadelphia — which had sent me to St Andrews the first time — to see about applying for their graduate degree scholarship. It was less money, but still enough to cover tuition. Unfortunately, that was 2004, when America's multiple war spending habits sent the dollar to its lowest point in decades compared to the British pound. The St Andrews Society cut back their scholarship program, and eliminated their graduate scholarship. Strike two.

It was March by this point, graduation was about two months away, and I suddenly had the next 60 or so years of my life free — a little less if I took up smoking. So when a friend suggested we should pool some money and start selling "Not Penn State" t-shirts on campus, I agreed.

We each put in about $150, bought 100 shirts, sold them in a few days, bought 100 more, sold them in a few days, and the proverbial lightbulb went off in my head: this is what I should be doing, something creative.

After graduation, I traveled between Boston and DC, selling shirts out of a bag on particularly busy street corners or college campuses. I was selling cheap goods to kids at Columbia, Harvard, Brown, and NYU. I'd moved from being one *of* those kids to being someone those kids deal with. But for someone who had always dreamed of doing something creative, there is no better feeling than to take something you have made and have a complete stranger give you money for it.

Through 2004, the shirts I was selling were getting a good reception, but I was running into basic business problems — having other people produce the shirts was an issue, not having a home base for shipping was an issue, not having a niche market was an issue.

I had visited dozens and dozens of stores, and started to develop an idea for a store and production space of my own. The main issue was location. Stay in Philly? Move to New York? Boston? Providence?

My 2005 move back to Iowa was a surprise to my friends at Penn — why would I leave the cultural mecca? More importantly, it was a surprise to my girlfriend still studying at St Andrews. I had gone from being an Ivy League guy planning on getting a masters degree in the UK to a traveling t-shirt salesman with dreams of one day (if I played my cards right!) opening a store in Des Moines, Iowa.

This thing had *Death of a Salesman* written all over it.

But Des Moines seemed like the best environment for me. A lot of the Midwestern stereotypes are true.

First of all, the people are nice and supportive. Soon after opening my store, I bumped into a guy looking through the Dumpsters in the alley who said, "Boy, it sure is turning cold early this year." Not long back from Philly, here I was thinking, "Wow, even the bums here are polite and good natured."

Second, if I were going to stay in New York, I'd not only be competing against kids from New York, but I'd be competing against a bunch of kids from Iowa who'd moved to New York.

Des Moines seemed wide open, more full of possibility.

Friendly people and less competition would allow me to grow unhindered and figure out what I wanted to do. As Des Moines entrepreneur Mike Wagner said to me, "Iowa is the Zen garden of America; you go there to think and get your bearings."

In the summer of 2005, I was printing shirts in my parents' basement, building the retail space that would become RAYGUN, and, most impressively, convincing my girlfriend to move from London to Iowa to join me. It might have helped that the English are even worse with Midwestern geography than Easterners — she thought Des Moines was located on a body of water.

Only five years before, Iowa had been the epitome of a place to leave. Heading back, I kind of felt like a pioneer. Not only because I had left the East for the great unknown, but also because I was wearing my coonskin hat, driving a team of oxen who pulled my Conestoga wagon, and half of my party died of dysentery.

Mike Wagner
Columbus, Nebraska

" 'Iowa is the Zen garden of America; you go there to think and get your bearings.' "

Stranger than moving back to Iowa was meeting dozens of others who were moving back to Iowa from cities like Austin, Denver, New York, or LA for the same reasons I was: to take advantage of the opportunities in the city.

People who had grown up in a suburbanized America were now eager to connect with something like urban areas, local stores, local foods.

I didn't even realize that I myself was a part of the new energy in the Midwest. St Louis, once the example of urban decay, also holds examples of revitalization. Not only are more residents moving back to city centers, but farmers markets such as the Soulard Farmers Market — the oldest market west of the Mississippi River — are more popular than ever. And on the local store side, STL-Style is a clothing store

Jeff and Randy Vines
St Louis, Missouri

opened in 2001 that designs St Louis-based products that celebrate a city that, the founders Jeff and Randy Vines explain, "is overflowing with idiosyncrasies, and that unique flavor should be a source of pride, not embarrassment."

This power of t-shirts should not be underestimated. Once I opened in Des Moines, the core of the business connected designs to my city and state. STL-Style took a similar tack in St Louis, but there are dozens across the Midwest: Ork Posters in Chicago, the Social Department in Ohio ("handmade silkscreen goods done up in the Midwest USA!"), Hammer Press in Missouri ("handmade with love in Kansas City"), Ink Detroit ("Detroit Loves Me"), Fargo Stuff ("I've Been to Fargo. Really."), CLE Clothing out of Cleveland ("Hello from Beautiful & Fabulous Cleveland Ohio!"), M-22 in Northern Michigan, "Michigan Awesome," and "Duluth is a Cool City."

Jenny Beorkrem
founder of Ork Posters
Bettendorf, Iowa

Paul Marcial
cofounder of Ink Detroit
Royal Oak, Michigan

Steven Mansour
cofounder of Ink Detroit
Royal Oak, Michigan

Mike Kubinski
cofounder of CLE Clothing
born in Akron, Ohio,
raised in Sharon Center, Ohio

Jeffery Rees
cofounder of CLE Clothing
born in Cleveland, Ohio,
raised in Granger, Ohio

T-shirts hold a special place in America. They are one of the only products acceptable to shoot out of cannons into crowds at sporting events. Fans will then struggle over this free piece of $2 cotton, not even knowing if it will fit them. When the *Los Angeles Times* asked *Girls Gone Wild* creator Joe Francis how he got girls to take off their tops for him on camera, he said that all he had to do was offer them free t-shirts. And in 2010, *Vanity Fair* reported that, "President Obama and Rahm Emanuel would joke that, when [the presidency] was all over, they were going to open a t-shirt stand on a beach in Hawaii."

That's right: I am living Barack Obama's dream. Only on a street in Iowa, not a beach in Hawaii.

T-shirts are probably the most visible aspect of renewed local pride. But they are the tip of the renaissance iceberg.

RANDOM LIST OF PEOPLE FROM THE MIDWEST:

Warren Buffett (Omaha, Nebraska) Esteemed money manager.

James Dean (Marion, Indiana) Cultural icon from *Rebel Without a Cause*.

Macy Gray (Canton, Ohio) Beloved R&B singer.

John Malkovich (Christopher, Illinois) Famed actor.

Dick Van Dyke (raised in Danville, Illinois) Famed American actor from *Mary Poppins* and *Chitty Chitty Bang Bang*.

Dan Patrick (Mason, Ohio) Best commentator on ESPN.

Fred Astaire (Omaha, Nebraska) Dance sensation and one of the greatest male stars of all time.

Don Johnson (born in Flat Creek, Missouri and raised in Wichita, Kansas) *Miami Vice*'s man in the white blazer, and writer of one of the worst pop songs of all time.

Neil Armstrong (Wapakoneta, Ohio) First man on the moon and true American hero.

Elliot Ness (Chicago, Illinois) Famous crime fighter at the head of "The Untouchables."

Ernest Hemingway (Oak Park, Illinois) Famed American writer.

Sam Walton (raised in Columbia, Missouri) Founder of Wal-Mart.

Amelia Earhart (Atchison, Kansas) Pioneering female aviator.

Harry Caray (St Louis, Missouri) Large-spectacle-clad announcer for the Chicago Cubs.

Charles Lindbergh (Little Falls, Minnesota) Pilot, American hero, Midwesterner.

Erin Brockovich (Lawrence, Kansas) The real Erin Brockovich.

Orson Welles (Kenosha, Wisconsin) and **Francis Ford Coppola** (Detroit, Michigan) Two of the greatest American directors, with films like *Citizen Kane* and *The Godfather*.

PEOPLE

The Midwest has produced some pretty memorable people, but that's not to say that everywhere outside the Midwest hasn't also produced a couple noteworthy folks. We break it down for you here with a totally random collection of some people from the Midwest and some people not from the Midwest ... Yup, totally random ... Just pulled some names out a hat, and this is what we came up with. Seriously. We're as surprised as you with the results.

RANDOM LIST OF PEOPLE *NOT* FROM THE MIDWEST:

Adolf Hitler (Braunau am Inn, Austria) German dictator behind the Second World War and Holocaust.

Pol Pot (Kampong Thom Province, French Indochina) Leader of Cambodia's Khmer Rouge that brought executions, malnutrition, and forced labor that killed 21% of the Cambodian population.

Osama Bin Laden (Riyadh, Saudi Arabia) International terrorist behind the 9/11 bombings.

Ke$ha (Los Angeles, California) Pop singer who experimented through the early 2000s with new forms of audio torture like "Tik Tok" and "We R Who We R."

Joseph Stalin (Gori, Tiflis Governorate) Brutal Russian dictator who killed or imprisoned thousands during his various, nondietary purges.

Kim Jong-il (Vyatskoye, Soviet Union) "Supreme leader" of North Korea who enjoyed watching his own people starve, running his country into the ground, long walks on the beach, and Hollywood blockbusters.

The Kardashians (Los Angeles, California) Yup.

WE'RE #1 BY A WIDER MARGIN THAN USUAL!

'AT LAST DETROIT HAS ITS NOVEL.

WHAT DUBLIN GOT FROM JAMES JOYCE ... DETROIT HAS FROM NATIVE SON EUGENIDES' [*MIDDLESEX*]'

Calling the Midwest's current era a "Renaissance" may not be the right word. "New Regionalism" is more accurate.

The first Regionalism refers to a short-lived artistic movement led by Grant Wood in Iowa, Thomas Hart Benton in Missouri, and John Steuart Curry in Kansas. These artists moved away from the abstract modernism of the time and toward the realistic celebration of their homeland.

Wood started painting at an art school in Minneapolis in 1910, then at the Art Institute of Chicago in 1913, and finally on trips to Europe between 1920 and 1928. In 1932, he founded the Stone City Art Colony near his hometown of Cedar Rapids and began teaching, lecturing, and helping artists through the Great Depression. In 1935 he wrote *Revolt Against the City,* a rejection of the idea that Americans needed to look to Paris or the East Coast for their art and their inspiration. "[I decry] the domination exercised over art and letters and over much of our thinking," Wood writes, "by Eastern capitals of finance and politics."

Wood believed Regional artists should embrace their hometowns, interpret their landscape, physical geography, industries, and psychology, because these elements are the base of American culture.

He hoped that people would see artistic inspiration in everything around them, diffusing art to "the whole people."

Regionalism reached a great height when Benton's self portrait was on the cover of *Time* in 1934, in an issue devoted to the illustrations of painters in the Regionalist movement. It was the first time that the Midwest had been portrayed, on the national level, as an engine of art.

In fact, regional pride and innovation permeated the Midwest in the early Twentieth century.

Chicago's road to modern greatness started at the same point that I put the start of regional pride: the 1871 Great Chicago Fire. At the time, the Midwest was still taking shape. The Civil War ended in 1865, Nebraska joined the Union in 1867, and settlers still fought over county seats in 1868 when Naperville and Wheaton got into their tussle. And although devastating, the Chicago Fire ushered in massive growth in Chicago, and led to a Midwestern style that started with William Le Baron Jenney's Home Insurance Building, the first metal frame "skyscraper," and the first major work of the Chicago School.

Jenney's building used Midwestern steel and clean, simple lines. This style caught on, and in 1889, Dankmar Adler and Louis Sullivan's Auditorium Building became the first mixed-use building in America, with a hotel, offices, and theater.

The Chicago School's simple, straight lines and utilitarian style may have been an economic choice. University of Illinois professor John Garner argues that costs had to be kept down. "The most prominent Manhattan skyscrapers," writes Garner, "were corporate headquarters requiring more lavish treatments to heighten corporate identity, while in Chicago, entirely speculative office buildings, for which such treatments were irrelevant, predominated."

The crowning achievement of these architects was the 1893 Columbian Exhibition in Chicago — "The White City" along the shores of Lake Michigan. It demonstrated how far Chicago had come since the Fire, and it introduced Chicago to the rest of the country as a symbol of modernity and an example of what a city could look like. The "City Beautiful" movement started out of the Columbian Exhibition.

That same year, Frank Lloyd Wright left Adler and Sullivan's firm to start his own, envisioning Chicago as "the New Athens."

Wright, years before Grant Wood, recognized the importance of drawing from your surroundings. He took the solid, simple lines used in the steel skyscrapers of Chicago, he used local materials in houses, he tried to blend his works with natural features, and he called this, "The Prairie Style."

Like Grant, Wright didn't see art as something to be squirreled away or appreciated by a single class, but wanted to create a beautiful, "living city."

A PLACE TO SIT WHILE YOU ADMIRE OUR GREATNESS:
One of the many inspired by Frank Lloyd Wright was Charles Eames (St Louis, Missouri) who studied architecture at the Cranbrook Academy of Art in Bloomington, Michigan. Later he teamed up with the Herman Miller company in Zeeland, Michigan, to pioneer modern American furniture with legendary pieces like the "Eames Lounge" chair and ottoman.

In 1911, three years after Ford introduced the Model T, Wright opened The Prairie School in Spring Green, Wisconsin. Nine years later, in 1920, Sinclair Lewis published *Main Street* and opened the Midwest further to the rest of the country as he became the first American writer to win the Nobel Prize for Literature. "Whether (Lewis) has 'got' the Middle West," E.M. Forster noted, "only the Middle West can say, but he has made thousands of people all over the globe alive to its existence, and anxious for further news."

Ten years after *Main Street,* in 1930, Wood's *American Gothic* debuted in Chicago. Cryptic in its meaning, *American Gothic* is possibly the most famous American painting of all time. As Twain and Hemingway epitomized "American" literature, as Carson epitomized "American" humor, Grant's painting epitomized "American" art.

The years that followed 1950 aren't what I'd call a "decline," but attention to local surroundings certainly slipped. The Civil Rights movement and Vietnam War focused attention on national issues and national identity. Large brands, national retail stores, and chain restaurants began to push out local competitors. A sign of status was to shun local stores or brands, and purchase national or international products. Downtowns withered; suburbs prospered.

More than 70 years after the initial rise of regionalism, the pendulum is swinging back.

In 2011, Rob Russell cofounded *Midwest Gothic,* a literary journal, in Ann Arbor. Only six years before, he had left the Midwest (and America) to study at Oxford Brookes University after graduating from Michigan State. There, he began studying regional writers and said he "noticed there was a severe lack of Midwestern literature, no real national push like there was with Southern, Eastern, or even Western lit." This became the main impetus for him to move back to Michigan and publishing.

"Our main focus," Rob explains, "is to really draw attention to the region, the little details, the people, and show others how we already see it, not just as the Corn Belt or Rust Belt or whatever."

Rob is on the ground level when it comes to a resurgence in Midwestern writers, from Charles Baxter and Steve Amick to some of the biggest modern American writers: David Foster Wallace (*Infinite Jest*), Jeffrey Eugenides (*The Virgin Suicides* in

Rob Russell
Kentwood, Michigan

Charles Baxter
Minneapolis, Minnesota

Steve Amick
Ann Arbor, Michigan

David Foster Wallace
raised in Champaign/Urbana, Illinois

Jeffry Eugenides
Detroit, Michigan

1993 and *Middlesex* in 2002), Chad Harbach (*The Art of Fielding* in 2011) and Jonathan Franzen, whose novels such as 2001's *The Corrections* and 2010's *Freedom* landed him on the cover of *Time* — the first author to do so in more than a decade.

All of the above set their works in the Midwest. *The Detroit Free Press* said of *Middlesex* that, "At last Detroit has its novel. What Dublin got from James Joyce ... Detroit has from native son Eugenides." Franzen's first major novel, 1988's *The Twenty-Seventh City,* was set in St Louis and documented life as the city was falling from grace — the title subtly alluding to when St Louis had been the seventh-largest city in 1930 before falling in the size rankings. Franzen's most recent novel, *Freedom,* documents life in St Paul. "Maybe I'm doomed as a novelist never to do anything but stories about Midwestern families," Franzen commented.

These works add to a growing Midwestern-centric art: the Coen brothers' 1996 film *Fargo* and 2009's *A Serious Man* (set in their hometown of St Louis Park, Minnesota), filmmaker Alexander Payne's 1999 movie *Election* and 2002's *About Schmidt* (both set in Omaha); Diablo Cody's 2007 and 2011 films *Juno* and *Young Adult* (both set in Minnesota). These films weave the region into the plots, rather than use it as a stereotypical backdrop. Likewise, innovative bands such as the Detroit-bred White Stripes and the Akron-bred Black Keys base much of their material and sound on their home region. All these names closely tie their works to the Midwest, and have gone on to influence artists across the country.

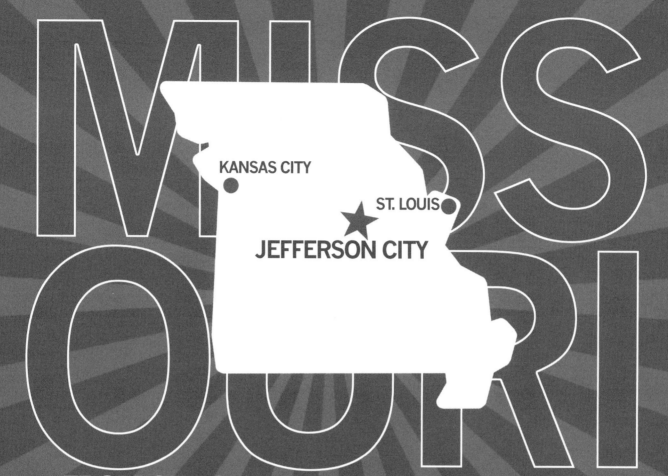

MISSOURI

KANSAS CITY

ST. LOUIS

★ JEFFERSON CITY

FROM ST LOUIS TO KANSAS CITY WITH ALABAMA IN BETWEEN!

CAPITAL: Jefferson City **SIZE:** 69,704 square miles **POPULATION:** 6,010,688 **ADMISSION TO THE UNION:** August 10, 1821 **I'LL SEE YOU YOUR MAINE, AND RAISE YOU A MISSOURI:** Missouri was admitted as a slave state and was balanced by Maine, which was freed from the yoke of Massachusetts and admitted as a free state. **MOST FAMOUS ANIMAL:** The "Missouri Mule." Shown off at the 1904 St Louis World's Fair, this animal proved its supremacy in the world of mules, becoming the mule of choice during the Boer War. **ST LOUIS, DC?** In the late 1800s, St Louis journalist Logan Reavis campaigned for the national capital to relocate from DC to St Louis. Close, but no cigar, Missouri. **SURPRISE! I'M FROM MISSOURI:** Maya Angelou, TS Eliot, Tennessee Williams, Rusty Wallace, Yogi Bera, JC Penney, Sam Walton, Jesse James, Walt Disney, Betty Grable, Jon Hamm, Brad Pitt, Dick Van Dyke, Charlie Parker, Miles Davis, Bob Barker, Harry Caray, Walter Cronkite.

5.5 THE MIDWEST: THE CHINA BEFORE CHINA

"WHERE CHINA IS HEADED ... THE MIDWEST HAS ALREADY BEEN."

Why is this reconnection mentioned earlier happening? Sit down, Midwest, and let this not-particularly-qualified 29-year-old tell you. America in general, you're gonna need to sit down too.

Reconnection to local products and production seems to happen when there is a major transition. So before you wash down a handful of Prozac with a bottle of Templeton Rye, know that this has happened before. At the time of the American Revolution, the colonies questioned (to say the least) their relationship with Britain. That led to breaking of traditional roles and a hyper-local mentality. "Independence" applied to all facets of life. Colonists stopped drinking tea from Britain and looked for beverages that could be made in America, such as hard cider. On George Washington's inauguration, he wore a suit made by a small factory in Hartford, not by some European tailor.

These were small demonstrations of self-assurance. In a time of change, the colonists needed no one but one another to succeed. Early Twentieth century regionalism came at a time when America was rising to power, and it wanted to define and demonstrate its self-assurance to the world.

Now, as America moves into the post-Industrial world, there is a reconnection to local production, but also anxiety.

Why are we getting acne? Why is our voice cracking? Will we always be so nervous around girls? Are we losing productive capacity and rare-metal mining to China?

That last one comes up a lot nowadays. It used to be that "China" was just a word on the bottom of your Hot Wheels, but now it's all over the news.

China, China, China!

Where China is headed, though, the Midwest has already been. One recent example of China's dominance is Foxconn, the Chinese factory that turns out 40% of the word's smart phones from a facility that employs somewhere between 200,000 and 400,000 and has hanging nets that are either to help cut down on suicide jumps from dormitory

PREVIOUS PAGE:
Templeton Rye
Templeton, Iowa

THIS PAGE:
River Rouge
Dearborn, Michigan

Express
Columbus, Ohio

windows or to help burn excess calories with some bouncing! The scale seems staggering, but in proportional terms, Foxconn is still one quarter the size of Henry Ford's River Rouge plant in 1930.

River Rouge was Ford's largest complex. It was a mile and a half long and one mile wide. It included 93 buildings, 16 million square feet, 100 miles of interior railroad track, and its own channel and docks. It had its own power plant, it processed its own ore on site, and employed more than 100,000 workers. In 1930, 100,000 workers was .08% of the U.S. population — all working at one plant in southern Michigan. By comparison, the highest estimates put Foxconn at only .02% of the Chinese population.

Ford was making a product that he had designed, a product that his employees could buy. China is still making American-designed products, and no Foxconn worker is using an iPhone to update his friends on the great new shirt he just bought on sale at Express.

The Midwest was very productive during the Second World War. It turned out more war material — equipment, munitions, food — than the rest of the world combined. Michigan alone produced one-eighth of all the U.S. military equipment — turning out aircraft faster than they could be shot down. It could be argued that the industrial capacity of the Midwest has never been surpassed.

Ford was working at the height of that Second Industrial revolution. Those are days many look back on fondly. Even at the time, Ford was revered. In Aldous Huxley's 1932 novel about the future *Brave New World,* he envisions that years will be denoted not in A.D. but "A.F." – After Ford.

But things weren't all peaches and high-fructose corn syrup back then. In the early 1940s, British journalist Alistair Cooke spent a year traveling the U.S. and kept a private manuscript that was published in 2006 as *The American Home*

MIKE TELLS THE COUNTRY HOW IT IS

"YOU GUYS ARE JUST STRUGGLING WITH ANXIETY ABOUT YOUR FUTURE ROLE IN THE WORLD."

"SHIIIIT."

"I SEEEEE."

Front. It's one of the best guides to America in the '40s — and to Americans in general.

Cooke enjoys most of the Midwest, but also describes south Chicago as "solid miles of some of the world's most reeking slums." He describes those who came of age in the Depression-era 1930s as "one generation that never had a job." The layoffs were massive — steel mills closed, coal mines had nothing but skeleton shifts. He said no one wanted to discuss the region before 1939.

And Cooke highlights the major change in the region at the time. "The cheap mass production of automobiles," writes Cooke, "killed off the little craftsmen ... who came to practice European skills in a peaceful place. While they taught their sons to carve wood or later to build an adding machine or vacuum cleaner, Henry Ford's discovery decided that those same sons should grow up and put a bolt in #39 on an automobile assembly line."

NOT SO FAST, CHINA! Just when China thought it had pulled a fast one on America, Rob Gifford discovered that the Midwest had infiltrated the Great Red Threat of Asia with our secret weapon: the pyramid scheme. Gifford recalled in *China Road* of being deep in the Gobi Desert when he met two Chinese men in suits who showed him their bag that had, "the Chinese characters An Li on it, and below them, the English name of the company, Amway." Yes indeed, one of Grand Rapids, Michigan's, most famous exports, a "direct selling" company that may or may not be a pyramid scheme is on the inside!

So 40 years after Chicago started the "City Beautiful" movement, it was still plagued by mass poverty and inequality. Only two decades before America hit its industrial peak, hoards of people were out of work. And the massive industrialization that many applauded now had its downside: low-skill jobs destroying small craftsmen, overcrowded cities and company towns draining small towns, a handful of industrialists dominating the economy. But the industrialization that produced Ford grew out of agricultural industrialization. Fewer hands needed on the farm sent many into cities looking for work.

Those industries, like the farms before them, are now streamlining, requiring fewer hands. The Midwest, especially, has to blaze a new trail, to figure out what

" the Midwest isn't behind, it's in the lead ... The path for China is charted for them - they can go where we have already been. "

economy will rise in the Third Industrial Revolution. On the one hand, we have lost resources like coal and copper. On the other hand, much of the Midwest sits on newly valuable resources such as natural gas. How should the Midwest use its natural resources in a way that avoids costly ecological disasters like the Dust Bowl or pollution in Treece? On the one hand, vacant buildings blight a city. On the other hand, they are inexpensive real estate to start up in. How do we transition industry-centric cities to non-industry-centric cities?

> " What China will look like in 30 years is what the Midwest looked like 100 years ago, if China's lucky. "

In answering these questions, the Midwest isn't behind, it's in the lead. China is good at making the products that we design and purchase, but still lacks innovation. The path for China is charted for them — they can go where we have already been.

In the coming decades, China will deplete its resources in industrial expansion. Its natural pollution may be even wider and more expensive than what the Midwest saw. The labor unrest seen across the Midwest starting in the late 1800s is a fraction of the unrest China will see in the coming decades as their populace grows smarter and wealthier. What China will look like in 30 years is what the Midwest looked like 100 years ago, if China's lucky.

For America, though, what the Midwest looks like in 25 years will determine what America looks like in 25 years.

"I love this state, the trees are the right height." · Mitt Romney ·

ISHPEMING

LANSING
★

DETROIT

WHERE THE TREES ARE *JUUUUST* THE RIGHT HEIGHT

CAPITAL: Lansing **SIZE:** 96,716 square miles **POPULATION:** 9,876,187 **ADMISSION TO THE UNION:** January 26, 1837 **STATE ROCK:** Petoskey Stone **IF YOU SEEK A PLEASANT PENINSULA, HOLY SHIT, YOU'RE IN LUCK:** Michigan is made up of not one, but two of the largest inland peninsulas. And the distance from Detroit to Houghton (on the UP) is greater than from Detroit to Baltimore. **TREE HEIGHT:** Perfect. **RIVAL STATE:** Ohio. This is a big one. Similar to Kansas and Missouri, Michigan and Ohio were actually involved in a border war — the Toledo War in 1836. Then the football rivalry between the two schools escalated with Michigan's Bo Schembechler facing off against Ohio State's Woody Hayes in what was dubbed the "Ten-Year War." Over 108 meetings, Michigan leads 58-43-6. M go blue! **SURPRISE! I'M FROM MICHIGAN:** Henry Ford, Iggy Pop, Larry Page, Herman Miller, Francis Ford Coppola, Sojourner Truth, Jerry Bruckheimer, Casey Kasem, Al Green, Diana Ross, and Jack "Dr Death" Kevorkian.

WE ARE HERE

5.6 WAVE THE NEXT TIME YOU FLY OVER

From organized religion to the Office Max rewards program, I've never been much of a joiner, but sometimes I've had no choice. In the spring of 2002 I was rejected as a tour guide for high school students visiting Penn. It was an unpaid position, but even so, Penn determined that they didn't want me as the face of their organization.

So in the spring of 2009, when my wife suggested we join a community garden in downtown Des Moines, I was dubious. For one thing, we lived in a loft and had managed to kill every photosynthetic organism from orchids to a tiny cactus — apparently our living room is a harsher environment than the Mojave Desert. For another thing, I worried that joining a community garden would open me up to barbecue invitations, competition with neighboring plots for yields, and the Midwestern passive-aggressive comments that would come when — as happens with so many groups I've been a part of — my attendance started to flag.

My wife thinks that she's different from me, but she's just as bad when it comes to being a productive member of a group. And once another humid Iowa summer set in, her interest in walking over to the garden regularly waned. My work ethic — which involves avoiding manual labor to keep my hands soft — couldn't make up for that loss. Two weeks absent turned into a month, then two months.

After that long, even when we wanted to go, we'd worry about what our fellow gardeners would think. We'd be the rednecks of downtown's community garden: our weed-filled plot the equivalent to parking three dead cars and four dead air conditioners in front of a trailer.

Finally, I worked up the courage to head over to our plot. "Courage" may be the wrong word since I went at 6 a.m. on a Sunday, knowing no one would be there to see my brutal slash-and-destroy approach to de-gardening my ten-by-ten-foot farm.

Amazingly, our tiny garden was filled with store-ready produce. It had plenty of weeds too, but the bounty of tomatoes blew my mind. Three months, no work, and I had been rewarded! The God that I don't believe in certainly does work in mysterious ways.

In a technological world, it's easy to forget that life depends on water and food. Well, I haven't tried drinking an iPad, so I guess I can't say for sure it won't sustain me.

Though the Southwestern United States has been a popular destination for companies and people looking to move, there is no way the Southwest can actually sustain that much life. There isn't enough water, there isn't a way to grow enough food. There is no country in the world with the climate of the Southwest (and no oil) that has the population of the Southwest.

The Southwest can only be sustained through a free-trade agreement with the rest of America.

The Midwest, by contrast, is built to sustain life. The climate is so geared toward growing food that even the most irresponsible can stay alive off the land. And in a world with shrinking water supplies, the Midwest's Great Lakes contain a fifth of the world's freshwater supply.

When I talked to Dick Longworth, author of *Caught in the Middle* and a senior fellow at Global Midwest, he explained to me that, "The water thing is big. Infrastructure is needed for growth, and water is an important part of that. Whether it's agriculture or computer chips, every industry needs water."

But when I asked him what he thought would be the next big industry, he, like almost everyone I spoke with, admitted that, "I can't say what could be something like the next car industry."

After all, in 1900, it would have been difficult to predict that in 50 years, the car would symbolize culture in the United States. At that time, automotive technology was worse than horses and there were no roads to drive on.

Alternative energy. Services. Bioscience. There are certainly many fields and directions in which the economy could move — but no clear winner. The advantage the Midwest has is in the people.

The term "Flyover Country" defines the Midwest. The economy ranges wildly from agriculture to heavy industry, the people range wildly from western Nebraska to inner-city Chicago, and the landscape varies more ... well, modestly. Hey, not every category can range wildly.

But we all share the idea that, going back to the late Nineteenth century, our

"I'm from Iowa, I only work in outer space." -Captain James T Kirk

AMES

IOWA CITY

DES MOINES

ON SECOND THOUGHT, YEAH, THIS IS HEAVEN.

CAPITAL: Des Moines **SIZE:** 56,272 square miles **POPULATION:** 2,062,309 **ADMISSION TO THE UNION:** December 28, 1846 **STATE ROCK:** Geode **CHANCES YOU'LL ACTUALLY SEE A GEODE IN IOWA:** 0% **PIGS:** Went a little overboard here. There are about 17 million pigs in Iowa. That is almost six times as many people. Although the people don't have to live in birthing crates. **RIVAL:** Minnesota. This is kind of a one-way rivalry, though. Minnesota may not even be aware of it, really, which is part of the problem! They're so goddam sure of themselves up there. With their esteemed arts centers, their professional sports teams, their nationally broadcast NPR shows. **SURPRISE! I'M FROM IOWA:** Tom Arnold, Herbert Hoover, Ashton Kutcher, Bill Bryson, Johnny Carson, John Wayne, Buffalo Bill, George Gallup, and James T Kirk **JON STEWART ON IOWA'S FAMOUS PEOPLE:** "In Iowa, this is true, they are so hard up for celebrities, there's actually a sign that says, 'Home of the future birthplace of Captain Kirk.'"

region was one that was, at best, something to be driven through on the way to somewhere else. That can really infiltrate the psyche of young minds — that everything is happening in LA or New York.

This hit me the hardest when I spent a few days in Washington, DC in 2009 lobbying for health care reform on behalf of small businesses. I spoke in front of the Ways and Means Committee; I met with senators, representatives, and some White House officials. Much of it was a letdown (so many of our elected officials are really old and hard of hearing); it was also a rush — not only to see people in real life that I'd seen on TV, but to know that the news would be about what I had been a part of that day — legislation, meetings, committees.

Washington is Hollywood for ugly people because this news coverage feeds self-worth. When the national news pays attention to you, it makes you think the rest of the country is hanging on your every move.

I never had that feeling growing up in Iowa. Getting onto the local news was a big deal. The national news, needless to say, was not hanging on our every move. Usually, the national news only showed up if enough people died or if someone from either coast was spending a considerable amount of time here.

It's always been this way and always will be this way. Jean Shepherd's observations that the "Midwesterner is by definition a born audience member" came from a man who was born almost 100 years ago. Likewise, in 1949, an Iowa editorial lamented that, "Washington has assumed the role of spokesman for our affairs, both public and private. The nation's gossip is dispensed out of New York, giving prominence to people of little use or importance. Our manners — God save the mark — are portrayed by Hollywood. The quoted opinions regarding the state of business come from Eastern Seaboard economists, and the dicta as to what we shall wear, read and think issue from the same area. The interior of the country is strictly a benchwarmer in the national lineup."

"But being flown over is what makes a Midwesterner a Midwesterner."

But being flown over is what makes a Midwesterner a Midwesterner. It not only gives us a sense of modesty, it endows us with some pretty keen powers of observation: Midwesterner Mark Twain coined "The Gilded Age" to describe his era, and F Scott Fitzgerald coined "The Jazz Age" to describe his. Likewise, Midwestern filmmakers such as the Coen brothers and Alexander Payne have perfectly captured other regions of the country with their works including *O Brother Where Art Thou?, Sideways,* and *The Descendants.* Johnny Carson's humor was built on a sly modesty — he was able to make anyone he was speaking with feel like the star. He had the confidence needed for comedy, but it did not rise to arrogance.

When Kurt Vonnegut looked back on his life, he owed all he had to growing up in Indiana. And he saw growing up in the Midwest as opening up a world of possibilities. "Participation in an art," he wrote in 1999, "although unrewarded by wealth or fame, as the Midwest has encouraged so many of its young to discover for themselves, is a way to make one's soul grow. No artist from anywhere, not even Shakespeare, not even Beethoven, not even James Whitcomb Riley, has changed the course of so many lives all over the planet as have four hayseeds in Ohio — two in Dayton [the Wright Brothers] and two in Akron ... Dr Robert Holbrook Smith and William Griffith Wilson were in Akron in 1935 when they devised the twelve steps to sobriety of Alcoholics Anonymous. By comparison with Smith and Wilson, Sigmund Freud was a piker when it came to healing dysfunctional minds and lives. Beat that! Let the rest of the world put that in their pipes and smoke it."

Being flown over encourages people to keep their head down and work. The world isn't hanging on our every move, so we have time to work quietly, building.

As America transitions and heads for uncharted territory, different regions and different states will play different roles. When it comes to which region will really lead the way in the twenty-first century, my money's on the one that has already given us the car, the computer, and rock and roll.

HUGE LIST OF MIDWESTERNERS

Believe it or not, this book contains over 500 Midwesterners. Woooooowwww. We've indexed them all below, in what may very well be the largest index of Midwesterners every compiled in a book written by RAYGUN.

A

George Ade	Kentland, IN	page 68
Tim Allen	Birmingham, MI	page 68
Will Allen	Milwaukee, WI	page 206
Sparky Anderson	Bridgewater, SD	page 38
Johnny Appleseed	*Indiana*	*page 99*
Steve Amick	Ann Arbor, MI	page 217
Marc Andreesen	*Cedar Falls, IA*	*page 200*
Maya Angelou	Missouri	page 218
Neil Armstrong	Wapakoneta, OH	page 26, 75
Tom Ashbrook	Bloomington, IL	page 86
Fred Astaire	Nebraska	page 67
Atmosphere	Minneapolis, MN	page 111
Kate Austen	Ames, IA	page 21
Bill Ayers	*Glen Ellyn, IL*	*page 176*

from Johnny Appleseed *to* Marc Andreesen *(the founder of Netscape) and ending with* Bill Ayers? *it's hard to top the A's*

B

Catherine Bach	Cleveland, OH	page 133
Bob Barker	South Dakota	page 59
L Frank Baum	Aberdeen, SD	page 52
Charles Baxter	Minneapolis, MN	page 217
Charles Beaumont	Chicago, IL	page 176
Bix Beiderbecke	Davenport, IA	page 106
The Bellville Three	Bellville, MI	page 106
John Belushi	Wheaton, IL	page 68, 187
Jack Benny	Chicago, IL	page 68
Thomas Hart Benton	Neosha, MO	page 215
Jenny Beorkrem	Bettendorf, IA	page 212
Yogi Bera	St Louis, MO	page 70
Victor Berger	Milwaukee, WI	page 146
Chuck Berry	St Louis, MO	page 104
Halle Berry	Cleveland, OH	page 31

Larry Bird	Indiana	page 99
The Black Keys	Akron, OH	page 111
Rod Blagojevich	Chicago, IL	page 183
Bill Blass	Fort Wayne, IN	page 54
Roy Blunt, Jr	Indianapolis, IN	page 68
Wade Boggs	Omaha, NE	page 67
Bon Iver	Eau Claire, WI	page 111
Bone Thugs N Harmony	Cleveland, OH	page 111
Sunny Bono	Detroit, MI	page 200
John Bosley	Slater, IA	page 9
Jason Bourne	Nixa, MO	page 21
Ray Bradbury	Waukegon, IL	page 70, 176
Omar Bradley	Clark, MO	page 125
James Brady	Centralia, IL	page 142
Marlon Brando	Omaha, NE	page 31
Bright Eyes	Omaha, NE	page 111
Jessica Brinck	Moulton, IA	page 9
Christie Brinkley	Monroe, MI	page 31
Douglas Brinkley	Perrysburg, OH	page 60
Erin Brockovich	Kansas	page 53
Tom Brokaw	Webster, SD	page 60
Herb Brooks	St Paul, MN	page 187
Sam Brownback	Garnett, KS	page 87
Jerry Bruckheimer	Detroit, MI	page 154
William Jennings Bryan	Salem, IL	page 54
Bill Bryson	Des Moines, IA	page 229
Tom Buchanan	Chicago, IL	page 149
Larry Buendorf	Wells, MN	page 141
Warren Buffett	Omaha, NE	page 54, 181
Sitting Bull	South Dakota	page 38
Chester "Howlin Wolf" Burnett	Chicago, IL	page 104
Ken Burns	*Ann Arbor, MI*	
Ambrose Burnside	*Liberty, IN*	*page 118*
William S Burroughs	St Louis, MO	page 53, 175
Dick Butkus	Chicago, IL	page 75

C

Harry Caray	St Louis, MO	page 213
Danny Carey	Lawrence, KS	page 109
Drew Carey	Cleveland, OH	page 60
Dale Carnegie	Pumpking Center, MO	page 55
Johnny Carson	Corning, IA	page 26

finally Ken Burns
next to Ambrose
Burnside

George Washington Carver	Diamond, MO	page 131
Dick Cavett	Gibbon, NE	page 70
Anton Cermak	Chicago, IL	page 141
John Chancellor	Chicago, IL	page 60
Octave Chanute	Chicago, IL	page 124
Tracy Chapman	Cleveland, OH	page 111
Don Cheadle	Kansas City, MO	page 31
Cheap Trick	Illinois	page 111
Leonard Chess	Chicago, IL	page 106
Jesus Christ	Kirksville, MO	page 24
Hillary Clinton	Chicago, IL	page 27
Buffalo Bill Cody	*Fort Leavenworth, KS*	*page 98*
Diablo Cody	*Lemont, IL*	*page 218*
The Coen Brothers	St Louis Park, MN	page 70, 218
Common	Chicago, IL	page 106
Doc Cook	Detroit, MI	page 111
Jay Cooke	Sandusky, OH	page 182
Alice Cooper	Detroit, MI	page 107
Francis Ford Coppola	Detroit, MI	page 150
Suzanne Corum-Rich	Pella, IA	page 9
John Corzine	Willey Station, IL	page 181
Blake Crabb	Lawrence, KS	page 9
Cindy Crawford	DeKalb, IL	page 31
Walter Cronkite	St Joseph, MO	page 60
Edward "Team Edward!" Cullen	Chicago, IL	page 21
John Steuart Curry	Dunavant, KS	page 53, 215
John Cusack	Illinois	page 173
William Cushing	Delafield, WI	page 118
George Custer	New Rumley, OH	page 118
Leon Czolgosz	Detroit, MI	page 138

D

Jeffrey Dahmer	West Allis, WI	page 141
Richard M Daley	Chicago, IL	page 183
Miles Davis	St Louis, MO	page 106
Tom Davis	St Paul, MN	page 68
Jack "King of the World!" Dawson	Chippewa Falls, WI	page 21
James Dean	Marion, IN	page 99, 213
Eugene Debs	Terre Haute, IN	page 85, 145
John Deere	Grand Detour, IL	page 30
Donald DeFreeze	Cleveland, OH	page 176
Walter Deubener	St Paul, MN	page 127

Buffalo Bill Cody *and* Diablo Cody: *both explored young adult dysfunction in a post-modern world*

234

Devo	Akron, OH	page 111
Bo Diddley	Chicago, IL	page 104
Walt Disney	Marceline, MO	page 132, 172
Bernadine Dohrn	Milwaukee, WI	page 176
Bob Dole	Kansas	page 53
Phil Donahue	Cleveland, OH	page 60
Steve "I'm a Talking Penis" Doocy	Kansas	page 53
The Dorsey Brothers	Detroit, MI	page 111
Jack Dorsey	St Louis, MO	page 200
Stephen Douglas	Jacksonville, IL	page 116
Alex Doumak	Illinois	page 164
Don Draper	small town, IL	page 21
Mike Draper	Van Meter, IA	page 8
Duesenberg Brothers	Des Moines, IA	page 126
Finely Peter Dune	Chicago, IL	page 68
Bob Dylan	Duluth, MN	page 70, 106

E

Charles Eames	St Louis, MO	page 216
Amelia Earhart	Atchison, KS	page 53, 125
Wyatt Earp	Kansas	page 53
Roger Ebert	Urbana, IL	page 60
Harold Edgarton	Fremont, NE	page 127
Thomas Edison	Milan, OH	page 26, 126
Dwight Eisenhower	Abilene, KS	page 125
TS Eliot	St Louis, MO	page 104
Rahm Emanuel	Chicago, IL	page 201
Dan Emmett	Mount Vernon, OH	page 131
Jeffry Eugenides	Detroit, MI	page 217
The Everly Brothers	Shenandoah, IA	page 111

F

Fall Out Boy	Chicago, IL	page 111
The Faint	Omaha, NE	page 111
Chris Farley	Madison, WI	page 68
Michael Feldman	Milwaukee, WI	page 86
Clay Felker	Webster Groves, MO	page 133
Mike Ferrari	Dayton, OH	page 202
Eugene Field	St Louis, MO	page 55
Marshall Field	Chicago, IL	page 54
Harvey Firestone	Columbiana, OH	page 126
Carl Fisher	Greensburg, IN	page 171

F Scott Fitzgerald	St Paul, MN	page 149
Larry Flynt	Dayton, OH	page 132, 177
Axel "Beverly Hills Cop" Foley	Detroit, MI	page 21
Henry Fonda	Grand Island, NE	page 146
Gerald Ford	*Omaha, NE*	*page 67, 137*
Harrison Ford	*Chicago, IL*	*page 31*
Henry Ford	*Greenfield Twnshp, MI*	*page 26*
Red Foxx	St Louis, MO	page 68
Thomas Frank	Mission Hills, KS	page 87
Al Franken	St Louis Park, MN	page 68
Jonathan Franzen	St Louis, MN	page 218
Alan Freed	Cleveland, OH	page 99
Glen Frey	Detroit, MI	page 111
Betty Friedman	Peoria, IL	page 176
Esther and Pauline Friedman	Sioux City, IA	page 56
Arthur Fry	Minnesota	page 127

now THIS is how you do people with the last name of "Ford!"

G

Clark Gable	Cadiz, OH	page 20
John Wayne Gacey	Chicago, IL	page 141
Jim Gaffigan	Chesterton, IN	page 68
George Gallup	Jefferson, IA	page 229
James Garfield	Moreland Hills, OH	page 137
Hamlin Garland	West Salem, WI	page 40
Elbert Gary	Wheaton, IL	page 126
Jon Gaskell	Des Moines, IA	page 202
Ina May Gaskin	Marshall County, IA	page 84
Jay Gatsby	small town, ND	page 21
Ed Gein	La Crosse, WI	page 141
Martha Gellhorn	St Louis, MO	page 151
John Glenn	Cambridge, OH	page 125
Sonari Glinton	Chicago, IL	page 86
Benny Goodman	Chicago, IL	page 106
Jeff Gordon	Indiana	page 99
Berry Gordy	Detroit, MI	page 106
God	Sheboygan, WI	page 27
Don Gonyea	Monroe, MI	page 86
Betty Grable	Missouri	page 218
Grand Funk Railroad	Flint, MI	page 106
Jane Grant	Joplin, MO	page 133
Ulysses S Grant	Point Pleasant, OH	page 118
Macy Gray	Akron, OH	page 111

Al Green	Michigan	page 225
Bob Griese	Indiana	page 99
Ken Griffey Jr	Ohio	page 113

H

Charles Hall	Thompson, OH	page 126
Joyce Clyde "Hallmark" Hall	David City, NE	page 54
Jon Hamm	St Louis, MO	page 31
Chad Harbach	Racine, WI	page 218
Warren G Harding	Blooming Grove, OH	page 137
William Henry Harrison	North Bend, OH	page 138
Tom Hayden	Detroit, MI	page 176
Elwood Haynes	Portland, IN	page 126
George Hearst	Sullivan, MO	page 150
Hugh Hefner	Chicago, IL	page 176
Ernest Hemingway	Oak Park, IL	page 26, 151
Paul Henning	Independence, MO	page 46
Joe Heuermann	Des Moines, IA	page 9
Hall Hibbard	Fredonia, KS	page 125
Van Holmgren	Johnston, IA	page 9
John Lee Hooker	Detroit, MI	page 111
Herbert Hoover	West Branch, IA	page 70, 138
Bob Hope	Cleveland, OH	page 68
Dennis Hopper	Kansas	page 53
Crazy Horse	South Dakota	page 38
William Hoskins	Chicago, IL	page 127
Harry Houdini	*Appleton, WI*	*page 98*
Terrence Howard	Chicago, IL	page 31
William Dean Howells	Martins Ferry, OH	page 66
L Ron Hubbard	*Tildan, NE*	*page 67*
Ernie Hudson	Benton Harbor, MI	page 165
Rock Hudson	*Winnetka, IL*	*page 31*
Clarenec Huebner	Bushton, KS	page 165
Howard Hughes, Sr	*Lancaster, MO*	*page 150*
John Hughes	*Lansing, MI*	*page 71*
Langston Hughes	*Joplin, MO*	*page 68*
Edward Hume	Chicago, IL	page 192
Hubert Humphry	Wallace, SD	page 38
Husker Du	Minneapolis, MN	page 111
Marjorie "Betty Crocker" Husted	Minneapolis, MN	page 164

believe it: Harry Houdini, L Ron Hubbard, *and* Rock Hudson, *then* John Hughes, Howard Hughes, Sr, *and* Langston Hughes! *the index alone is worth the price of admission.*

I

Steve Inskeep   Carmel, IN   page 86

J

The Jackson Five   Gary, IN   page 106
Phil Jackson   Williston, ND   page 70, 202
Jesse James   Missouri   page 218
Clarence Johnson   Ishpeming, MI   page 125
Don Johnson   Wichita, KS   page 53
Kristen Johnson   Whitefish Bay, WI   page 154
Adam Jones   Libertyville, IL   page 109
January Jones   Sioux Falls, SD   page 32
Scott Joplin   Sedalia, MO   page 104
Whitcomb Judson   Chicago, IL   page 127

K

Ted Kaczynski   Chicago, IL   page 141
Casey Kasem   Michigan   page 225
Buster Keaton   Piqua, KS   page 53
Anthony Kedis   Grand Rapids, MI
Maynard James Keenan   Ravenna, OH   page 109
Garrison Keillor   Anoka, MN   page 19
John Harvey Kellogg   Battle Creek, MI   page 164
Shawn Kemp   Indiana   page 99
Jack Kevorkian   Pontiac, MI   page 141
Brad Keywell   Detroit, MI   page 200
Kid Cudi   Cleveland, OH   page 111
Craig Kilborn   Kansas City, MO   page 69
Don King   Cleveland, OH   page 70
William King   Minnesota   page 87
Greg Kinnear   Indiana   page 99
James T Kirk   Riverside, IA   page 20
The Koch Brothers   Wichita, KS   page 88
Daniel Kraemer   Illinois   page 172
Ray Kroc   Oak Park, IL   page 170
Mike Kubinski   Akron, OH   page 212
Ashton Kutcher   Cedar Rapids, IA   page 202

L

Mike Lahti   Hancock, MI   page 115
Robert LaFollette   Primrose, WI   page 85, 140

Lois Lane	Pittsdale, KS	page 22
William Laughead	Minneapolis, MN	page 74
Ken Lay	Tyron, MO	page 183
Eric Lefkofsky	Detroit, MI	page 200
John Legend	Ohio	page 111
David Letterman	Indianapolis, IN	page 54
Delano Lewis	Arkansas City, KS	page 86
Sinclair Lewis	Sauk Centre, MN	page 150
Liberace	Milwaukee, WI	page 111
Rush Limbaugh	Cape Girardeau, MO	page 111, 178
Abraham Lincoln	Perry County, IN	page 26
Charles Lindbergh	Little Falls, MN	page 125
John Lithgow	Lakewood, OH	page 153
Harold Lloyd	Burchard, NE	page 20
Dick Longworth	Boone, IA	page 191
Jim Lovell	Cleveland, OH	page 125
Low	Duluth, MN	page 111
Lupe Fiasco	Chicago, IL	page 111
Lex Luthor	Smallville, KS	page 168

M

Bernie Mac	Chicago, IL	page 68
Thomas MacDonald	Iowa	page 171
James MacGillivray	Oscoda, MI	page 74
Madonna	Detroit, MI	page 111
Thomas "PI" Magnum	Detroit, MI	page 21
John Malkovich	Illinois	page 173
David Mamet	*Chicago, IL*	*page 54*
Charles Manson	Cincinnati, OH	page 141
Steven Mansour	Royal Oak, MI	page 212
Marshal "Eminem" Mathers	St Joseph, MO	page 70, 106
Paul Marcial	Royal Oak, MI	page 212
Rebecca Mark-Jusbasche	Kirksville, MO	page 183
Frank Mars	Hancock, MN	page 164
Dean Martin	Steubenville, OH	page 111
Glen Martin	Salina, KS	page 124
Stevens T Mason	Michigan	page 185
Don Mattingly	Indiana	page 99
Curtis Mayfield	Chicago, IL	page 106
Floyd "Money" Mayweather, Jr	Grand Rapids, MI	page 70
Joe McCarthy	Grand Chute, WI	page 87
Tim McCarthy	Ashburn, IL	page 142

"coffee is for closers ONLY!"

William McKinley	Niles, OH	page 54, 137
Jim McKelvey	St Louis, MO	page 200
McKinney's Cotton Pickers	Detroit, MI	page 111
Ed McMahon	Detroit, MI	page 68
Timothy McVeigh	Terre Haute, IN	page 87
MC5	Detroit, MI	page 111
John Cougar Mellancamp	Indiana	page 111
Seth Meyers	Evanston, IL	page 68
Tim Meadows	Highland Park, MI	page 68
Herman Miller	Michigan	page 225
Ben Milne	Cedar Falls, IA	page 202
Jen Mitchard	Sheldahl, IA	page 9
Irving Moore	Chicago, IL	page 132
Michael Moore	Flint, MI	page 195
Tom Morello	Libertyville, IL	page 111
Toni Morrison	Ohio	page 113
Bill Murray	Wilmette, IL	page 68, 187

N

The Naked Cowboy	*Ohio*	*page 113*
Connor Neeson	Detroit, MI	page 127
Elliot Ness	Chicago, IL	page 75
Bob Newhart	Oak Park, IL	page 68
Paul Newman	*Ohio*	*page 113*
Terry Nichols	Lapeer, MI	page 87
Nine Inch Nails	Cleveland, OH	page 111
Michele Norris	Minneapolis, MN	page 86
Seth Nosbusch	Jackson, MN	page 9
Robert Noyce	Burlington, IA	page 132, 200
Ted Nugent	*Detroit, MI*	*page 107*

The Naked Cowboy, Paul Newman, *and* Ted Nugent, *together at last*

O

Annie Oakley	North Star, OH	page 75, 98
Barack Obama	Chicago, IL	page 22
Michelle Obama	Chicago, IL	page 88
Ransom Olds	Geneva, OH	page 126
Floyd Olson	Minneapolis, MN	page 117
Norman Olson	Alanson, MI	page 87
PJ O'Rourke	Toledo, OH	page 68

P

Jack Paar	Canton, OH	page 66

Frederick Pabst	Wisconsin	page 205
Larry Page	Lansing, MI	page 200
Lawanda Page	Cleveland, OH	page 68
DD Palmer	Davenport, IA	page 81
Potter Palmer	Chicago, IL	page 127
Charlie Parker	Kansas City, MO	page 53, 106, 111
Ray Parker Jr	Detroit, MI	page 164
Craig Patrick	Detroit, MI	page 187
Dan Patrick	Mason, OH	page 213
Danica Patrick	Wisconsin	page 205
Art Paul	Chicago, IL	page 176
Les Paul	Milwaukee, WI	page 111
Hank Paulson	Barrington Hills, IL	page 181
Alexander Payne	Omaha, NE	page 218
James Cash Penney	Hamilton, MO	page 104
Edwin Perkins	Hasting, NE	page 164
John J Pershing	Laclede, MO	page 125
Pauline Pfeiffer	Parkersburg, IA	page 151
Liz Phair	Illinois	page 111
The Phelps Family	Topeka, KS	page 88
Mark Pincus	Chicago, IL	page 200
Brad Pitt	*Springfield, MO*	*page 26*
Iggy Pop	*Muskegon, MI*	*page 106*
CW Post	*Springfield, IL*	*page 164*
Prince	*Minneapolis, MN*	*page 111*
Jeff Probst	*Wichita, KS*	*page 53, 75*
Richard Pryor	*Peoria, IL*	*page 68*

Q

Dan Quayle	Indiana	page 99

R

Dennis Rader	Wichita, KS	page 141
Gilda Radnor	Detroit, MI	page 68, 187
Harold Ramis	Chicago, IL	page 164
Ronald Reagan	Tampico, IL	page 24, 137
Nick Reding	St Louis, MO	page 68
Jeffery Rees	Cleveland, OH	page 212
George Reeves	Woolstock, IA	page 20
REO Speedwagon	Illinois	page 111
Hadley Richardson	St Louis, MO	page 151
Andy Richter	Grand Rapids, MI	page 68

whoa. it's in this index, so it must be true, but who would've thought?

The Ringling Brothers	Baraboo, WI	page 97
James Ritty	Dayton, OH	page 127
RJD2	Columbus, OH	page 111
Jason Robards	Chicago, IL	page 192
Billy Robinson	Redfield, SD	page 124
Smokey Robinson	Detroit, MI	page 104
Kid Rock	Romeo, MI	page 54
John D Rockefeller	Strongsville, OH	page 126
Rodriguez	Detroit, MI	page 111
Joseph Rolette	Red River Valley, MN	page 117
Ann Romney	Bloomfield Hills, MI	page 88
Mitt Romney	Detroit, MI	page 84
Axl Rose	Lafayette, IN	page 79, 99
Diana Ross	Detroit, MI	page 106
Barney Rosset	Chicago, IL	page 176
David Lee Roth	Indiana	page 99
Brandon Routh	Norwalk, IA	page 20
Alan Ruck	Dayton, OH	page 71
Rudy	Indiana	page 99
Rob Russell	Kentwood, MI	page 217
George Ryan	Kankakee Co, IL	page 183
Paul Ryan	Janesville, WI	page 88
T Claude Ryan	Parsons, KS	page 125

S

Pat Sajak	Chicago, IL	page 36
DJ Jesse Saunders	Chicago, IL	page 106
Bo Schembechler	Barberton, OH	page 108
Joseph Schlitz	Wisconsin	page 205
Charles Schulz	*St Paul, MN*	*page 71*
Tom Scholz	*Toledo, OH*	*page 107*
Bob Seger	Detroit, MI	page 111
Frank Seiberlint	Summit Co, OH	page 126
Tom Selleck	Detroit, MI	page 21, 60
Lucy Shay	Chicago, IL	page 9
Martin Sheen	Dayton, OH	page 150
Jean Shepherd	Hammond, IN	page 26
William Tecumseh Sherman	Lancaster, OH	page 118
James Shortridge	Lawrence, KS	page 77
Joe Shuster	Cleveland, OH	page 20
Jerry Siegel	Cleveland, OH	page 20
Ben Silberman	Des Moines, IA	page 200

the creator of Snoopy and the creator of the band Boston. similar last name, exact same region.

Scott Simon	Chicago, IL	page 86
John Sinclair	Flint, MI	page 175
Oliver Sipple	Detroit, MI	page 142
Gene Siskel	Chicago, IL	page 60
Jeff Skilling	*Aurora, IL*	*page 183*
Slipknot	*Des Moines, IA*	*page 111*
Smashing Pumpkins	Chicago, IL	page 111
Patti Smith	Chicago, IL	page 111
Roger Smith	Columbus, OH	page 195
Kathleen Soliah	Fargo, ND	page 176
David Spade	Birmingham, MI	page 68
Jerry Springer	Cincinnati, OH	page 178
Sufjan Stevens	Detroit, MI	page 111
Potter Stewart	Jackson, MI	page 160
Tony Stewart	IN	page 99
AT Still	Kirksville, MO	page 81
William Stout	Quincy, IL	page 125
Joseph Strauss	Cincinnati, OH	page 132
Charles Strite	Iowa	page 127
Styx	Illinois	page 111
Jenny "Mrs Mark Sanford" Sullivan	Winnetka, IL	page 117
Superman	Smallville, KS	page 20

T

William Howard Taft	Cincinnati, OH	page 140
Booth Tarkington	Indiana	page 99
Art Tatum	Toledo, OH	page 106
Chuck Taylor	Indiana	page 99
George "Damn Dirty Apes!" Taylor	Fort Wayne, IN	page 21
George Taylor	Flat Rock, IL	page 164
Kent Taylor	Nashua, IA	page 20
Maxwell Taylor	Keytesville, MO	page 164
Frederick Terman	English, IN	page 132
John Thain	Antioch, IL	page 182
Sister Rosetta Tharpe	Chicago, IL	page 107
Paul Michael Thomas	Columbus, OH	page 132
Three-Eleven	Omaha, NE	page 111
James Thurber	Columbus, OH	page 66, 133
Paul Tibbits	Quincy, IL	page 165
Cheryl Rae Tiegs	Breckenridge, MN	page 132
Tilly and the Wall	Omaha, NE	page 111
David Tod	Youngstown, OH	page 119

what do Enron and heavy metal have in common? that's right: the Midwest.

Lily Tomlin   Detroit, MI   page 68
Calvin Trillin   Kansas City, MO   page 66
Harry S Truman   Lamar, MO   page 137
Sojourner Truth   Michigan   page 225
Ike Turner   St Louis, MO   page 104
Ted Turner   Cincinnati, OH   page 44
Tom Turpin   Kansas City, MO   page 104
Mark Twain   Hannibal, MO   page 54

U

Seriously? No one with a last name starting with the letter U?

V

Dick Van Dyke   Danville, IL   page 213
Jesse "The Body" Ventura   Minneapolis, MN   page 84
Jeff and Randy Vines   St Louis, MO   page 212
The Violent Femmes   Milwaukee, WI   page 111
Kurt Vonnegut   Indianapolis, IN   page 29

W

Ric Waite   Sheboygan, WI   page 192
Mike Wagner   Columbus, NE   page 211
Scott Walker   Delavan, WI   page 88
David Foster Wallace   Champaign, IL   page 217
Rusty Wallace   Missouri   page 218
Joe Walsh   Wichita, KS   page 111
Sam Walton   Columbia, MO   page 213
The Warner Brothers   Youngstown, OH   page 132
Bill Watterson   Chagrin Falls, OH   page 71
Brian "Marilyn Manson" Warner   Canton, OH   page 107
John Wayne   Winterset, IA   page 54
Freddie Webster   Cleveland, OH   page 111
Lawrence Welk   *North Dakota*   *page 111*
Orson Welles   *Kenosha, WI*   *page 54*
Peter Weller   Stevens Point, WI   page 192
Roger Welsch   Lincoln, NE   page 66
Mary Welsh   Minnesota   page 151
Kanye West   Chicago, IL   page 106
Matt Whitacre   Morrow, OH   page 168
Jack White   Detroit, MI   page 54

whoa!

The White Stripes	Detroit, MI	page 111
William Allen White	Emporia, KS	page 111
HJ Whitley	Chicago, IL	page 132
Grace Lee Whitney	Ann Arbor, MI	page 62
Diane Wiest	Kansas City, MO	page 192
Oprah Winfrey	Milwaukee, WI	page 70
Gene Wilder	Milwaukee, WI	page 68
Wendell Wilkie	Indiana	page 99
George Will	Champaign, IL	page 27
Benjamin Willard	Toledo, OH	page 21
Andy Williams	*Wall Lake, IA*	*page 46*
Evan Williams	Clarks, NE	page 200
Robin Williams	*Chicago, IL*	*page 68*
Tennessee Williams	*Missouri*	*page 218*
Paul Willis	Thornton, IA	page 203
Phyllis Willis	Ventura, IA	page 203
Sarah Willis	Thornton, IA	page 203
James "Tama Jim" Wilson	Traer, IA	page 63
Stevie Wonder	Saginaw, MI	page 106
John Wooden	Indiana	page 99
Tom Wopat	Lodi, WI	page 133
Frank Lloyd Wright	Richland Center, WI	page 26
The Wright Brothers	Dayton, OH	page 30
Grant Wood	Cedar Rapids, IA	page 22, 215

only the best Williams are Midwestern Williams.

X

Malcolm X	Omaha, NE	page 67

Y

First the letter U and now Y? Not even a Mr Young in this book?

Z

Robert Zemeckis	Chicago, IL	page 50
William Zoster	Chicago, IL	page 147

SOURCES

Well, that pretty much wraps it up. Hope you've enjoyed reading! You may be wondering the same thing as some friends of RAYGUN who have read through parts or drafts of this book as we all worked on it: "Is this true?"

Yes! These are all facts. Sure, they're arranged in such a way as to prove a broader point, and I throw in plenty of subjective hyperbole when it comes to other regions or historical generalizations. But hey, I'm an Ivy League history major, so I've learned from the best when it comes to using facts to distort the truth.

Since this book is filled with facts, it took waaaaaaaaaaaaay longer to write and finish than any of us expected. We started off as a t-shirt company, which means that this project was the biggest thing we've ever done by a long shot. If we had known how much work this thing was going to be, we never would have gotten into it.

The months started with a lot of research, much of which comes from the "general books" below — though most of what is covered in there didn't make it into the final text. I spent a ton of time on Wikipedia to find the more trivial hometowns, but whether it came from a book or Wikipedia, I tried to identify a second source.

I thought about going the Stephen Ambrose route and just plagiarizing the shit out of other books, but I wanted to set a good example for academia instead, which means everything above is from the minds of me or someone at RAYGUN.

And "The Midwest," apparently, is a pretty enormous topic. There is a ton more that could have gone in, so if your favorite Midwestern feature is missing, just email us and maybe it can get crammed into the Second Edition (assuming this thing actually sells). There is no way this book can be topped (it will surely be studied for generations to come!), but if you're looking to read more about the Midwest, below are some great places to start.

GENERAL BOOKS:

The American Midwest (edited by Richard Sisson, Christian Zacher, and Andrew Cayton) There was a lot more we could have covered in our book, and The American Midwest really hammers that point home. Clocking in at 1,890 pages, and weighing nine pounds, this monster has almost everything you could ever want to know about the Midwest. Carrying it will also increase muscle mass.

The Encyclopedia of the Midwest (Allan Carpenter) The original Midwest encyclopedia! This guy was written in 1989, so a few things in there are sliiiiightly out of date. But at least the history never changes. And at only 544 pages, it was a lot more manageable than *The American Midwest*.

Historical Atlas of the United States (edited by National Geographic) If you like words but don't want them bigger than your pictures, this is a great collection.

Caught in the Middle (Dick Longworth) This is a great book on the Midwestern economy today, and Dick was nice enough to talk to me about it!

The Middle West (James Shortridge) Great short book on the naming of the Midwest, how the Midwest has been viewed over time, etc.

MORE SPECIFIC BOOKS:

The American Home Front (Alistair Cooke) One of the best observations of America.

American Road (Pete Davies)

Best of the Midwest (Dan Kaercher)

China Road (Rob Gifford)

City Life (Witold Rybczynski)

The End of Detroit (Micheline Maynard)

Hollowing out the Middle (Patrick Carr and Maria Kefalas)

It Happened in Wisconsin (Michael Bie) I grabbed this at Boswell Book Company in Milwaukee, and it has some really entertaining stories about the great cheese state of the north.

The Illustrated Man (Ray Bradbury)

The Know-It-All (AJ Jacobs)

Little Heathens (Mildred Kalish)

How to Talk Minnesota (Howard Mohr) I only read a little bit of this book, but what I did read was funny!

The Martian Chronicles (Ray Bradbury)

Methland (Nick Reding) Not exactly welcome sign material, but *Methland* is a really informative book, and a great read. Pretty unforgettable stuff.

Nature's Metropolis (William Cronon) This is a biiiiig book about the development of Chicago. Pretty dry stuff. I skimmed it.

Righteous Porkchop (Nicolette Niman)

Russell Baker's Book of American Humor (edited by Russell Baker)

The Short Stories of F Scott Fitzgerald (edited by Matthew Bruccoli)

Some Sort of Epic Grandeur (Matthew Bruccoli)

This is NPR (edited by NPR) Is it not enough for you to steadily listen to NPR every day? Why not read a whole book about it!

Variations on a Theme Park (edited by Michael Sorkin)

What's the Matter with Kansas? (Thomas Frank) This is a phenomenal book about American politics in general, and a little about Kansas. Frank is also a contributor for *Harper's*.

The Worst Hard Time (Timothy Egan)

Wry Harvest (edited by Chris Lamb)

INTERVIEWS + LIFE EXPERIENCE:

Over the years I've had contact with several people in this book, including Ben Milne of Dwolla, Paul Willis of Niman Ranch, Don Gonyea of NPR, Jenny Beorkrem at Ork Posters, my wife, and my grandparents. I was born and raised in central Iowa, and traveled the state growing up to visit relatives or with my high school football team. I spent a lot of my summers up in Leelanau County in Michigan, and (since apparently my parents really liked having me out of the house) I spent some time after Michigan at a camp on Whitefish Lake in northern Minnesota. Before starting on this book, I'd been to every major city in the Midwest at least once.

To fill in the geography gaps, which were mainly the Dakotas, I swung through South and North Dakota to check things out and do some writing ("hi" to Joe and Greg in Fargo!). I've casually talked to plenty of other people, like the guys at CLE Clothing and STL-Style. To fill in the life experience or interview gaps, I reached out to a couple people in various fields outside of t-shirts.

Dick Longworth (author of *Caught in the Middle*) An Iowa native now in Chicago, Dick is one of the foremost experts on the modern Midwestern economy. A Pulitzer Prize-winning journalist, Dick's view is a little more balanced than this book. He was gracious enough to talk with me at length about the Midwestern economy.

Dustin Dwyer (Michigan Public Radio) A reporter out of Grand Rapids for Michigan Public Radio and one of the founders of the now-defunct Midwestern-topic website, Changing Gears. Though a Florida native, Dustin is a fantastic observer of the Midwest economy and culture, and was a phenomenal guy to talk to.

Rob Russell (founder of *Midwest Gothic*) Another Michigander, in Ann Arbor. He offered some great insight on art and writing in the Midwest.

Geoff Wood (Silicon Prairie News) COO of Silicon Prairie News, Geoff has thought a lot about tech in the Midwest and is a great voice for this emerging field.

Henry Adams (author of *Tom and Jack*) The god I don't believe in shines on me steadily, because it turns out that a high school classmate of my dad's is one of the leading experts on Regionalism. He works in Cleveland, but just as I was writing the section on Regionalism, he came to give a talk in Des Moines and met with me since my dad was out of town. He had some great insights into the birth of Regionalism and art today.

MAGAZINES + NEWSPAPERS:

As you might have been able to tell, I read a lot of *The New York Time*s, *Harper's*, and *Vanity Fair*. Since deciding to write this book about a year ago, stories started to jump out at me, like an expose about Treece, Kansas, in *The Times*, La Leche League in *Harper's*, and the Obama/Emanuel t-shirt anecdote in *Vanity Fair*. Just more proof that the Midwest is everywhere.

FILM + TELEVISION, ETC:

This is a category I've been classically trained in. From greats like *The Simpsons* and *Ren and Stimpy* to daytime television like The *Price Is Right* and *Magnum P.I.* and *The A-Team* reruns, I covered a lot of ground as a kid. By age fourteen, my favorite movie was *Fargo*, and I had almost memorized the entire screenplay.

So this book is littered with references or allusions to a lot of TV (especially *The Daily Show*) and movies. And it was a good excuse to rewatch *Food, Inc*, *Robocop* (although I didn't rewatch *Footloose*). I also watched some new stuff like *The Pruitt-Igoe Myth*, a great documentary about public housing in general, and St Louis' Pruitt-Igoe in particular.

WIKIPEDIA:

I could kiss you! Thank you for existing. When it comes to quickly scanning just about anyone you can think of to see if they have some connection to the Midwest, there is no better place. And for all you haters out there, anything that made it into the book was double-checked elsewhere.

I should point out that I found as many errors in the printed books we used as I found in Wikipedia. However, the errors in the books were pretty minor. *The American Midwest*, for instance, misspelled the shopping bag inventor's name. Wikipedia, on the other hand, had a couple big ones slip through their network of editors, like the claim that Chevrolet was started in Alaska in 1911.

THANKS AND OTHER STUFF

There are a lot of people who have helped bring this together. If I started at the beginning I'd need to thank my parents for moving back to the Midwest from Boston, and thank the good folks at Lutheran Hospital in Des Moines for catching me when I was born back in 1982. Without those two things, it is pretty unlikely this book would have happened.

After that, I should probably thank the subjects of history and art, the only two I wasn't shitty at. I had some great history teachers over the years, from my dad at home, to Mrs Sayer, Mrs Merical, and Mrs Garvey in elementary school, to Mr Sittner and Mr Parks in high school at Van Meter and Central Academy, to Dr Steinberg, Dr Fawn, Dr Childers, and Dr Beeman (who later made it onto *The Daily Show* twice) at Penn and St Andrews. And the only official art teacher I've ever had was Mr Swearngin at Van Meter (heckuva job, Jim!).

Thanks to the Thouron people for rejecting me in 2004. Without them, I may have ended up in academia, consulting, or banking (ah!). Instead, I started selling t-shirts back in Des Moines, having more fun than at any point in my life.

Which brings me to the greatest city in the gol-dang universe: Des Moines. I thank the gods of skinny punks that Des Moines and everyone in it has been so supportive of the store over the years. When you start a small company by yourself, it is painfully apparent how every dollar, every small purchase, really counts. Back in 2005, when the store first opened, there were times when only two people would walk through the door all day (not two *customers*, but just two people, and sometimes they were a couple!). But Des Moines is a phenomenal city, with a phenomenal population of good looking people, and an even more phenomenal network outside of Iowa (a lot of people move away from here). RAYGUN has grown from a one-man operation in 2005 to a multinational corporation (maybe not) in just a couple of years. The city that houses our headquarters has a lot to do with that growth.

Outside Des Moines, the company has found stores and partners and fans all over the place: Iowa City, Ames, Decorah, Cedar Falls, Grinnell, Hampton (Orange Possum!), Mason City, Clear Lake, Davenport, Elkader, Kansas City, Fargo, Minot, Bismarck, Sioux Falls, Eau Claire, Waussau, Chicago, northern Michigan, Minnesota, and beyond!

Thanks to all the staff here at RAYGUN for showing up (most of the time) and working hard (hard-ish), and thanks for not suing me for the bizarre things I'll say in the course of a day. Thanks to my wife for letting me write stories about her (though she'll read them for the first time after the book is in print, so I hope this book moves enough copies for me to afford a new couch for her to smooth out any marital hiccups). Thanks to my two kids, you guys didn't really do much (in fact, now that I think about it, because of my younger son, there were very few nights during this whole thing that I slept for over 6 hours in a row), but you did reinforce the fact that I need to work harder to get more money for you. Thank you Internet (what did I do before you?), and thank you Kombucha Energy shots/Five Hour Energy/iced tea/iced coffee/asprin with caffeine/Excedrin with caffeine (without all of you I would have had to get back into Mountain Dew or experiment with meth).

Thanks to you for having bought this book. Or thanks to the person who gave you this book as a gift. Or if you're standing in a store just reading this, don't just put it back on the shelf, this isn't a fucking library, get out your wallet and hand the person at the register some money!

And for those who ask if I'm serious about the Midwest being so great: yes, I am 100% serious. If you've been here and don't think the powers above shower us with adulation, you are mentally ill.

Mike (July 2012)